The Legitimate Corporation

Essential Readings in Business Ethics and Corporate Governance

EDITED BY BRENDA SUTTON

BLACKWELL
Business

Copyright © Basil Blackwell Ltd 1993

First published 1993

Blackwell Publishers
238 Main Street, Suite 501
Cambridge, Massachusetts 02142
USA

108 Cowley Road
Oxford OX4 1JF
UK

Library of Congress Cataloging-in-Publication Data
The Legitimate corporation: essential readings in business ethics and
corporate governance / edited by Brenda Sutton.
p.   cm.
Includes bibliographical references and index.
ISBN 0-631-18747-2 (alk. paper). — ISBN 0-631-18748-0 (pbk.:
alk. paper)
1. Business ethics.   2. Corporate governance.   3. Corporations—
Social aspects.   I. Sutton, Brenda.
HF5387.L44   1993   173'.4—dc20   92-47388

British Library Cataloguing in Publication Data
A CIP catalogue record for this book is available from
the British Library.

Typeset in 11 on 13 pt Ehrhardt
by Best-set Typesetter Ltd., Hong Kong
Printed in Great Britain by
Hartnolls Ltd., Bodmin

This book is printed on acid-free paper

To the invisible college

Contents

List of Contributors

Ahmet Aykaç is IMD Faculty, Economics and Quantitative Methods. He is currently Programme Director of the International Programme for Senior Executives (IPSE) and the Programme for Executive Development (PED). He is a former faculty member at INSEAD in France, and works as consultant to governments and industry.

Adolph A. Berle and **Gardiner C. Means** were both professors at Columbia University at the time that *The Modern Corporation and Private Property* was published in 1932 – Dr Berle in the Department of Law, and Dr Means in the Department of Economics. Both went on to have influential careers as critics and theorists of the American capitalist system. Dr Berle, a member of President Roosevelt's New Deal "brain trust" during the Depression, is probably best known for his books *The 20th Century Capitalist Revolution* (1954), and *The American Economic Republic* (1963). Dr Means, also an advisor to President Roosevelt, developed the theory of "administered prices" in the 1950s, and is the author of *Pricing Power and the Public Interest* (1962), and *The Modern Economy in Action* (1936), co-authored with economist Caroline Ware.

Kenneth Boulding is a social philosopher, as well as an economist comparable to John Kenneth Galbraith or Milton Friedman in terms of innovation in economic thought. His work in economics is not limited to the techniques of societal provisioning, but has raised wider questions of social, political, and ethical concerns. Educated at Oxford and the University of Chicago, Dr Boulding is currently with the Institute of Behavioral Science at the University of Colorado in Boulder. His many publications include *The Organizational Revolution* (1954); *Principles of Economic Policy* (1958); *The Impact of the Social*

Sciences (1966); *Beyond Economics* (1968); *Stable Peace* (1978); *Evolutionary Economics* (1981); and *The World as a Total System* (1985).

Barry Bozeman is Director of the Technology and Information Policy Program and Professor of Public Administration at the Maxwell School of Citizenship and Public Affairs, Syracuse University. He received his BA degree in political science from Florida Atlantic University in 1968, and his Ph.D. in political science from Ohio State University in 1973. Bozeman's research in the fields of organizational theory and public management has focused on scientific and technical institutions. His books include *Public Management and Policy Analysis* (1979) and *Strategic Management of Industrial R&D* (1983, with Albert Link and Michael Crow).

Ada Demb is Vice Provost for International Studies at the Ohio State University. She received her Ed.D. from Harvard, and a degree in Economics from Brandeis University. Dr Demb was formerly Programme Director of IMD's International Programme for Board Members, and is the author of numerous articles and papers on the subject of enhanced board behavior and performance. She recently authored (with F. Neubauer) the book *Corporate Boards: Confronting the Paradoxes* (New York, Oxford University Press, 1992).

Michael Gordy is consultant to Digital Equipment Corporation on issues of social change and the "knowledge age", as well as to academic institutions on executive programme design. He received his Ph.D. in Philosophy from the University of Texas at Austin. Formerly Professor for Ethics in the Professions at Boston University, Dr Gordy currently works in France as a wine merchant and as board member of Nice Beverages Company. He is the author of numerous articles on ethics, aesthetics, political theory and the philosophy of history. He lives in France with his wife and two chidren.

Jürgen Habermas is Professor of Philosophy at the University of Frankfurt, Germany. He was educated at the Universities of Bonn and Göttingen, and is a former director of the Max Planck Institute. His brilliant and often controversial analyses of the capitalist system earned him an early reputation as a socio-economic theorist. Many of his works have been translated from German and are available in other languages; these include *Theorie und Praxis* (1963); *Theorie des* *kommunikativen Handelns* (1981); and *Der Philosophische Diskürs ober Moderne* (1985).

Willis Harman is Director of the Institute of Noetic Sciences, Sausalito California, a non-profit research and educational organiz- ation. He is also a founding member of the World Business Academy and emeritus professor of Engineering-Economics at Stanford Univer- sity. Dr Harman's most recent books include *Global Mind Change: The Promise of the Last Years of the Twentieth Century* (Knowledge Systems, 1988) and *Creative Work: The Constructive Role of Business in a Trans- forming Society* (Knowledge Systems, 1989).

Edward S. Mason joined the Harvard University faculty in 1923, becoming Professor of Economics in 1936. He served as Dean of Harvard's Graduate School of Public Administration from 1947 to 1958, during which time (1954–5) he directed an eight-man team which drew up a plan for the economic development of Pakistan. During the 1950s and 60s he worked on many such committees for the World Bank and other organizations, and is best known for his research on the problems of monopoly in the United States, aspects of world trade issues, and economic development.

Robert A. G. Monks is President of Institutional Shareholder Partners in Washington DC, a firm that acts with shareholders to create long- term value. He is also the founder of Institutional Shareholder Ser- vices, which advises institutions on how to vote their proxies. He is author of the recent book *Power and Accountability* (with Nell Minow, Harper Collins, 1991). An attorney, Mr Monks has been an indus- trialist, the chair of a leading Boston investment firm, a two-time candidate for a Republican senatorial seat, and a top adviser to the Reagan administration.

F.-Friedrich Neubauer is IMD Faculty of Multinational Corporate Strategy and Planning. He received his Dipl. Kfm. at Frankfurt University, and his Dr rer. pol. at the University of Warzburg. Dr Neubauer is current programme Director of the International Programme for Board Members at IMD, and acts as consultant to the top management of several multinational corporations. He is the author of *Strategic Portfolio Management* (Kluwer, 1990) and co-author with Dr Demb of *Corporate Boards: Confronting the Paradoxes* (Oxford University

Press, 1992). He is currently working on two books, the first of which addresses the phenomenon of the "European Manager", and the second which explores vision and visioning in the management process.

Joseph Schumpeter was born in 1883 in Moravia (then a part of Austria). He studied law and economics at the University of Vienna, which at the time was dominated by the "Austrian School": economists who allied themselves with the British *laissez-faire* theorists as opposed to the current Germanic schools of thought (another famous alumnus from this period was Friedrich von Hayek). Schumpeter published his first book on economic theory while working as an attorney in Cairo, and held subsequent academic posts at the Universities of Graz and Czernovitz in Austria. In 1911 he published *The Theory of Economic Development*, widely viewed as his basic contribution to economic theory. After several disappointing forays into finance and politics, he returned to academic life, first at the University of Bonn, and then to Harvard University in 1932. While in the United States, he published *Business Cycles: A Theoretical, Historical and Statistical Analysis of the Capitalist Process* (1939) and *Capitalism, Socialism, and Democracy*, which is excerpted in this volume. He died in 1950.

Brenda Sutton is an independent writer and consultant, and has researched and authored works centering on corporate governance, ownership structures, and the problems of corporate legitimacy in the post-modern context. Formerly affiliated with IMI/IMD, she now directs a consulting and research service devoted to the socio-political environment of business. She is based in Geneva, Switzerland.

Preface

The end of the East–West confrontation is having an increasing and pervasive effect on the social, political, economic and managerial debate, an effect that will be maintained in forthcoming years. The so-called world order, accepted ideas, and even legislation have heretofore been so heavily influenced by the organizing principles emanating from the Cold War period that it is difficult, without the perspective of time, to assess the magnitude of the theoretical and practical vacuum we now face. These changes are also related to a globalization of the economy, the regionalization of markets, the emergence of complex alliances, and rapid technological change. The latter of these trends, while transforming the economy and the nature and practice of work, at the same time are beginning to pose deep and intractable ethical dilemmas in a pluralistic world.

Indeed, plurality, diversity, and heterogeneous systems increasingly characterize a world accustomed to a more monolithic structure, uniform cultures, and single comprehensive views of reality.

An even deeper trend is emerging in the socio-political and economic domain as we witness the end of the scientific determinism of the 17th century. Monolithic views of socialist or capitalist forms of society are unmistakenly an expression of this determinism.

The impact of these tectonic shifts, a sort of post-modernism, is felt everywhere. The change in geopolitical alignments is the first, and most visible, of these impacts.

For corporations, the change is in many respects more complex, more profound, and also less apparent. This is because market economies and capitalism will need to derive their legitimacy, their social acceptance, from their own merits as opposed to the faults of other systems – and without the benefit of self-censorship that such confrontation inevitably creates.

Which market economy, rather than *whether* market economy, is the forthcoming debate which is now open, especially as Europe seeks to build a new collaborative entity, and the various national economies learn to compete globally. Confronting the challenges of growth, employment and environmental viability needs to be done in the context of markets, outside of the alternative theoretical or historical models which have polarized the political system and which serve to cloud the real issues in the heat of purely ideological confrontations.

The question will remain whether or not this can actually occur without converting many aspects of the behaviour of market economies into a sort of religion, with its own rites and inquisitions. It will be an important test to see how democracy is capable of evolving in the absence of an ideologically competitive entity, both within nation-states and on a global level.

All of these issues are important to the role and function of corporations, of their management, of the owners of capital and labor, and to how each of these will interrelate in this new context.

These new challenges offer a taste of the coming managerial and social debate that has just begun to reach beyond a close circle of specialists. This book prepared by Brenda Sutton provides a significant framework for a discussion that is not limited to governance or stake-holders, but, more appropriately, is about social models and indeed about a key aspect of our future societies.

Dr Juan F. Rada
Director of Strategies and New Initiatives
Digital Equipment International

Acknowledgements

I would like to express my appreciation to the following people for their support, assistance and contributions during the course of editing this collection. Special thanks go to Dr Juan Rada, former Director General of IMI-Geneva and IMD International, for his conviction that embracing change and ambiguity is wiser than trying to fight it. Thanks also go to my colleagues and mentors Ahmet Aykaç, Yury Boshyk, Fred Neubauer, Ada Demb, and Mike Gordy; to Doctoral Fellows Thomas J. Cummings and Charles Després; and to librarians and documentalists Nicole Vautier, Eliane Bartelme, and Catherine Thiessens. Finally, I would like to thank the senior executives I have met and worked with over the years, who have expressed a continuous interest in creating the legitimate corporation.

Introduction: The Legitimate Corporation

Brenda Sutton

Although "corporate legitimacy" is not a term used widely by the general populace, most people have an opinion – informed or otherwise – on the scale and appropriateness of business activity.

These viewpoints, which range from radical conspiracy theories to a comprehensive attitude of *laissez-faire*, have an impact on commercial organizations in much the same way that perceptions of validity or invalidity can, in the long run, stabilize or weaken political institutions.

Legitimacy theory originated in the philosophy of law and politics, and since the late Middle Ages has acted as a yardstick of "political morality": a measure of the right and wrong uses of power. For the purposes of this inquiry, legitimacy provides a framework within which different perceptions of corporate power can be more clearly captured and defined – more clearly, that is, than with some of the less socially-oriented analyses of economic organization and control that prevail today. This is because a judgement of legitimacy is informed by the *total context* within which a system operates, balancing such subjective elements as beliefs and ethics with the more material constructs of the institutional environment.

Applied thoughtfully, the concept of legitimacy allows a comprehesive investigation into the impact of the public's perception of corporate power and accountability on business activity. The importance of this exercise is directly related to the atmosphere of change, complexity and uncertainty that typifies the current business environment. Probably the most important task facing today's leaders is the development of effective responses to their rapidly evolving social, economic, and geopolitical surroundings; an understanding of corporate legitimacy is one facet of that development.

BRENDA SUTTON

How Legitimacy Works

The term "legitimacy" can be used in a number of different ways. This is somewhat inevitable in fact, as the word, and the concepts behind it, have emerged from a variety of disciplines and semantic traditions. Adding to the confusion in the present context is the fact that while the "legitimating function" of senior management and the board of directors is often mentioned in the growing avalanche of governance literature each year, a thorough explanation of this concept's origins and implications is very often neglected in these venues. It may be helpful, then, to try and clarify some of those meanings before further exploring their applicability in the corporate environment.

Legitimacy is inherent in every authority and power relationship, from the family unit to the world political order. While "legitimate" can also mean "legal", or in accord with an accepted set of rules, the legitimacy of *power* is a notion of political morality that also implies *rightness* – rightness, that is, as it is defined in a given context by groups or individuals.

According to (primarily) Western political ideals, power is legitimate when it is granted by the consent of the governed (tacit or open, by some process of political selection) or by contractual agreement. In some cases, it can be legitimized by both means.[1] Legitimacy crises – which can range from proxy battles to revolutions, depending on the situation – usually arise over conflicting claims to sovereignty or authority; it is difficult to separate the notion of legitimacy from the idea of crisis, in fact, as this is often the only time that constituents in a power system will consciously assert where they believe authority should be concentrated, and how it should be used.

When the validity of social and political systems (and the institutions that represent them) is taken more or less for granted, emerging conflicts are generally negotiated in public forums (e.g., courtrooms or legislatures), or between groups. These negotiations may result either in some type of power-sharing agreement – such as coalition governments or collective bargaining – or in the setting of new standards and oversight. It is only when a great number of people realize that profound changes are necessary to their survival, and believe that their basic values are being threatened by the existing system, that an advanced stage of crisis is realized.

This process may take quite some time to develop; as Berger points out, "The old order in Europe did not suddenly collapse when Louis

XVI lost his head under the guillotine; the dramatic events of the French Revolution merely ratified a loss of legitimacy that had already taken place."[2] Even then, it took France another century to decide just what kind of *régime* it wanted in place of the dynasty so enthusiastically dispatched.

If a structure or system is sufficiently flexible, however, conflicts can be good for that system: discord between groups allows changing norms to be thematized and expressed, lessening the overall pressure. Periods of crisis, in turn, create an opportunity to test the ability of established systems to adapt and respond to trends as they arise.

Just as legitimacy is a notion difficult to divorce from crisis, so any discussion of legitimacy most pivot on the fundamental issue of context. Stillman's statement that "A government is legitimate if and only if the results of governmental output are consistent with the value pattern of the society" holds equally true for corporations.[3] In any discussion of legitimacy it is essential to bear in mind questions of national purpose and priority, political philosophy and process, dominant traditions and belief systems, and other elements that shape the socio-political "life-space".

The "legitimacy crisis" many analysts have ascribed to the current corporate system is directly related to perceived inconsistencies between the way firms do business and the changing goals and priorities of people in society. It is, in other words, a questioning of corporate power and authority, and of how that authority is being used.

Legitimacy and Corporate Power

Where there is no power, or no access to power, there is no need for a debate on legitimacy. Similarly, when systems of power and authority[4] are generally perceived of as valid, there is little stimulus for debate. The questions of corporate legitimacy addressed in this collection arise, therefore, from a set of (currently rather ill-defined) conflicts sparked not only by the *fact* of corporate power, but to a greater extent by how that power is exercised vis-à-vis changing public values. The following brief overview of corporate development may help to illuminate the current status of corporate power.

John Davis wrote in 1905 that "The most important and conspicuous feature of the development of society in Europe and America . . . during the past century . . . has been the growth of corporations".[5] In the transition from mercantile societies to complex commercial relationships, the corporation offered a locus of authority as well as an entity that was immortal, capable of entering into contractual relationships, and of exercising its rights as a "legal person". Thus the corporate form of organization and management, first created by the ancient Romans to undertake ongoing public-works projects, became the ideal vehicle for expanding networks of capitalist activity across the globe.

The first organizations that closely resembled the modern corporation were the joint-stock companies chartered by European sovereigns to explore new territory and to extract the wealth of existing colonies. These companies (such as the East India Company of Britain or the Casa di San Giorgio at Genoa) maintained legitimacy so long as the prevailing government, its authority and laws, were perceived as valid and acceptable.

Yet, even after the various monarchs and city-states lost hegemony, corporations continued to grow and gain influence – in North America, Europe, and other fast-developing areas. Although they lost certain of the trappings of overt political power (their private armies, for example), corporations became firmly entrenched as the primary agents for the advancement of capitalism, industrialism, and technical progress. Heilbroner sees this step as a central theme in the ascendancy of the capitalist system: "The creation of a broad sphere of social activity from which the exercise of traditional command was excluded bestowed on capitalism . . . an historical specificity, namely an 'economy', a semi-independent state within a state and *also extending beyond its borders*" [my emphasis].[6]

Corporate legitimacy – if indeed anyone questioned it – was protected by the sacred notion of "rights of property", a concept inextricably bound to the ideals of free markets and free societies. The professionalization of corporate administration, in turn, was legitimated by the shift from belief in the "divine right of kings" to the rational process of governance. This shift, which placed much of the responsibility for the provisioning of society into private rather than dynastic hands, marks an important turning point in both political and business legitimacy. As Mason wrote, "The eighteenth-century philosophers considered property ownership as essential to the full development of personality, to the maintenance of individual freedom from the encroachment of those power systems represented by church and state, and to the formation of a citizenry capable of self-government".[7]

This was not done, however, without certain reservations on the part of the political and economic theorists of the time, many of whom perceived the proliferation of the corporate organization as an overt promotion of "class privileges, inequality, and the limitations of individual activity."[8] In the final analysis, necessity triumphed over the newly-won democratic principles, and corporations flourished as the lesser of two evils – i.e., as being closer to individual rather than state control of the economic function.

Thus, whether *de facto* or tacitly, the business corporation is legitimate. As in many other realms of power, this legitimacy tends to be normative, and to reinforce itself over time. The gradual development of corporate networks of authority and power, while ostensibly consistent with political and social developments, ultimately arose from more of an historical *power* base than one of conscious consent – a distinction which has placed its legitimacy in potential conflict with democratic, pluralistic, and possibly even contractual ideals.

One school of thought in legitimacy theory contends that legitimation is a kind of retrospective process – in other words, as mentioned in the discussion on legitimacy crises, we don't question what we have until we are in danger of losing it. Transitions and recalibrations in the values and needs of many societies, coupled with (or, in some cases, caused by) global crises on a number of levels, have highlighted the contrasts between the justifications of corporate power and the "*volonté générale*"; the following section will describe a few of these changes in brief, and their potential impact on the perception of corporate legitimacy.

The Corporation as a Social Institution

The modern business corporation is generally perceived to be legitimate because it appears to fulfill its implicit contract with the public: to produce the goods, services, and utilities needed for the provisioning and prosperity of society. It is further validated by the products of those activities, including dividends for investors, employment, the development of new technologies, and wealth generation.

But the "business of business" is no longer conceived of in terms of such clear-cut expectations, and many of the outputs of business activity (pollution, for example) can no longer be considered beneficial. Questions about the legitimacy of capitalism and its institutions, most importantly corporations, signal a transformation in the social and ideological context that govern the role and function of organizations.

In an increasingly complex political and business environment, business leaders are being called upon to resolve a significant number of problems that were previously either relegated to the public sector (e.g., resource management, urban renewal, and economic development), or had not yet reached the proportions of today's challenges.

While individual business executives may not conceive of themselves as wielding a great deal of power, it would be difficult to deny that Western systems of rewards, recognition, status and values have been dominated by business for at least the past century.[9] This social domination is, however, merely symptomatic of the more telling phenomenon of sheer scale: the average transnational corporation can have operations in 60 countries, employ hundreds of thousands of people, control sums of wealth greater than many nations' GDP, and command vast amounts of resources. Growing numbers of analysts pose that our association with a corporation is becoming more important even than our identification with a particular nation-state – that, in time, the multinational corporation will eclipse the nation-state altogether. Again, returning to Mason, the situation begs the question: "Who selected these men, if not to rule over us, at least to exercise vast authority, and to whom are they responsible? The answer to the first question is quite clearly: they selected themselves. The answer to the second is, at best, nebulous. This, in a nutshell, constitutes the problem of legitimacy".[10]

Whether corporate managers desire or welcome the changing perception of their social role, the resolution of such inherent polemics is an essential factor in maintaining corporate legitimacy; according to Lewis Coser, "*Legitimacy* is a crucial intervening variable without which it is impossible to predict whether feelings of hostility ... will actually lead to conflict".[11]

Thus far, however, the social role of corporations has not really been a topic of open public debate. The effectiveness of the corporate system, its close identification with democratic and free market ideologies, and its symbolic position as adversary to the bogeyman of controlled economies (such as the ex-USSR) should have, in fact, forever banished its critics to the periphery which some conservative thinkers reserve for regulators, environmental fanatics and intellectual malcontents. Yet, in real terms, concerns over the legitimacy of corporate power have been growing steadily – both in the development of corporation law and public policy – since the turn of this century.

The corporation is currently experiencing the effects of a systemic crisis that gained momentum with the end of the Cold War, and will certainly not be ameliorated by the superabundance of economic, social, and political upheaval around the world. These crises – restrictions on resources, unchecked population growth in poor countries, religious and political tyranny, world hunger, ecological degradation and so on – simply cannot be resolved or even explained within the usual parameters of either political or business management.

It is clear that different groups within society hold widely divergent views on the impact and congruence of corporate operations, and the relationships between these groups have traditionally been adversarial rather than informative. As the gap widens between the general conception of the "public good" and the prevailing mandate of corporations, confidence in the business sector, and ultimately its legitimacy, is threatened.

This is perhaps best summarized by James Willard Hurst's statement that "An institution must be legitimated by its utility to some chosen end other than its own perpetuation. An institution which wields practical power – which compels men's wills or behavior – must be accountable for its purposes and its performance by criteria not wholly in control of the institution itself."[12]

The normative endowment of power which corporations enjoy – based both on the ideals surrounding private property and on its effectiveness in carrying out its tasks – has reached a kind of conceptual impasse; it is becoming increasingly necessary to redefine and examine the implications of that power in contraposition with fundamental changes in systems, interrelationships, and values.

Governing for Legitimacy in the Changing Corporate "Lifespace"

Again, the perception of legitimacy is a complex phenomenon, composed of factors in continual flux. Legitimacy has been described as a "syncretic" concept, or one which blends different ideas sharing a similar base in tradition. The interaction and interdependence of these ideas in possible situations support this description, and work together to define the legitimacy of an institution.

Some theorists have posed that the perception of legitimacy is a subjective phenomenon, based primarily on belief in the validity of a governance system (and its prevailing values) or even an extraordinary individual. Another stream of research suggests that legitimacy should derive from *rational* claims to validity that can be tested and examined independently of its social-psychological character, or the ruler–ruled relationship.

In considering the legitimacy of the corporation, the latter approach may prove more relevant in assessing changing public expectations and in defining performance measures which are, to some extent, "external to the mere floating 'conviction' of the majority".[13] The pluralism of belief in many societies, the transnational reach of large corporations, and the difficulty of identifying the actual locus of power within these organizations, necessitate a more objective view of legitimate corporate influence and control.

In addition to identifiable community, national, or regional boundaries, each corporation operates within an institutional environment that is defined by its own aims, strategies, and needs. Herbert Simon described this as follows: "We are not interested in describing some physically objective world in its totality, but only those aspects of the totality that have relevance as the 'life space' of the organism considered. Hence, what we call the 'environment' will depend upon the 'needs', 'drives,' or 'goals' of the organism, and upon its perceptual apparatus."[14]

Along with this internal perspective, the corporate environment is also defined by elements which are external to (but which have a distinct impact on) its own immediate organizational aspect: these include the characteristics of the labor force, legal and regulatory systems, consumer and capital markets, volunteer and pressure groups, governments, and extra-national agencies like the EC. All of these elements, internal and external, comprise the "lifespace" of the corporation. It is the job of the board of directors and senior management to understand and respond to changes in that lifespace, as Worthy and Neuschel point out in their definition of corporate governance:

> Governance ... is concerned largely, though ... not exclusively, with relating the corporation to the institutional environment within which it functions. Issues of governance include the legitimacy of corporate power, corporate accountability, to whom and for what the corporation is responsible, and by what standards it is to be governed and by whom.[15]

This duality of perspective – internal needs and goals versus external expectations and criteria – could be responsible for many of the gaps, perceived or actual, that occur between managers' definition of their role, and the evolving demands of society. Most managers are aware that organizational pressures are only part of the picture; yet, a thorough reconciliation between the needs of the organization and those of society presents a challenge that current business systems, and the traditional structures of management thinking, are largely unequipped to take on.

While corporate legitimacy cannot effectively be reduced to an accounting of the elements in a company's lifespace, this optic demonstrates that the investment and maintenance of an institution's authority and power is a complex mix of both rational and "gut-level" ingredients. In other words, institutions must base their claims to authority on both a task-based public mandate, and on a fundamental set of beliefs. The business corporation and its management have thus far operated relatively freely under both of these legitimating umbrellas: their activities were not only validated by a belief in free enterprise and the rights of property, but also by the effectiveness of this form of organization in meeting economic goals.

Although capitalist societies and systems have always had their critics, it was generally accepted that, overall, the good outweighed the bad – particularly in comparison to other systems and societies. This is no longer the immutable truth it once was, however. While no completely viable models have yet arisen to replace current systems, the steady emergence of conflicting interests and large-scale problems – and our seeming inability to adequately assimilate or address these issues on a systematic basis – have diminished our ability to rest on the performance, or the rationales, of the past.

What does this mean, ultimately, for the management and governance of large firms? Probably quite a lot; but, as Daniel Bell pointed out, feudalism did not disappear overnight. Processes of fundamental social and economic change evolve gradually, along with the ideas and material realities that drive them.

It is clearly in business's long-term interest to promote healthy, prosperous, and stable societies. If political and public-sector leaders continue to jettison their share of the burden in creating such a climate, corporations will have to pick up the pieces or suffer the results. This is already evidenced by companies' increased involvement in, for example, education and training programmes. The fundamental problem here lies in the fact that, in democratic societies, social tasks *should*, for the most part, be handled by capable public servants properly chosen in free elections. While the corporation is undeniably a dominant social institution, with proven organizational talents, it is neither desirable nor justifiable to expect industry to shape the future of societies according to its own needs alone.

Yet, corporations will continue to have a responsibility for, and a stake in, the health and well-being of societies, including developing countries and the natural environment. Rather than defaulting to some kind of ill-advised "corporatism", or, worse, adopting the "let them eat cake" philosophy of some past leaders, the maintenance of corporate legitimacy requires that managers engage actively in comprehensive information gathering, analysis, and reflection on changes in the social and business environment – a process which includes open and non-adversarial discourse with stakeholders before decision-making. This may, eventually, necessitate quite different corporate structures, and will certainly mean a reassessment of *how* information about the environment is gathered and categorized. As one educator writes, "[Corporate] survival is becoming contingent on the ability to see and manage many interrelationships, some going far beyond traditional commercial links".[16]

In terms of these interrelationships, and the challenges facing both public and private sector managers in the future, the world is getting bigger, not smaller; to understand and weather the changes that lie ahead, these leaders will need to rely on a strong fabric of perceived legitimacy in the lifespace of their organizations.

Summary of the Text

This collection of essays and excerpts on the subject of corporate legitimacy was compiled to help those interested in the implications of this notion – researchers, students, business executives, and others – understand some of the basic issues surrounding the phenomenon of modern corporate power. It is intended as an introduction to the topic and literature, and by no means does it, or could it, present every side of each argument concerning the legitimacy of the large corporation. The excerpts and reprinted articles were, rather, selected on the basis of their comprehensiveness, provocative ideas, and their representation of the various points of view to be found in these discussions.

The book is divided into three parts which loosely delineate the three main streams of literature regarding corporate legitimacy. I will briefly outline those sections here, but it will soon become evident to the reader, as he or she reads through the various pieces, how the ideas addressed within work interactively throughout the sections and chapters.

The first part, "The Context of Corporate Legitimacy", contains original chapters and excerpts from different authors which explore the changing nature of capitalism, some broad definitions or constructions of corporate legitimacy theory vis-à-vis corporations, and some of the contradictions inherent in economic systems which can lead to legitimacy problems.

Part II examines the ongoing debate over corporate control between managers and shareholders – owners – which has, I feel, solidified certain aspects of the study of corporate legitimacy in all areas; the literature that has emerged from this discussion still stands as some of the most telling on the general topic of the corporation and society.

Hurst maintains that, prior to the late nineteenth century, corporate legitimacy questions largely surrounded the power of government as it affected corporate activity. It was not until certain other concerns regarding that activity became worrisome to both the public and law-makers that the shift was made from questions of irresponsible *public* power to the unchecked or unmanageable use of *private* power; this latter issue being, in the final analysis, what all questions of corporate legitimacy boil down to. It was not until the 1930s, however, that those questions found their full voice, and they found it in the context of the owner/manager control debate – a conflict which continues to evolve, yet never resolve, as ownership structures change and modify over time (as evidenced by the piece from Robert Monks).

I should note that although this discussion, and others surrounding corporate legitimacy, could very easily be investigated within the parameters of Agency Theory (legitimacy crises being "agency problems" *in extremis*), several authors have already covered this ground pretty comprehensively elsewhere. Rather than end up being merely derivative of their work, I prefer to direct the reader to those authors and keep this set of readings within a more unstructured, social science type of framework.

Part III raises certain other legitimacy issues in more detail, issues that have arisen from the changing role of the corporation in global society. These essays demonstrate how legitimacy theory can aid our thinking about corporations and their governance, and far from being exhaustive, are more of a tease which will (hopefully) stimulate other researchers and analysts to use this optic in their explorations of the society and corporation interface.

A selected bibliography with occasional annotations is appended to the text of this book.

Notes

1 Parsons, Talcott 1960: *Structure and Process in Modern Societies*. New York: Free Press.
2 Berger, Peter 1981: New Attack on the Legitimacy of Business. *Harvard Business Review*, September/October, 82–9.
3 Stillman, Peter G. 1974: The Concept of Legitimacy. *Polity*, 10, 39–42.
4 Although I may use the terms "authority" and "power" synonymously on occasion, the two do not exactly describe the same phenomenon. Many theorists have debated the difference between these terms, so rather than revisiting that discussion in detail, I would like to simplify the distinction as follows: one may *take* power, but ultimately needs authority to *keep* it. Authority, then, implies access to legal and moral legitimacy in the view of the majority; the possession of power can, however, lead to a gradual investment of this authority over time, based on the normative and interactive characteristics of the legitimation process. I think one could safely say that, at this point in time, the business corporation is in possession of both power and authority. The reader who is interested in pursuing this debate further should refer to Hannah Arendt, *On Revolution*, Barbara Goodwin's *Using Political Ideas*, or David Held, *Political Theory and the Modern State*. Full references are in the bibliography.
5 Davis, John P. 1905: *Corporations: A Study of the Origin and Development of Great Business Combinations and of their Relation to the Authority of the State*. New York: G. P. Putnam's Sons (reprint by W. S. Hein, Buffalo New York). Quotation from Introduction.
6 Heilbroner, Robert 1988: *Behind the Veil of Economics*. New York: W. W. Norton, 44.
7 Mason, Edward S. 1959: *The Corporation in Modern Society*. Cambridge Mass: Harvard University Press, introduction.
8 Davis, introduction.
9 Bell, Daniel 1974: The Post-industrial Society. In Herman Kahn, *The Future of the Corporation*, New York: Mason & Lipscomb, 12–46.
10 Mason, 5.
11 Coser, Lewis 1956: *The Functions of Social Conflict*. New York: Free Press.
12 Hurst, James Willard 1970: *The Legitimacy of the Business Corporation in the Law of the United States 1780–1970*. Charlottesville VA: University of Virginia Press, 59.
13 Merquior, J. G. 1980: *Rousseau and Weber: Two Studies in the Theory of Legitimacy*. London: Routledge and Kegan Paul.
14 Simon, Herbert 1956: Rational Choice and the Structure of the Environment. *Psychological Review*, 63, 129–38.

15 Worthy, James C. and Neuschel, Robert P. 1983: *Emerging Issues in Corporate Governance*. Chicago: Northwestern University Press.

16 Aykaç, Ahmet 1991: Prospectus for IMD's International Programme for Senior Executives.

Part I

The Context of Corporate Legitimacy

1

Transformations of the Capitalist Institutional Framework

JOSEPH A. SCHUMPETER

There is the capitalist art and the capitalist style of life. If we limit ourselves to painting as an example, both for brevity's sake and because in that field my ignorance is slightly less complete than it is in others, and if (wrongly, as I think) we agree to start an epoch with Giotto's Arena frescoes and then follow the line (nothing short of damnable though such "linear" arguments are) Giotto–Masaccio–Vinci–Michelangelo–Greco, no amount of emphasis on mystical ardors in the case of Greco can obliterate my point for anyone who has eyes that see. And Vinci's experiments are offered to doubters who wish, as it were, to touch the capitalist rationality with their fingertips. This line if projected (yes, I know) could be made to land us (though perhaps gasping) in the contrast between Delacroix and Ingres. Well, and there we are; Cézanne, Van Gogh, Picasso or Matisse will do the rest. Expressionist liquidation of the object forms an admirably logical conclusion. The story of the capitalist novel (culminating in the Goncourt novel: "documents written up") would illustrate still better. But that is obvious. The evolution of the capitalist style of life could be easily – and perhaps most tellingly – described in terms of the genesis of the modern lounge suit.

There is finally all that may be grouped around the symbolic centerpiece of Gladstonian liberalism. The term Individualist Democracy would do just as well – better in fact because we want to cover some things that Gladstone would not have approved and a moral and spiritual attitude which, dwelling in the citadel of faith, he actually hated. At that I could leave this point if radical liturgy did not consist largely in picturesque denials of what I mean to convey. Radicals may insist that the masses are crying for salvation from intolerable sufferings and rattling their chains in darkness and despair, but of course there never was so much personal freedom of mind and body *for all*, never so much readiness to bear with and even to finance the mortal enemies of the leading class, never so much active sympathy with real and faked sufferings, never so much readiness to accept burdens, as there is in modern capitalist society; and whatever democracy there was, outside of peasant communities, developed historically in the wake of both modern and ancient capitalism. Again plenty of facts can be adduced from the past to make up a counterargument that will be effective but is irrelevant in a discussion of present conditions and future alternatives.[1] If we do decide to embark upon historical disquisition at all, then even many of those facts which to radical critics may seem to be the most eligible ones for their purpose will often look differently if viewed in the light of a comparison with the corresponding facts of pre-capitalist experience. And it cannot be replied that "those were different times." For it is precisely the capitalist process that made the difference.

Two points in particular must be mentioned. I have pointed out before that social legislation or, more generally, institutional change for the benefit of the masses is not simply something which has been forced upon capitalist society by an ineluctable necessity to alleviate the ever-deepening misery of the poor but that, besides raising the standard of living of the masses by virtue of its automatic effects, the capitalist process also provided for that legislation the means "and the will." The words in quotes require further explanation that is to be found in the principle of spreading rationality. The capitalist process rationalizes behavior and ideas and by so doing chases from our minds, along with metaphysical belief, mystic and romantic ideas of all sorts. Thus it reshapes not only our methods of attaining our ends but also these ultimate ends themselves. "Free thinking" in the sense of materialistic monism, laicism and pragmatic acceptance of the world this side of the grave follow from this not indeed by logical necessity but nevertheless very naturally. On the one hand, our inherited sense of duty, deprived of its traditional basis, becomes focused in utilitarian ideas about the betterment of mankind which, quite illogically to be sure, seem to withstand rationalist criticism better than, say, the fear of God does. On the other hand, the same rationalization of the soul rubs off all the glamour of super-empirical sanction from every species of classwise rights. This then, together with the typically capitalist enthusiasm for Efficiency and Service – so completely different from the body of ideas which would have been associated with those terms by the typical knight of old – breeds that "will" within the bourgeoisie itself. Feminism, an essentially capitalist phenomenon, illustrates the point still more clearly. The reader will realize that these tendencies must be understood "objectively" and that therefore no amount of anti-feminist or anti-reformist talk or even of temporary opposition to any particular measure proves anything against this analysis. These things are the very symptoms of the tendencies they pretend to fight.

Also, capitalist civilization is rationalistic "and anti-heroic." The two go together of course. Success in industry and commerce requires a lot of stamina, yet industrial and commercial activity is essentially unheroic in the knight's sense – no flourishing of swords about it, not much physical prowess, no chance to gallop the armored horse into the enemy, preferably a heretic or heathen – and the ideology that glorifies the idea of fighting for fighting's sake and of victory for victory's sake understandably withers in the office among all the columns of figures. Therefore, owning assets that are apt to attract the robber or the tax gatherer and not sharing or even disliking warrior ideology that conflicts with its "rational" utilitarianism, the industrial and commercial bourgeoisie is fundamentally pacifist and inclined to insist on the application of the moral precepts of private life to international relations. It is true that, unlike most but like some other features of capitalist civilization, pacifism and international morality have also been espoused in non-capitalist environments and by pre-capitalist agencies, in the Middle Ages by the Roman Church for instance. Modern pacifism and modern international morality are nonetheless products of capitalism.

In view of the fact that Marxian doctrine – especially Neo-Marxian doctrine and even a considerable body of non-socialist opinion – is, as we have seen in the first part of this book, strongly opposed to this proposition it is necessary to point out that the latter is not meant to deny that many a bourgeoisie has put up a splendid fight for hearth and home, or that almost purely bourgeois commonwealths were often aggressive when it seemed to pay – like the Athenian or the Venetian commonwealths – or that no bourgeoisie ever disliked war profits and advantages to trade accruing from conquest or refused to be trained in warlike nationalism by its feudal masters or leaders or by the propaganda of some specially interested group. All I hold is, first, that such instances of capitalist combativeness are not, as Marxism has it, to be explained – exclusively or primarily – in terms of class interests or class situations that systematically engender capitalist wars of conquest; second, that there is a difference between doing that which you consider your normal business in life, for which you prepare yourself in season and out of season and in terms of which you define your success or failure, and doing what is not in your line, for which your normal work and your mentality do not fit you and success in which will increase the prestige of the most unbourgeois of professions; and third, that this difference steadily tells – in international as well as in domestic affairs – against the use of military force and for peaceful arrangements, even where the balance of pecuniary advantage is clearly on the side of war which, under modern circumstances, is not in general very likely. As a matter of fact, the more completely capitalist the structure and attitude of a nation, the more pacifist – and the more prone to count the costs of war – we observe it to be. Owing to the complex nature of every individual pattern, this could be fully brought out only by detailed historical analysis. But the bourgeois attitude to the military (standing armies), the spirit in which and the methods by which bourgeois societies wage war, and the readiness with which, in any serious case of prolonged warfare, they submit to non-bourgeois rule are conclusive in themselves. The Marxist theory that imperialism is the last stage of capitalist evolution therefore fails quite irrespective of purely economic objections.

But I am not going to sum up as the reader presumably expects me to. That is to say, I am not going to invite him, before he decides to put his trust in an untried alternative advocated by untried men, to look once more at the impressive economic and the still more impressive cultural achievement of the capitalist order and at the immense promise held out by both. I am not going to argue that achievement and that promise are in themselves sufficient to support an argument for allowing the capitalist process to work on and, as it might easily be put, to lift poverty from the shoulders of mankind.

There would be no sense in this. Even if mankind were as free to choose as a businessman is free to choose between two competing pieces of machinery, no determined value judgement necessarily follows from the facts and relations between facts that I have tried to convey. As regards the economic performance, it does not follow that men are "happier" or even "better off" in the industrial society of today than they were in a medieval manor or village. As regards the cultural performance, one may accept every word I have written and yet hate it – its utilitarianism and the wholesale destruction of Meanings incident to it – from the bottom of one's heart. Moreover, one may care less for the efficiency of the capitalist process in producing economic and cultural values than for the kind of human beings that it turns out and then leaves to their own devices, free to make a mess of their lives. There is a type of radical whose adverse verdict about capitalist civilization rests on nothing except stupidity, ignorance or irresponsibility, who is unable or unwilling to grasp the most obvious facts, let alone their wider implications. But a completely adverse verdict may also be arrived at on a higher plane.

However, whether favorable or unfavorable, value judgements about capitalist performance are of little interest. For mankind is not free to choose. This is not only because the mass of people are not in a position to compare alternatives rationally and always accept what they are being told. There is a much deeper reason for it. Things economic and social move by their own momentum and the ensuing situations compel individuals and groups to behave in certain ways whatever they may wish to do – not indeed by destroying their freedom of choice but by shaping the choosing mentalities and by narrowing the list of possibilities from which to choose. If this is the quintessence of Marxism then we all of us have got to be Marxists. In consequence, capitalist performance is not even relevant for prognosis. Most civilizations have disappeared before they had time to fill to the full the measure of their promise. Hence I am not going to argue, on the strength of that performance, that the capitalist intermezzo is likely to be prolonged. In fact, I am now going to draw the exactly opposite inference.

I. The Obsolescence of the Entrepreneurial Function

In our discussion of the theory of vanishing investment opportunity, a reservation was made in favor of the possibility that the economic wants of humanity might some day be so completely satisfied that little motive would be left to push productive effort still further ahead. Such a state of satiety is no doubt very far off even if we keep within the present scheme of wants; and if we take account of the fact that, as higher standards of life are attained, these wants automatically expand and new wants emerge or are created,[2] satiety becomes a flying goal, particularly if we include leisure among consumers' goods. However, let us glance at that possibility, assuming, still more unrealistically, that methods of production have reached a state of perfection which does not admit of further improvement.

A more or less stationary state would ensue. Capitalism, being essentially an evolutionary process, would become atrophic. There would be nothing left for entrepreneurs to do. They would find themselves in much the same situation as generals would in a society perfectly sure of permanent peace. Profits and along with profits the rate of interest would converge toward zero. The bourgeois strata that live on profits and interest would tend to disappear. The management of industry and trade would become a matter of current administration, and the personnel would unavoidably acquire the characteristics of a bureaucracy. Socialism of a very sober type would almost automatically come into being. Human energy would turn away from business. Other than economic pursuits would attract the brains and provide the adventure.

For the calculable future this vision is of no importance. But all the greater importance attaches to the fact that many of the effects on the structure of society and on the organization of the productive process that we might expect from an approximately complete satisfaction of wants or from absolute technological perfection can also be expected from a development that is clearly observable already. Progress itself may be mechanized as well as the management of a stationary economy, and this mechanization of progress may affect entrepreneurship and capitalist society nearly as much as the cessation of economic progress would. In order to see this it is only necessary to restate, first, what the entrepreneurial function consists in and, secondly, what it means for bourgeois society and the survival of the capitalist order.

We have seen that the function of entrepreneurs is to reform or revolutionize the pattern of production by exploiting an invention or, more generally, an untried technological possibility for producing a new commodity or producing an old one in a new way, by opening up a new source of supply of materials or a new outlet for products, by reorganizing an industry and so on. Railroad construction in its earlier stages, electrical power production before the First World War, steam and steel, the motorcar, colonial ventures afford spectacular instances of a large genus which comprises innumerable humbler ones – down to things as making a success of a particular kind of sausage or toothbrush. This kind of activity is primarily responsible for the recurrent "prosperities" that revolutionize the economic organism and the recurrent "recessions" that are due to the disequilibrating impact of the new products or methods. To undertake such new things is difficult and constitutes a distinct economic function, first, because they lie outside of the routine tasks which everybody understands and, secondly, because the environment resists in many ways that vary, according to social conditions, from simple refusal either to finance or to buy a new thing, to physical attack on the man who tries to produce it. To act with confidence beyond the range of familiar beacons and to overcome that resistance requires aptitudes that are present in only a small fraction of the population and that define the entrepreneurial type as well as the entrepreneurial function. This function does not essentially consist in either inventing anything or otherwise creating the conditions which the enterprise exploits. It consists in getting things done.

This social function is already losing importance and is bound to lose it at an accelerating rate in the future even if the economic process itself of which entrepreneurship was the prime mover went on unabated. For, on the one hand, it is much easier now than it has been in the past to do things that lie outside familiar routine – innovation itself is being reduced to routine. Technological progress is increasingly becoming the business of teams of trained specialists who turn out what is required and make it work in predictable ways. The romance of earlier commercial adventure is rapidly wearing away, because so many more things can be strictly calculated that had of old to be visualized in a flash of genius.

On the other hand, personality and will power must count for less in environments which have become accustomed to economic change – best instanced by an incessant stream of new consumers' and producers' goods – and which, instead of resisting, accept it as a matter of course. The resistance which comes from interests threatened by an innovation in the productive process is not likely to die out as long as the capitalist order persists. It is, for instance, the great obstacle on the road toward mass production of cheap housing which presupposes radical mechanization and wholesale elimination of inefficient methods of work on the plot. But every other kind of resistance – the resistance, in particular, of consumers and producers to a new kind of thing because it is new – has well-nigh vanished already.

Thus, economic progress tends to become depersonalized and automatized. Bureau and committee work tends to replace individual action. Once more, reference to the military analogy will help to bring out the essential point.

Of old, roughly up to and including the Napoleonic Wars, generalship meant leadership and success meant the personal success of the man in command who earned corresponding "profits" in terms of social prestige. The technique of warfare and the structure of armies being what they were, the individual decision and driving power of the leading man – even his actual presence on a showy horse – were essential elements in the strategical and tactical situations. Napoleon's presence was, and had to be, actually felt on his battlefields. This is no longer so. Rationalized and specialized office work will eventually blot out personality, the calculable result, the "vision". The leading man no longer has the opportunity to fling himself into the fray. He is becoming just another office worker – and one who is not always difficult to replace.

Or take another military analogy. Warfare in the Middle Ages was a very personal affair. The armored knights practiced an art that required lifelong training and every one of them counted individually by virtue of personal skill and prowess. It is easy to understand why this craft should have become the basis of a social class in the fullest and richest sense of that term. But social and technological change undermined and eventually destroyed both the function and the position of that class. Warfare itself did not cease on that account. It simply became more and more mechanized – eventually so much so that success in what now is a mere profession no longer carries that connotation of individual achievement, which would raise not only the man but also his group into a durable position of social leadership.

Now a similar social process – in the last analysis the same social process – undermines the role and, along with the role, the social position of the capitalist entrepreneur. His role, though less glamorous than that of medieval warlords, great or small, also is or was just another form of individual leadership acting by virtue of personal force and personal responsibility for success. His position, like that of warrior classes, is threatened as soon as this function in the social process loses its importance, and no less if this is due to the cessation of the social needs it served than if those needs are being served by other, more impersonal, methods.

But this affects the position of the entire bourgeois stratum. Although entrepreneurs are not necessarily or even typically elements of that stratum from the outset, they nevertheless enter it in case of success. Thus, though entrepreneurs do not *per se* form a social class, the bourgeois class absorbs them and their families and connections, thereby recruiting and revitalizing itself currently while at the same time the families that sever their active relation to "business" drop out of it after a generation or two. Between, there is the bulk of what we refer to as industrialists, merchants, financiers and bankers; they are in the inter- mediate stage between entrepreneurial venture and mere current administration of an inherited domain. The returns on which the class lives are produced by, and the social position of the class rests on, the success of this more or less active sector – which of course may, as it does in this country [US], form over 90 percent of the bourgeois stratum – and of the individuals who are in the act of rising into that class. Economically and sociologically, directly and indirectly, the bourgeoisie therefore depends on the entrepreneur and, as a class, lives and will die with him, though a more or less prolonged transitional stage – eventually a stage in which it may feel equally unable to die and to live – is quite likely to occur, as in fact it did occur in the case of the feudal civilization.

To sum up this part of our argument: if capitalist evolution – "progress" – either ceases or becomes completely automatic, the economic basis of the industrial bourgeoisie will be reduced eventually to wages such as are paid for current administrative work excepting remnants of quasi-rents and monopoloid gains that may be expected to linger on for some time. Since capitalist enterprise, by its very achievements, tends to automatize progress, we conclude that it tends to make itself superfluous – to break to pieces under the pressure of its own success. The perfectly bureaucratized giant industrial unit not only ousts the small or medium-sized firm and "expropriates" its owners, but in the end it also ousts the entrepreneur and expropriates the bourgeoisie as a class which in the process stands to lose not only its income but also what is infinitely more important, its function. The true pacemakers of socialism were not the intellectuals and agitators who preached it but the Vanderbilts, Carnegies and Rockefellers. This result may not in every respect be to the taste of Marxian socialists, still less to the taste of socialists of a more popular (Marx would have said, vulgar) description. But so far as prognosis goes, it does not differ from theirs.

II.   The Destruction of the Protecting Strata

So far we have been considering the effects of capitalist process upon the economic bases of the upper strata of capitalist society and upon their social position and prestige. But effects further extend to the institutional framework that protected them. In showing this we shall take the term in its widest acceptance so as to include not only legal institutions but also attitudes of the public mind and policies.

1. Capitalist evolution first of all destroyed, or went far toward destroying, the institutional arrangements of the feudal world – the manor, the village, the craft guild. The facts and mechanisms of this process are too familiar to detain us. Destruction was wrought in three ways. The world of the artisan was destroyed primarily by the automatic effects of the competition that came from the capitalist entrepreneur; political action in removing atrophic organizations and regulations only registered results. The world of the lord and the peasant was destroyed primarily by political – in some cases revolutionary – action and capitalism merely presided over adaptive transformations say, of the German manorial organizations into large-scale agricultural units of production. But along with these industrial and agrarian revolutions went a no less revolutionary change in the general attitude of legislative authority and public opinion. Together with the old economic organization vanished the economic and political privileges of the classes or groups that used to play the leading role in it, particularly the tax exemptions and the political prerogatives of the landed nobility and gentry and of the clergy.

Economically all this meant for the bourgeoisie the breaking of so many fetters and the removal of so many barriers. Politically it meant the replacement of an order in which the bourgeois was a humble subject by another that was more congenial to his rationalist mind and to his immediate interests. But, surveying that process from the standpoint of today, the observer might well wonder whether in the end such complete emancipation was good for the bourgeois and his world. For those fetters not only hampered, they sheltered. Before proceeding further we must carefully clarify and appraise this point.

2. The related process of the rise of the capitalist bourgeoisie and of the rise of national states produced, in the sixteenth, seventeenth and eighteenth centuries, a social structure that may seem to us amphibial though it was no more amphibial or transitional than any other. Consider the outstanding instance that is afforded by the monarchy of Louis XIV. The royal power had subjugated the landed aristocracy and at the same time conciliated it by proferring employment and pensions and by conditionally accepting its claim to a ruling or leading class position. The same royal power had subjugated and allied itself with the clergy.[3] It had finally strengthened its sway over the bourgeoisie, its old ally in the struggle with the territorial magnates, protecting and propelling its enterprise in order to exploit it the more effectively in turn. Peasants and the (small) industrial proletariat were likewise

managed, exploited and protected by public authority – though the protection was in the case of the French *ancien régime* very much less in evidence than for instance in the Austria of Maria Theresa or of Joseph II – and, vicariously, by landlords or industrialists. This was not simply a government in the sense of nineteenth-century liberalism, i.e., a social agency existing for the performance of a few limited functions to be financed by a minimum of revenue. On principle, the monarchy managed everything, from consciences to the patterns of the silk fabrics of Lyons, and financially it aimed at a maximum of revenue. Though the king was never really absolute, public authority was all-comprehensive.

Correct diagnosis of this pattern is of the utmost importance for our subject. The king, the court, the army, the church and the bureaucracy lived to an increasing extent on revenue created by the capitalist process, even purely feudal sources of income being swelled in consequence of contemporaneous capitalist developments. To an increasing extent also, domestic and foreign policies and institutional changes were shaped to suit and propel that development. *As far as that goes*, the feudal elements in the structure of the so-called absolute monarchy come in only under the heading of atavisms which in fact is the diagnosis one would naturally adapt at first sight.

Looking more closely, however, we realize that those elements meant more than that. The steel frame of that structure still consisted of the human material of feudal society and this material still behaved according to precapitalist patterns. It filled the offices of state, officered the army, devised policies – it functioned as a *class dirigente* and, though taking account of bourgeois interests, it took care to distance itself from the bourgeoisie. The centerpiece, the king, was king by the grace of God, and the root of his position was feudal, not only in the historical but also in the sociological sense, however much he availed himself of the economic possibilities offered by capitalism. All this was more than atavism. It was an active symbiosis of two social strata, one of which no doubt supported the other economically but was in turn supported by the other politically. Whatever we may think of the achievements or shortcomings of this arrangement, whatever the bourgeois himself may have thought of it at the time or later – and of the aristocratic scapegrace or idler – it was of the essence of that society.

3. Of *that* society only? The subsequent course of things, best exemplified by the English case, suggests the answer. The aristocratic element continued to rule the roost *right to the end of the period of intact*

and vital capitalism. No doubt that element – though nowhere so effectively as in England – currently absorbed the brains from other strata that drifted into politics; it made itself the representative of bourgeois interests and fought the battles of the bourgeoisie; it had to surrender its last legal privileges; but with these qualifications, and for ends no longer its own, it continued to man the political engine, to manage the state, to govern.

The economically operative part of the bourgeois strata did not offer much opposition to this. On the whole, that kind of division of labor suited them and they liked it. Where they did revolt against it or where they got into the political saddle without having to revolt, they did not make a conspicuous success of ruling and did not prove able to hold their own. The question arises whether it is really safe to assume that these failures were merely due to lack of opportunity to acquire experience and, with experience, the attitudes of a politically ruling class.

It is not. There is a more fundamental reason for those failures such as are instanced by the French or German experiences with bourgeois attempts at ruling – a reason which again will best be visualized by contrasting the figure of the industrialist or merchant with that of the medieval lord. The latter's "profession" not only qualified him admirably for the defense of his own class interest – he was not only able to fight for it physically – but it also cast a halo around him and made of him a ruler of men. The first was important, but more so were the mystic glamor and the lordly attitude – that ability and habit to command and to be obeyed that carried prestige with all classes of society and in every walk of life. That prestige was so great and that attitude so useful that the class position outlived the social and technological conditions which had given rise to it and proved adaptable, by means of a transformation of the class function, to quite different social and economic conditions. With the utmost ease and grace the lords and knights metamorphosed themselves into courtiers, administrators, diplomats, politicians and into military officers of a type that had nothing whatever to do with that of the medieval knight. And – most astonishing phenomenon when we come to think of it – a remnant of that old prestige survives even to this day, and not only with our ladies.

Of the industrialist and merchant the opposite is true. There is surely no trace of any mystic glamor about him which is what counts in the ruling of men. The stock exchange is a poor substitute for the Holy Grail. We have seen that the industrialist and merchant, as far as they are entrepreneurs, also fill a function of leadership. But economic leadership of this type does not readily expand, like the medieval lord's military leadership, into the leadership of nations. On the contrary, the ledger and cost calculation absorb and confine.

I have called the bourgeois rationalist and unheroic. He can only use rationalist and unheroic means to defend his position or to bend a nation to his will. He can impress by what people may expect from his economic performance, he can argue his case, he can promise to pay out money or threaten to withhold it, he can hire the treacherous services of a *condottiere* or politician or journalist. But that is all and all of it is greatly overrated as to its political value. Nor are his experiences and habits of life of the kind that develop personal fascination. A genius in the business office may be, and often is, utterly unable outside of it to say boo to a goose – both in the drawing room and on the platform. Knowing this he wants to be left alone and to leave politics alone.

Again exceptions will occur to the reader. But again they do not amount to much. Aptitude for, and interest and success in, city management is the only important exception in Europe, and this will be found to strengthen our case instead of weakening it. Before the advent of the modern metropolis, which is no longer a bourgeois affair, city management was akin to business management. Grasp of its problems and authority within its precincts came naturally to the manufacturer and trader, and the local interests of manufacturing and trading supplied most of the subject matter of its politics which therefore lent itself to treatment by the methods and in the spirit of the business office. Under exceptionally favorable conditions, exceptional developments sprouted from those roots, such as the developments of the Venetian or Genoese republics. The case of the Low Countries enters into the same pattern, but it is particularly instructive by virtue of the fact that the merchants' republic invariably failed in the great game of international politics and that in practically every emergency it had to hand over the reins to a warlord of feudal complexion. As regards the United States, it would be easy to list the uniquely favorable circumstances – rapidly waning – that explain its case.

4.   The inference is obvious: barring such exceptional conditions, the bourgeois class is ill equipped to face the problems, both domestic and international, that have normally to be faced by a country of any importance. The bourgeois themselves feel this in spite of all the

phraseology that seems to deny it, and so do the masses. Within a protective framework not made of bourgeois material, the bourgeoisie may be successful, not only in the political defensive but also in the offensive, especially as an opposition. For a time it felt so safe as to be able to afford the luxury of attacking the protective frame itself; such bourgeois opposition as there was in imperial Germany illustrates this to perfection. But without protection by some non-bourgeois group, the bourgeoisie is politically helpless and unable not only to lead its nation but even to take care of its particular class interest. Which amounts to saying that it needs a master.

But the capitalist process, both by its economic mechanics and by its psycho-sociological effects, did away with this protecting master or, as in this country, never gave him, or a substitute for him, a chance to develop. The implications of this are strengthened by another consequence of the same process. Capitalist evolution eliminates not only the king *Dei Gratia* but also the political entrenchments that, had they proved tenable, would have been formed by the village and the craft guild. Of course, neither organization was tenable in the precise shape in which capitalism found it. But capitalist policies wrought destruction much beyond what was unavoidable. They attacked the artisan in reservations in which he could have survived for an indefinite time. They forced upon the peasant all the blessings of early liberalism – the free and unsheltered holding and all the individualist rope he needed in order to hang himself.

In breaking down the pre-capitalist framework of society, capitalism thus broke not only barriers that impeded its progress but also flying buttresses that prevented its collapse. That process, impressive in its relentless necessity, was not merely a matter of removing institutional deadwood, but of removing partners of the capitalist stratum, symbiosis with whom was an essential element of the capitalist schema. Having discovered this fact which so many slogans obscure, we might well wonder whether it is quite correct to look upon capitalism as a social form *sui generis* or, in fact, as anything else but the last stage of the decomposition of what we have called feudalism. On the whole, I am inclined to believe that its peculiarities suffice to make a type and to accept that symbiosis of classes which owe their existence to different epochs and processes as the rule rather than the exception – at least it has been the rule these 6,000 years, i.e., ever since primitive tillers of the soil became the subjects of mounted nomads. But there is no great objection that I can see against the opposite view alluded to.

III. The Destruction of the Institutional Framework of Capitalist Society

We return from our digression with a load of ominous facts. They are almost, though not quite, sufficient to establish our next point, viz., that the capitalist process in much the same way in which it destroyed the institutional framework of feudal society also undermines its own.

It has been pointed out above that the very success of capitalist enterprise paradoxically tends to impair the prestige or social weight of the class primarily associated with it and that the giant unit of control tends to oust the bourgeoisie from the function to which it owed that social weight. The corresponding change in the meaning, and the incidental loss in vitality, of the institutions of the bourgeois world and of its typical attitudes are easy to trace.

On the one hand, the capitalist process unavoidably attacks the economic standing ground of the small producer and trader. What it did to the pre-capitalist strata it also does – and by the same competitive mechanisms – to the lower strata of capitalist industry. Here of course Marx scores. It is true that the facts of industrial concentration do not quite live up to the ideas the public is being taught to entertain about it. The process has gone less far and is less free from setbacks and compensatory tendencies than one would gather from many a popular exposition. In particular, large-scale enterprise not only annihilates but also, to some extent, creates space for the small producing, and especially trading, firm. Also, in the case of the peasants and farmers, the capitalist world has at last proved both willing and able to pursue an expensive but on the whole effective policy of conservation. In the long run, however, there can be little doubt about the fact we are envisaging, or about its consequences. Outside of the agrarian field, moreover, the bourgeoisie has shown but little awareness of the problem[4] or its importance for the survival of the capitalist order. The profits to be made by rationalizing the organization of production and especially by cheapening the tortuous way of commodities from the factory to the ultimate consumer are more than the mind of the typical businessman can resist.

Now it is important to realize precisely what these consequences consist in. A very common type of social criticism which we have already met laments the "decline of competition" and equates it to the decline of capitalism because of the virtues it attributes to competition and the vices it attributes to modern industrial "monopolies." In this schema of interpretation, monopolization plays the role of arteriosclerosis and reacts upon the fortunes of the capitalist order through increasingly unsatisfactory economic performance. We have seen the reasons for rejecting this view. Economically neither the case for competition nor the case against concentration of economic control is anything like as strong as this argument implies. And, whether weak or strong, it misses the salient point. Even if the giant concerns were all managed so perfectly as to call forth applause from the angels in heaven, the political consequences of concentration would still be what they are. The political structure of a nation is profoundly affected by the elimination of a host of small and medium-sized firms the owner-managers of which, together with their dependents, henchmen and connections, count quantitatively at the polls and have a hold on what we may term the foreman class that no management of a large unit can ever have; the very foundation of private property and free contracting wears away in a nation in which its most vital, most concrete, most meaningful types disappear from the moral horizon of the people.

On the other hand, the capitalist process also attacks its own institutional framework – let us continue to visualize "property" and "free contracting" as *partes pro toto* – within the precincts of the big units. Excepting the cases that are still of considerable importance in which a corporation is practically owned by a single individual or family, the figure of the proprietor and with it the specifically proprietary interest have vanished from the picture. There are the salaried executives and all the salaried managers and submanagers. There are the big stockholders. And then there are the small stockholders. The first group tends to acquire the employee attitude and rarely if ever identifies itself with the stockholding interest even in the most favorable cases, i.e., in the cases in which it identifies itself with the interest of the concern as such. The second group, even if it considers its connection with the concern as permanent and even if it actually behaves as financial theory would have stockholders behave, is at one remove from both the functions and the attitudes of an owner. As to the third group, small stockholders often do not care much about what for most of them is but a minor source of income and, whether they care or not, they hardly ever bother, unless they or some representatives of theirs are out to exploit their nuisance value; being often very ill used and still more often thinking themselves ill used, they almost regularly drift into an attitude hostile to "their" corporations, to big business in general and, particularly when things look bad, to the capitalist order as such. No element of any of those three groups into which I schematized the typical situation unconditionally takes the attitude characteristic of that curious phenomenon, so full of meaning and so rapidly passing, that is covered by the term Property.

Freedom of contracting is in the same boat. In its full vitality it meant individual contracting regulated by individual choice between an indefinite number of possibilities. The stereotyped, unindividual, impersonal and bureaucratized contract of today – this applies much more generally, but *a potiori* we may fasten upon the labor contract – which presents but restricted freedom of choice and mostly turns on a *c'est à prendre ou à laisser*, has none of the old features the most important of which become impossible with giant concerns dealing with other giant concerns or impersonal masses of workmen or consumers. The void is being filled by a tropical growth of new legal structures – and a little reflection shows that this could hardly be otherwise.

Thus the capitalist process pushes into the background all those institutions, the institutions of property and free contracting in particular, that expressed the needs and ways of the truly "private" economic activity. Where it does not abolish them, as it already has abolished free contracting in the labor market, it attains the same end by shifting the relative importance of existing legal forms – the legal forms pertaining to corporate business for instance as against those pertaining to the partnership or individual firm – or by changing their contents or meanings. The capitalist process, by substituting a mere parcel of shares for the walls of and the machines in a factory, takes the life out of the idea of property. It loosens the grip that once was so strong – the grip in the sense of the legal right and the actual ability to do as one pleases with one's own; the grip also in the sense that the holder of the title loses the will to fight, economically, physically, politically, for "his" factory and his control over it, to die if necessary on his steps. And this evaporation of what we may term the material substance of property – its visible and touchable reality – affects not only the attitude of holders but also that of the workmen and of the public in general. Dematerialized, defunctionalized and absentee ownership does not impress and call forth moral allegiance as the vital form of property did. Eventually there will be nobody left who really cares to stand for it – nobody within and nobody without the precincts of the big concerns.

IV. The Social Atmosphere of Capitalism

From the [preceding] analysis, it should not be difficult to understand how the capitalist process produced that atmosphere of almost universal hostility to its own social order to which I have referred at the threshold of this part. The phenomenon is so striking and both the Marxian and popular explanations are so inadequate that it is desirable to develop the theory of it a little further.

1. The capitalist process, so we have seen, eventually decreases the importance of the function by which the capitalist class lives. We have also seen that it tends to wear away protective strata, to break down its own defenses, to disperse the garrisons of its entrenchments. And we have finally seen that capitalism creates a critical frame of mind which, after having destroyed the moral authority of so many other institutions, in the end turns against its own; the bourgeois finds to his amazement that the rationalist attitude does not stop at the credentials of kings and popes but goes on to attack private property and the whole scheme of bourgeois values.

The bourgeois fortress thus becomes politically defenseless. Defenseless fortresses invite aggression especially if there is rich booty in them. Aggressors will work themselves up into a state of rationalizing hostility[5] – aggressors always do. No doubt it is possible, for a time, to buy them off. But this last resource fails as soon as they discover that they can have all. In part, this explains what we are out to explain. So far as it goes – it does not go the whole way of course – this element of our theory is verified by the high correlation that exists historically between bourgeois defenselessness and hostility to the capitalist order: there was very little hostility on principle as long as the bourgeois position was safe, although there was then much more reason for it; it spread *pari passu* with the crumbling of the protecting walls.

2. But, so it might well be asked – in fact, so it is being asked in naïve bewilderment by many an industrialist who honestly feels he is doing his duty by all classes of society – why should the capitalist order need any protection by extra-capitalist powers or extra-rational loyalties? Can it not come out of the trial with flying colors? Does not our own previous argument sufficiently show that it has plenty of utilitarian credentials to present? And those industrialists will assuredly not fail to point out that a sensible workman, in weighing the pros and cons of his contract with, say, one of the big steel or automobile concerns, might

well come to the conclusion that, everything considered, he is not doing so badly and that the advantages of this bargain are not all on one side. Yes – certainly, only all that is quite irrelevant.

For, first, it is an error to believe that political attack arises primarily from grievance and that it can be turned by justification. Political criticism cannot be met effectively by rational argument. From the fact that the criticism of the capitalist order proceeds from a critical attitude of mind, i.e., from an attitude which spurns allegiance to extra-rational values, it does not follow that rational refutation will be accepted. Such refutation may tear the rational garb of attack but can never reach the extra-rational driving power that always lurks behind it. Capitalist rationality does not do away with sub- or super-rational impulses. It merely makes them get out of hand by removing the restraint of sacred or semi-sacred tradition. In a civilization that lacks the means and even the will to discipline and to guide them, they will revolt. And once they revolt it matters little that, in a rationalist culture, their manifestations will in general be rationalized somehow. Just as the call for utilitarian credentials has never been addressed to kings, lords and popes in a judicial frame of mind that would accept the possibility of a satisfactory answer, so capitalism stands its trial before judges who have the sentence of death in their pockets. They are going to pass it, whatever the defense they may hear; the only success victorious defense can possibly produce is a change in the indictment. Utilitarian reason is in any case weak as a prime mover of group action. In no case is it a match for the extra-rational determinants of conduct.

Second, the success of the indictment becomes quite understandable as soon as we realize what acceptance of the case for capitalism would imply. That case, were it even much stronger than it actually is, could never be made simple. People at large would have to be possessed of an insight and a power of analysis which are altogether beyond them. Why, practically every nonsense that has ever been said about capitalism has been championed by some professed economist. But even if this is disregarded, rational recognition of the economic performance of capitalism and of the hopes it holds out for the future would require an almost impossible moral feat by the have-not. That performance stands out only if we take a long-run view; any pro-capitalist argument must rest on long-run considerations. In the short run, it is profits and inefficiencies that dominate the picture. In order to accept his lot, the leveler or the chartist of old would have had to comfort himself with hopes for his great-grandchildren. In order to identify himself with the capitalist system, the unemployed of today would have completely to forget his personal fate and the politician of today his personal ambition. The long-run interests of society are so entirely lodged with the upper strata of bourgeois society that it is perfectly natural for people to look upon them as the interests of that class only. Like Louis XV, they feel *après nous le déluge,* and from the standpoint of individualist utilitarianism they are of course being perfectly rational if they feel like that.

Third, there are the daily troubles and expectations of trouble everyone has to struggle with in any social system – the frictions and disappointments, the greater and smaller unpleasant events that hurt, annoy and thwart. I suppose that every one of us is more or less in the habit of attributing them wholly to that part of reality which lies without his skin, and emotional attachment to the social order – i.e., the very thing capitalism is constitutionally unable to produce – is necessary in order to overcome the hostile impulse by which we react to them. If there is no emotional attachment, then that impulse has its way and grows into a permanent constituent of our psychic setup.

Fourth, the ever-rising standards of life and particularly the leisure that modern capitalism provides for the fully employed workman . . . well, there is no need for me to finish the sentence or to elaborate one of the tritest, oldest and most stodgy of all arguments which unfortunately is but too true. Secular improvement that is taken for granted and coupled with individual insecurity that is acutely resented is of course the best recipe for breeding social unrest.

1.   Faced by the increasing hostility of the environment and by the legislative, administrative and judicial practice born of that hostility, entrepreneurs and capitalists – in fact the whole stratum that accepts the bourgeois scheme of life – will eventually cease to function. Their standard aims are rapidly becoming unattainable, their efforts futile. The most glamorous of these bourgeois aims, the foundation of an industrial dynasty, has in most countries become unattainable already, and even more modest ones are so difficult to attain that they may cease to be thought worth the struggle as the permanence of these conditions is being increasingly realized.

Considering the role of bourgeois motivation in the explanation of the economic history of the last two or three centuries, its smothering by the unfavorable reactions of society or its weakening by disuse no doubt constitutes a factor adequate to explain a flop in the capitalist process – should we ever observe it as a permanent phenomenon – and one that is much more important than any of those that are presented by the Theory of Vanishing Investment Opportunity. It is hence interesting to observe that that motivation not only is threatened by forces external to the bourgeois mind but that it also tends to die out from internal causes. There is of course close interdependence between the two. But we cannot get at the true diagnosis unless we try to disentangle them.

One of those "internal causes" we have already met with. I have dubbed it Evaporation of the Substance of Property. We have seen that, normally, the modern businessman, whether entrepreneur or mere managing administrator, is of the executive type. From the logic of his position he acquires something of the psychology of the salaried employee working in a bureaucratic organization. Whether a stockholder or not, his will to fight and to hold on is not and cannot be what it was with the man who knew ownership and its responsibilities in the fullblooded sense of those words. His system of values and his conception of duty undergo a profound change. Mere stockholders of course have ceased to count at all – quite independently of the clipping of their share by a regulating and taxing state. Thus the modern corporation, although the product of the capitalist process, socializes the bourgeois mind; it relentlessly narrows the scope of capitalist motivation; not only that, it will eventually kill its roots.[6]

2.   Still more important however is another "internal cause," viz., the disintegration of the bourgeois family. The facts to which I am referring are too well known to need explicit statement. To men and women in modern capitalist societies, family life and parenthood mean less than they meant before and hence are less powerful molders of behavior; the rebellious son or daughter who professes contempt for "Victorian" standards is, however incorrectly, expressing an undeniable truth. The weight of these facts is not impaired by our inability to measure them statistically. The marriage rate proves nothing because the term Marriage covers as many sociological meanings as does the term Property, and the kind of alliance that used to be formed by the marriage contract may completely die out without any change in the legal construction or in the frequency of the contract. Nor is the divorce rate more significant. It does not matter how many marriages are dissolved by judicial decree – what matters is how many lack the content essential to the old pattern. If in our statistical age readers insist on a statistical measure, the proportion of marriages that produce no children or only one child, though still inadequate to quantify the phenomenon I mean, might come as near as we can hope to come to

indicating its numerical importance. The phenomenon by now extends, more or less, to all classes. But it first appeared in the bourgeois (and intellectual) stratum and its symptomatic as well as causal value for our purposes lies entirely there. It is wholly attributable to the rationalization of everything in life, which we have seen is one of the effects of capitalist evolution. In fact, it is but one of the results of the spread of that rationalization to the sphere of private life. All the other factors which are usually adduced in explanation can be readily reduced to that one.

As soon as men and women learn the utilitarian lesson and refuse to take for granted the traditional arrangements that their social environment makes for them, as soon as they acquire the habit of weighing the individual advantages and disadvantages of any prospective course of action – or, as we might also put it, as soon as they introduce into their private life a sort of inarticulate system of cost accounting – they cannot fail to become aware of the heavy personal sacrifices that family ties and especially parenthood entail under modern conditions and of the fact that at the same time, excepting the cases of farmers and peasants, children cease to be economic assets. These sacrifices do not consist only of the items that come within the reach of the measuring rod of money but comprise in addition an indefinite amount of loss of comfort, of freedom from care, and opportunity to enjoy alternatives of increasing attractiveness and variety – alternatives to be compared with joys of parenthood that are being subjected to a critical analysis of increasing severity. The implication of this is not weakened but strengthened by the fact that the balance sheet is likely to be incomplete, perhaps even fundamentally wrong. For the greatest of the assets, the contribution made by parenthood to physical and moral health – to "normality" as we might express it – particularly in the case of women, almost invariably escapes the rational searchlight of modern individuals who, in private as in public life, tend to focus attention on ascertainable details of immediate utilitarian relevance and to sneer at the idea of hidden necessities of human nature or of the social organism. The point I wish to convey is, I think, clear without further elaboration. It may be summed up in the question that is so clearly in many potential parents' minds: "Why should we stunt our ambitions and impoverish our lives in order to be insulted and looked down upon in our old age?"

While the capitalist process, by virtue of the psychic attitudes it creates, progressively dims the values of family life and removes the conscientious inhibitions that an old moral tradition would have put in the way toward a different scheme of life, it at the same time implements the new tastes. As regards childlessness, capitalist inventiveness produces contraceptive devices of ever-increasing efficiency that overcome the resistance which the strongest impulse of man would otherwise have put up. As regards the style of life, capitalist evolution decreases the desirability of, and provides alternatives to, the bourgeois family home. I have previously adverted to the Evaporation of Industrial Property. I have now to advert to the Evaporation of Consumers' Property.

Until the later decades of the nineteenth century, the town house and the country place were everywhere not only pleasant and convenient shells of private life on the higher levels of income, but they were indispensable. Not only hospitality on any scale and in any style, but even the comfort, dignity, repose and refinement of the family depended upon its having an adequate *foyer* of its own that was adequately staffed. The arrangements summarized by the term Home were accordingly accepted as a matter of course by the average man and woman of bourgeois standing, exactly as they had looked upon marriage and children – the "founding of a family" – as a matter of course.

Now, on the one hand, the amenities of the bourgeois home are becoming less obvious than its burdens. To the critical eye of a critical age it is likely to appear primarily as a source of trouble and expense which frequently fail to justify themselves. This would be so even independently of modern taxation and wages and of the attitude of modern household personnel, all of which are typical results of the capitalist process and of course greatly strengthen the case against what in the near future will be almost universally recognized as an outmoded and uneconomical way of life. In this respect as in others we are living in a transitional stage. The average family of bourgeois standing tends to reduce the difficulties of running the big house and the big country place by substituting for it small and mechanized establishments plus a maximum of outside service and outside life – hospitality in particular being increasingly shifted to the restaurant or club.

On the other hand, the home of the old type is no longer an indispensable requirement of comfortable and refined living in the bourgeois sphere. The apartment house and the apartment hotel represent a rationalized type of abode and another style of life which when fully developed will no doubt meet the new situation and provide all the essentials of comfort and refinement. To be sure, neither that style nor its shell are fully developed anywhere as yet and they proffer cost advantage only if we count in the trouble and annoyance incident to running a modern home. But other advantages they proffer already – the facility of using to the full the variety of modern enjoyments, of travel, of ready mobility, of shifting the load of the current little things of existence to the powerful shoulders of highly-specialized organizations.

It is easy to see how this in turn bears, in the upper strata of capitalist society, upon the problems of the child. Again there is interaction: the passing of the spacious home – in which alone the rich life of a numerous family can unfold[7] – and the increasing friction with which it functions supply another motive for avoiding the cares of parenthood; but the decline of philoprogenitivity in turn renders the spacious home less worth while.

I have said that the new style of bourgeois life does not as yet offer any decisive cost advantage. But this refers only to the current or prime costs of servicing the wants of private life. As to overhead, even the purely pecuniary advantage is obvious already. And inasmuch as the outlay on the most durable elements of home life – especially the house, the pictures, the furniture – used to be financed mainly from previous earnings we may say that the need for accumulation of "consumers' capital" is drastically reduced by that process. This does not mean of course that demand for "consumers' capital" is at present, even relatively, smaller than it was; the increasing demand for durable consumers' goods from small and medium incomes more than counterbalances this effect. But it does mean that, so far as the hedonistic component in the pattern of acquisitive motives is concerned, the desirability of incomes beyond a certain level is reduced. In order to satisfy himself of this, the reader need only visualize the situation in a thoroughly practical spirit: the successful man or couple or the "society" man or couple who can pay for the best available accommodation in hotel, ship and train, and for the best available qualities of the objects of personal comsumption and use – which qualities are increasingly being turned out by the conveyor of mass production[8] – will, things being what they are, as a rule have all they want with any intensity *for themselves*. And it is easy to see that a budget framed on those lines will be far below the requirements of a "seignioral" style of life.

3. In order to realize what all this means for the efficiency of the capitalist engine of production we need only recall that the family and

the family home used to be the mainspring of the typically bourgeois kind of profit motive. Economists have not always given due weight to this fact. When we look more closely at their idea of the self-interest of entrepreneurs and capitalists we cannot fail to discover that the results it was supposed to produce are really not at all what one would expect from the rational self-interest of the detached individual or the childless couple who no longer look at the world through the windows of a family home. Consciously or unconsciously they analyzed the behavior of the man whose views and motives are shaped by such a home and who means to work and to save primarily for wife *and children*. As soon as these fade out from the moral vision of the businessman, we have a different kind of *homo oeconomicus* before us who cares for different things and acts in different ways. For him and from the standpoint of his individualistic utilitarianism, the behavior of that old type would in fact be completely irrational. He loses the only sort of romance and heroism of *navigare necesse est, vivere non necesse est* ["Seafaring is necessary, living is not necessary." Inscription on an old house in Bremen.]. And he loses the capitalist ethics that enjoins working for the future irrespective of whether or not one is going to harvest the crop oneself.

The last point may be put more tellingly. In the preceding chapter it was observed that the capitalist order entrusts the long-run interests of society to the upper strata of the bourgeoisie. The bourgeoisie worked primarily in order to invest, and it was not so much a standard of consumption as a standard of accumulation that the bourgeoisie struggled for and tried to defend against governments that took the short-run view.[9] With the decline of the driving power supplied by the family motive, the businessman's time horizon shrinks, roughly, to his own life expectation. And he might now be less willing than he was to fulfill that function of earning, saving and investing even if he saw no reason to fear that the results would but swell his tax bills. He drifts into an anti-saving frame of mind and accepts with an increasing readiness antisaving *theories* that are indicative of a short-run *philosophy*.

But anti-saving theories are not all that he accepts. With a different attitude to the concern he works for and with a different scheme of private life he tends to acquire a different view of the values and standards of the capitalist order of things. Perhaps the most striking feature of the picture is the extent to which the bourgeoisie, besides educating its own enemies, allows itself in turn to be educated by them. It absorbs the slogans of current radicalism and seems quite willing to undergo a process of conversion to a creed hostile to its very existence. Haltingly and grudgingly it concedes in part the implications of that creed. And this again becomes fully understandable as soon as we realize that the social conditions which account for its emergence are passing.

This is verified by the very characteristic manner in which particular capitalist interests and the bourgeoisie as a whole behave when facing direct attack. They talk and plead – or hire people to do it for them; they snatch at every chance of compromise; they are ever ready to give in; they never put up a fight under the flag of their own ideals and interests – in this country there was no real resistance anywhere against the imposition of crushing financial burdens during the last decade or against labor legislation incompatible with the effective management of industry. Now, as the reader will know by this time, I am far from overestimating the political power of either big business or the bourgeoisie in general. Moreover, I am prepared to make large allowances for cowardice. But still, means of defense were not entirely lacking as yet and history is full of examples of the success of small groups who, believing in their cause, were resolved to stand by their guns. The only explanation for the meekness we observe is that the bourgeois order no longer makes any sense to the bourgeoisie itself, and that, when all is said and done, it does not really care.

Thus the same economic process that undermines the position of the bourgeoisie by decreasing the importance of the functions of entrepreneurs and capitalists, by breaking up protective strata and institutions, by creating an atmosphere of hostility, also decomposes the motor forces of capitalism from within. Nothing else shows so well that the capitalist order not only rests on props made of extra-capitalist material but also derives its energy from extracapitalist patterns of behavior which at the same time it is bound to destroy.

We have rediscovered what from different standpoints and, so I believe, on inadequate grounds has often been discovered before: there is inherent in the capitalist system a tendency toward self-destruction which, in its earlier stages, may well assert itself in the form of a tendency toward retardation of progress.

The capitalist process not only destroys its own institutional framework but it also creates the conditions for another. Destruction may not be the right word after all. Perhaps I should have spoken of transformation. The outcome of the process is not simply a void that could be filled by whatever might happen to turn up; things and souls are transformed in such a way as to become increasingly amenable to the socialist form of life. With every peg from under the capitalist structure vanishes an impossibility of the socialist plan. In both these respects Marx's *vision* was right.

... [T]he various components of the tendency we have been trying to describe, while everywhere discernable, have as yet nowhere fully revealed themselves. Things have gone to different lengths in different countries but in no country far enough to allow us to say with any confidence how far they will go, or to assert that their "underlying trend" has grown too strong to be subject to anything more serious than temporary reverses. Industrial integration is still far from being complete. Competition, actual and potential, is still a major factor in any business situation. Enterprise is still active, the leadership of the bourgeois group still the prime mover of the economic process. The middle class is still a political power. Bourgeois standards and bourgeois motivations though being increasingly impaired are still alive. Survival of traditions – and family ownership of controlling parcels of stock – still make many an executives behave as the owner-manager did of old. From the standpoint of immediate practice as well as for the purposes of short-run forecasting – and in these things, a century is a "short-run" – all this surface may be more important than the tendency toward another civilization that slowly works deep down below.

Notes

Excerpted from *Capitalism, Socialism, and Democracy* by J. Schumpeter. Reproduced by kind permission of Unwin Hyman Publishers, London, all rights reserved.

1   Even Marx, in whose time indictments of this kind were not anything like as absurd as they are today, evidently thought it desirable to strengthen his case by dwelling on conditions that even then were either past or visibly passing.

2   Wilhelm Wundt called this the Heterogony of Aims (Heterogonie der Zwecke).

3   Gallicanism was nothing else but the ideological reflex of this.

4   Although some governments did: the government of imperial Germany did much to fight this particular kind of rationalization, and there is now a strong tendency to do the same in this country.

5   It is hoped that no confusion will arise from my using the verb "to rationalize" in two different meanings. An industrial plant is being "rationalized" when its productive efficiency per unit of expenditure is being increased. We "rationalize" an action of ours when we supply ourselves and others with reasons for it that satisfy our standard of values regardless of what our true impulses may be.

6   Many people will deny this. This is due to the fact that they derive their impression

from past history and from the slogans generated by past history during which the institutional change brought about by the big corporation had not yet asserted itself. Also they may think of the scope which corporate business used to give for illegal satisfactions of the capitalist motivation. But that would cut my way: the fact that personal gain beyond salary and bonus cannot, in corporate business, be reaped by executives except by illegal or semi-illegal practices shows precisely that the structural idea of the corporation is averse to it.

7 Modern relations between parents and children are of course partly conditioned by the crumblimg of that steady frame of family life.

8 Effects on consumers' budgets of the increasing eligibility of mass-produced articles are enhanced by the price difference between them and the corresponding custom-made articles which increases owing to the increase in wages *pari passu* with the decrease in the relative desirability of the latter; the capitalist process democratizes consumption.

9 It has been said that in economic matters "the state can take the longer view." But excepting certain matters outside of party politics such as conservation of natural resources, it hardly ever does.

2

Crisis Tendencies and Legitimation in Liberal Capitalism

JÜRGEN HABERMAS

System Crisis Elucidated Through the Example of the Liberal-Capitalist Crisis Cycle

In liberal capitalism, crises appear *in the form* of unresolved economic steering problems. Dangers to system integration *are* direct threats to social integration, so that we are justified in speaking of economic crisis. In primitive social formations, a similarly close association exists, for the familial principle of organization does not permit separation of system and social integration. Functional differentiation, which developed in traditional societies, is not revoked in the transition to the modern. But in liberal capitalism, there occurs a peculiar transfer of socially integrative tasks to the separate, unpolitical steering system of the market in such a way that the elements of tradition that are effective (at first for the middle class) for legitimation (rational–natural law, utilitarianism) become dependent on an ideology that is itself built into the economic basis – namely, the exchange of equivalents. In traditional societies, crises appear when, and only when, steering problems cannot be resolved within the possibility space circumscribed by the principle of organization and therefore produce dangers to system integration that threaten the identity of the society. In liberal-capitalist societies, on the other hand, crises become endemic because temporarily unresolved steering problems, which the process of economic growth produces at more or less regular intervals, *as such* endanger social integration. With the persistent instability of accelerated social change, periodically recurring, socially disintegrating steering problems produce the objective foundation for a crisis consciousness in the bourgeois class and for revolutionary hopes among wage labourers. No

45

previous social formation lived so much in fear and expectation of a sudden system change, even though the idea of a temporally condensed transformation – that is, of a revolutionary leap – is oddly in contrast to the form of motion of system crisis as a permanent crisis [*Dauerkrise*].

The transfer of *socially* integrative functions to a subsystem that primarily fulfills *system* integrative functions is possible only because in liberal capitalism the class relationship is institutionalized through the labor market and is thereby depoliticized. Since the source of social wealth – that is, the labor power of the worker – becomes a commodity, and social capital is reproduced under conditions of wage labor, labor and exchange processes take on the double character analyzed by Marx: in producing use values, labor processes serve to produce exchange values. By regulating the allocation of labor power and of goods through the money mechanism, exchange processes serve the formation and self-realization of capital. The market thereby assumes a double function: on the one hand, it functions as a steering mechanism in the system of social labor, which is controlled through the medium of money; on the other, it institutionalizes a power relation between owners of the means of production and wage laborers. Because the *social power* of the capitalist is institutionalized as an exchange relation in the form of the private labor contract and the siphoning off of privately available surplus value has replaced *political dependency*, the market assumes, together with its cybernetic function, an ideological function. The class relationship can assume the anonymous, unpolitical form of wage dependency.

In Marx, therefore, theoretical analysis of the value form has the double task of uncovering both the steering principle of commerce in a market economy and the basic ideology of bourgeois class society. The theory of value serves, at the same time, the functional analysis of the economic system and the critique of ideology of a class domination that can be unmasked, even for the bourgeois consciousness, through the proof that in the labour market equivalents are not exchanged. The market secures for the owners of the means of production the power, sanctioned in civil law, to appropriate surplus value and to use it privately and autonomously. Naturally, in its crisis-ridden course, the process of accumulation surrenders the secret of the "contradiction" embedded in this mode of production. Economic growth takes place through periodically recurring crises because the class structure, transplanted into the economic steering system, has transformed *the contradiction of class interests into a contradiction of system imperatives.* In choosing this formulation we employ the concept of contradiction in two different theoretical frameworks. In order to prevent misunderstanding, I would like to insert a conceptual clarification.

The concept of contradiction has undergone such attrition that it is often used synonymously with "antagonism", "opposition", or "conflict". According to Hegel and Marx, however, "conflicts" are only the form of appearance, the empirical side of a fundamentally logical contradiction. Conflicts can be comprehended only with reference to the operatively effective rules according to which incompatible claims or intentions are produced within an action system. But "contradictions" cannot exist between claims or intentions in the same sense as they can between statements; the system of rules according to which utterances [*Ausserungen*] – that is, opinions and actions in which intentions are incorporated – are produced is obviously different in kind from the system of rules according to which we form statements and transform them without affecting their truth value. In other words, the deep structures of a society are not logical structures in a narrow sense. Propositional contents, on the other hand, are always used in utterances. The logic that could justify speaking of "social contradictions" would therefore have to be a logic of the employment of propositional contents in speech and in action. It would have to extend to communicative relations between subjects capable of speaking and acting; it would have to be universal pragmatics rather than logic.[1]

We can speak of the "fundamental contradiction" of a social formation when, and only when, its organizational principle necessitates that individuals and groups repeatedly confront one another with claims and intentions that are, in the long run, incompatible. In class societies this is the case. As long as the incompatibility of claims and intentions is not recognized by the participants, the conflict remains latent. Such forcefully integrated action systems are, of course, in need of an ideological justification to conceal the asymmetrical distribution of chances for the legitimate satisfaction of needs (that is, repression of needs). Communication between participants is then systematically distorted or blocked. Under conditions of forceful integration, the contradiction cannot be *identified* as a contradiction between the *declared* intentions of hostile parties and be settled in strategic action. Instead, it assumes the ideological form of a contradiction between the intentions that subjects believe themselves to be carrying out and their, as we say, unconscious motives or fundamental interests. As soon as incompatibility becomes conscious, conflict becomes manifest, and irreconcilable interests are recognized as antagonistic interests.[2]

Systems theory, too, is concerned with the logic of a system of rules according to which incompatibilities can be produced. When more problems are posed in a given environment than the system's steering capacity can solve, logically derivable contradictions appear that require, on pain of ruin, an alteration of system structures – alteration or surrender of elements that up to that point belonged to its "structural continuity" [Bestand]. These "contradictions" are introduced with reference to problems of system maintenance [Bestandserhaltungsprobleme]. They are not, therefore, as are dialectical problems, related from the start to communicative relations between subjects or groups of subjects capable of speaking and acting. Within the framework of systems theory, conflicts can be seen as the expression of unresolved systemic problems. But the continued employment of the term "contradiction" should not obscure the differences between the logic of self-regulated systems and the logic of ordinary language communication.

Conflicts that are described independently of communications theory or systems theory are empirical phenomena without relation to truth. Only when we conceive of such oppositions within communications theory or systems theory do they take on an immanent relation to logical categories. Problems of system integration admit of truth insofar as they are defined by a finite number of specifiable (and functionally equivalent) solutions. Naturally the truth relation of steering problems exists primarily for the observer (or systems theorist) and not necessarily for the participants of the action system in question. Problems of social integration (as whose expression conflicts can be conceived) likewise admit of truth; for competing claims can be understood as recommendations of (and warnings against) commonly binding norms of action on whose competing validity claims judgement could be passed in practical discourse. But the truth relation of systematically produced conflicts of interest exists, in this case, not for the sociologist, but for the members of the action system under analysis. In contrast to systems analysis, then, critique is related to the consciousness of addressees susceptible of enlightenment.[3]

The class structure determines which contradictions follow from the privileged appropriation of socially produced wealth. In traditional societies, such contradictions are manifested directly at the level of opposition of the interests of acting parties. In liberal capitalism, the class antagonism is reflected at the level of steering problems. The dynamic aspect thereby comes to the fore. Since, in the capitalist mode of production, the society acquires the capability to develop the forces of production relatively constantly, economic crisis designates the pattern of a *crisis-ridden course of economic growth*.

The accumulation of capital is, if we follow Marx's analysis, tied to the appropriation of surplus value. This means that economic growth is regulated through a mechanism that establishes and at the same time partially conceals a relation of social power. Because the production of value is controlled through the private appropriation of surplus value, a spiral of contradictions results that can be reconstructed within systems theory. The accumulation of total capital involves periodic devaluations of elements of capital. This form of development is the crisis cycle. *Under the aspect of the accumulation of capital*, the self-negating pattern of development is represented in such a way that, on the one hand, the mass of exchange and use values (that is capital and social wealth) accumulates by raising the relative surplus value, that is, by way of technical progress that is capital intensive and that, at the same time, cuts down expenses. But, on the other hand, at each new stage of accumulation, the composition of capital alters to the detriment of variable capital, which is alone productive of surplus value. From this analysis Marx derives the tendency to a falling rate of profit and the weakening impulse to continuation of the process of accumulation.

Under the aspect of the realization of capital, the same contradiction is represented in such a way that at each new stage of accumulation potential social wealth grows along with the increase in surplus value. On the other hand, however, the power of consumption of the masses, and therefore the chance to realize capital, can be strengthened to the same extent only if the owners of capital relinquish corresponding portions of their own surplus value. Hence, the process of accumulation must come to a standstill because of lack of *possibilities* of realization or because of lack of incentives to invest.

The interruption of the process of accumulation assumes the form of capital destruction. This is the economic form of appearance of the real social processes that expropriates individual capitalists (competition) and deprives the laboring masses of their means of subsistence (unemployment). Economic crisis is immediately transformed into social crisis; for, in unmasking the opposition of social classes, it provides a practical critique of ideology of the market's pretension to be free of power. The economic crisis results from contradictory system imperatives and threatens social integration. It is, *at the same time*, a social crisis in which the interests of acting groups collide and place in question the social integration of the society.

The economic crisis is the first (and perhaps only) example in world history of a system crisis characterized in the following way: namely, that the dialectical contradiction between members of an interaction context comes to pass *in terms of* structurally insoluble system contradictions or steering problems. Through this displacement of conflicts of interest to the level of system steering, systems crises gain an objectivity rich in contrast. They have the appearance of natural catastrophes that break forth from the centre of a system of purposive rational action. While in traditional societies antagonisms between social classes were mediated through ideological forms of consciousness and thus had the *fateful objectivity of a context of delusion*, in liberal capitalism, class antagonism is shifted from the intersubjectivity of the life-world into the substratum of this world. Commodity fetishism is both a secularized residual ideology and the actually functioning steering principle of the economic system. Economic crises thus lose the character of a fate accessible to self-reflection and acquire the objectivity of *inexplicable, contingent, natural events*. The ideological core has thus shifted to ground level. Before it can be destroyed by reflection, these events are in need of an objective examination of system processes.

On the Logic of Legitimation Problems

To the highest stage of moral consciousness there corresponds a universal morality, which can be traced back to fundamental norms of rational speech. Vis-à-vis competing ethics, universal morality makes a claim not only to *empirical* superiority (based on the ontogenetically observable hierarchy of stages of consciousness), but to *systematic* superiority as well (with reference to the discursive redemption of its claim to validity). In the present context, only this *systematic aspect* of the claimed truth relation of factually valid norms and values is of interest.

Max Weber's concept of legitimate authority[4] directs our attention to the connection between belief in the legitimacy of orders [*Ordnungen*] and their potential for justification, on one hand, and to their factual validity on the other. The basis of legitimacy reveals "the ultimate grounds of the 'validity' of a domination, in other words . . . those grounds upon which there are based the claims of obedience made by the master against the 'officials' and of both against the ruled".[5] Because the reproduction of class societies is based on the privileged appropriation of socially produced wealth, all such societies must resolve the problem of distributing the surplus social product inequitably and yet legitimately.[6] They do so by means of structural force, that is, by fixing in a system of observed norms the asymmetrical distribution of legitimate chances to satisfy needs. The factual recognition of such norms does not, of course, rest solely on belief in their legitimacy by those affected. It is also based on fear of, and submission to, indirectly threatened sanctions, as well as on simple compliance engendered by the individual's perception of his own powerlessness and the lack of alternatives open to him (that is, by his own fettered imagination). As soon, however, as belief in the legitimacy of an existing order vanishes, the latent force embedded in the system of institutions is released – either as manifest force from above (which is only a temporary possibility) or in the form of expansion of the scope for participation (in which case the key to the distribution of chances to legitimately satisfy needs, that is, the degree of repression, also changes).

> Naturally, the legitimacy of a system of domination may be treated sociologically only as the probability that to a relevant degree the appropriate attitudes will exist, and the corresponding practical conduct ensue. It is by no means true that every case of submissiveness to persons in positions of power is primarily (or even at all) oriented to this belief. Loyalty may be hypocritically simulated by individuals or by whole groups on purely opportunistic grounds, or carried out in practice for reasons of material self-interest. Or people may submit from individual weakness and helplessness because there is no acceptable alternative. But these considerations are not decisive for the classification of types of domination. What is important is the fact that in a given case the particular claim to legitimacy is to a significant degree, and according to its type, treated as "valid"; that this fact confirms the position of the persons claiming authority and that it helps to determine the choice of means of its exercise.[7]

In contemporary sociology, the usefulness of this concept of legitimation, which permits a demarcation of types of legitimate authority (in Weber's sense) according to the forms and contents of legitimation, is undisputed. What is controversial is the *relation of legitimacy to truth*. This relation to truth must be presumed to exist if one regards as possible a motivation crisis resulting from a systematic scarcity of the resource of "meaning". Non-contingent grounds for a disappearance of legitimacy can, that is, be derived only from an "independent" [*eigensinnigen*] – that is, truth-dependent – evolution of interpretive systems that systematically restricts the adaptive capacity of society.

Max Weber's Concept of Legitimation

The controversy over the truth-dependency of legitimations was ignited at the sociological level by Max Weber's ambiguous conception of "rational authority", that is, the legally formed and procedurally regulated type of authority characteristic of modern societies.

> Experience shows that in no instance does domination voluntarily limit itself to the appeal to material or affectual or ideal motives as a basis for its continuance. In addition every such system attempts to establish and to cultivate the belief in its legitimacy.[8]

Weber even affirms "the generally observable need of any power, or even of any advantage of life, to justify itself".[9] If belief in legitimacy is conceived as an empirical phenomenon without an immanent relation to truth, the grounds upon which it is explicitly based have only psychological significance. Whether such grounds can sufficiently stabilize a given belief in legitimacy depends upon the institutionalized prejudices and observable behavioral dispositions of the group in question. If, on the other hand, every effective belief in legitimacy is assumed to have an immanent relation to truth, the grounds on which it is explicitly based contain a rational validity claim that can be tested and criticized independently of the psychological effect of these grounds. In the first case, only the motivational function of the justificatory grounds can be the object of investigation. In the second, their motivational function cannot be considered independently of their logical status, that is, of their criticizable claim to *motivate rationally*. This is true even if this claim is, as it usually is, counterfactually raised and stabilized.

For the interpretation of rational authority,[10] this alternative means that in the first case an authority will be viewed as legitimate if at least two conditions are fulfilled: (*a*) the normative order must be established positively; and (*b*) those legally associated must believe in its legality, that is, in the formally correct procedure for the creation and application of laws. The belief in legitimacy thus shrinks to a belief in legality; the appeal to the legal manner in which a decision comes about suffices. In the case of the truth-dependency of belief in legitimacy, however, the appeal to the state's monopoly on the creation and application of laws obviously does not suffice. The procedure itself is under pressure for legitimation. At least *one* further condition must therefore be fulfilled: grounds for the legitimizing force of this formal procedure must be given (for example, that the procedural competency lies with a constitutionally established state authority).[11]

The first of the aforementioned positions is represented today by Niklas Luhmann:

> The law of a society is positivized when the legitimacy of pure legality is recognized, that is, when law is respected because it is made by responsible decision in accordance with definite rules. Thus, in a central question of human co-existence, arbitrariness becomes an institution.[12]

Luhmann is here following the decisionistic legal theory founded by Carl Schmitt:

> The positivization of law means that legitimate legal validity [*Rechtsgeltung*] can be obtained for any given contents, and that this is accomplished through a decision which confers validity upon the law and which can take the validity from it. Positive law is valid by virtue of decisions.[13]

The formal rules of procedure suffice as legitimizing premises of decision and require for their part no further legitimation, for they fulfill their function – to absorb uncertainty – in any case. They connect the uncertainty as to which decision will come about with the certainty that some decision will come about.[14] The abstract imperative validity [*Sollgeltung*] of norms that can do without a material justification beyond the following of correct procedure in their origin and application serves "to stabilize behavioral expectations against any disappointment and thereby to guarantee structures".[15] Normative validity can, of course, fulfill this function only as long as it remains latent and does not enter explicitly into the sense of the "ought": "Social processes for dealing with disappointment and for learning are presupposed in all norming of behavioral expectations. They cannot, however, by reflected in the normed meaning".[16]

It is meaningless to probe behind the factual belief in legitimacy and the validity claim of norms for criticizable grounds of validity. The fiction that one could do so if necessary belongs to the constituents of reliable counterfactual expectations. These, in turn, can be comprehended only from a functionalist point of view, that is, by treating validity claims as functionally necessary deceptions [*Täuschungen*]. The deception may not, however, be exposed if the belief in legality is not to be shaken.[17]

The *second* of the two positions mentioned above is represented by Johannes Winckelmann. He considers formal rationality in Weber's sense an insufficient foundation for legitimation: the belief in legality does not *per se* legitimize. Legal positivism requires, rather, a general consensus grounded in a rational orientation to value.[18] "The rational value-oriented postulates form the regulative principles for normative positing and its concretization. Only that positing is normatively legitimized ... which keeps within the bounds of the formal legal principles which are set in this way".[19] Legality can create legitimation when, and only when, grounds can be provided to show that certain formal procedures fulfill material claims to justice under certain institutional boundary conditions. "In principle, the concept of legal authority in Max Weber refers to the rational, and in fact rational *value-oriented*, statutory authority. Only in its degenerate form was this distorted into undignified, value-neutral, purely purposive-rational, formal legal authority".[20] Winckelmann's thesis is questionable from a hermeneutic point of view, because it leads systematically to the conclusion that the rational value-oriented foundations of the belief in legitimacy can be justified [*begründungsfähig*] and criticized.

This is incompatible with Max Weber's view of the rationally irresoluble pluralism of competing value systems and beliefs [*Glaubensmächte*].[21] This point is not important in the present context. But from a systematic point of view as well, the assumption of basic material norms capable of being justified leads to the difficulty that certain normative contents must be theoretically singled-out. Hitherto, philosophical efforts to rehabilitate traditional or – as Winckelmann himself seems inclined – modern natural law, in whatever version, have proved as unavailing as attempts to found a material value ethics (in the sense of Scheler or Nicolai Hartmann). Moreover, there is no need to accept such a burden of proof in order to demonstrate the criticizability of claims to appropriateness. Recourse to the fundamental norms of rational speech, which we presuppose in every discourse (including practical discourses), is sufficient.

In my debate with Luhmann, I derived the belief in legality from a belief in legitimacy that can be justified.

The unobjectionable manner in which a norm comes into being, that is, the legal form of a procedure, guarantees as such only that the authorities which the political system provides for, and which are furnished with certain competencies and recognized as competent within that system, bear the responsibility for valid law. But these authorities are part of a system of authority that must be legitimized as a whole if pure legality is to be able to count *as an indication* of legitimacy. In a fascist regime, for example, the legal form of administrative acts can have at best a masking function. This means that the technical legal form alone, pure legality, will not be able to guarantee recognition in the long run if the system of authority cannot be legitimized independently of the legal form of exercising authority. Luhmann admits that "special grounds are required in order for selection performances which rest only on decisions to be accepted." But he believes that through an institutionalized legal form of proceeding, that is, through procedures, "such additional grounds for the recognition of decisions are created and, in this sense, the power of decision is produced and legitimized, that is, made independent of concretely exercised force." A procedure can, however, legitimize only indirectly, through reference to authorities which, for their part, must be recognized. Thus, the written bourgeois constitutions contain a catalogue of basic rights, strongly immunized against alteration, which has legitimizing force in so far as, and only in so far as, it is understood in conjunction with an ideology of the system of authority. Moreover, the organs which are responsible for making and applying the laws are in no way legitimated by the legality of their modes of procedure, but likewise by a general interpretation which supports the system of authority as a whole.[22]

The discussion of the relation of truth to belief in legitimacy was sparked by Max Weber's conception of belief in legality. It has led meanwhile to problems concerning the possibility of justifying norms of action and evaluation in general: this problem cannot be resolved by sociological means. If the capacity of practical questions for truth could be disputed, the position I defended would be untenable.

Theorems of Legitimation Crisis

The concept of the rationality crisis is modeled after that of the economic crisis. According to that concept, contradictory steering imperatives assert themselves through the purposive-rational actions not of market-participants but of members of the administration; they manifest themselves in contradictions that directly threaten system integration and thus endanger social integration.

We have seen that an economic system crisis can be counted on only as long as political disputes (class struggles) maintain and do not change institutional boundary conditions of capitalist production (for example, the Chartist movement and the introduction of the normal working day). To the extent that the class relationship has itself been repoliticized and the state has taken over market-replacing as well as market-supplementing tasks (and made possible a "more elastic" form of production of surplus value), class domination can no longer take the anonymous form of the law of value. Instead, it now depends on factual constellations of power whether, and how, production of surplus value can be guaranteed through the public sector, and how the terms of the class compromise look. With this development, crisis tendencies shift, of course, from the economic into the administrative system. Indeed, the self-containment of exchange processes, mediated only through the market, is destroyed. But after the liberal-capitalist spell of commodity production is broken (and all participants have become, more or less, good practitioners of value theory), the unplanned, nature-like development of economic processes can re-establish itself, at least in secondary form, in the political system. The state must preserve for itself a residue of unconsciousness in order that there accrue to it from its planning functions no responsibilities that it cannot honor without overdrawing its accounts. Thus, economic crisis tendencies continue on the plateau of raising, and expending in a purposive-rational way, the requisite fiscal means.

But, if we do not wish to fall back on theorems of economic crisis, governmental activity can find a *necessary* limit only in available legitimations. As long as motivations remain tied to norms requiring justification, the introduction of legitimate power into the reproduction process means that the "fundamental contradiction" can break out in a questioning, rich in practical consequences, of the norms that still underlie administrative action. And such questioning will break out if the corresponding themes, problems, and arguments are not spared through sufficiently sedimented pre-determinations. Because the economic crisis has been intercepted and transformed into a systematic overloading of the public budget, it has put off the mantle of a natural fate of society. If governmental crisis management fails, it lags

behind programmatic demands *that it has placed on itself.* The penalty
for this failure is withdrawal of legitimation. Thus, the scope for action
contracts precisely at those moments in which it needs to be drastically
expanded.

Underlying this crisis theorem is the general reflection that a social
identity determined indirectly, through the capability of securing-system
integration, is constantly vulnerable on the basis of class structures.
For the problematic consequences of the processed and transformed
fundamental contradiction of social production for non-generalizable
interests are concentrated, as O'Connor tries to show, in the focal
region of the stratified raising and particularistic employment of the
scarce quantities of taxes that a policy of crisis avoidance exhausts
and overdraws. On the one hand, administrative and fiscal filtering
of economically conditioned crisis tendencies makes the fronts of
repeatedly fragmented class oppositions less comprehensible. The class
compromise weakens the organizational capacity of the latently con-
tinuing classes. On the other hand, scattered secondary conflicts also
become more palpable, because they do not appear as objective system
crises, but directly provoke questions of legitimation. This explains the
functional necessity of making the administrative system, as far as
possible, independent of the legitimating system.

This end is served by the separation of instrumental functions of
the administration from expressive symbols that release an unspecific
readiness to follow. Familiar strategies of this kind are the personalization
of substantive issues, the symbolic use of hearings, expert judgements,
juridical incantations, and also the advertising techniques (copied from
oligopolistic competition) that at once confirm and exploit existing
structures of prejudice and that garnish certain contents positively,
others negatively, through appeals to feeling, stimulation of unconscious
motives, etc.[23] The public realm, set up for effective legitimation, has
above all the function of directing attention to topical areas – that is, of
pushing *other* themes, problems, and arguments below the threshold of
attention and, thereby, of withholding them from opinion-formation.
The political system takes over tasks of ideology planning (Luhmann).
In so doing, maneuvering room is, to be sure, narrowly limited, for the
cultural system is peculiarly resistant to administrative control. *There is
no administrative production of meaning.* Commercial production and
administrative planning of symbols exhausts the normative force of
counterfactual validity claims. The procurement of legitimation is self-
defeating as soon as the mode of procurement is seen through.

Cultural traditions have their own, vulnerable, conditions of reproduction. They remain "living" as long as they take shape in an unplanned, nature-like manner, or are shaped with hermeneutic consciousness. (Whereby hermeneutics, as the scholarly interpretation and application of tradition, has the peculiarity of breaking down the nature-like character of tradition as it is handed on and, nevertheless, of retaining it at a reflective level.)[24] The critical appropriation of tradition destroys this nature-like character in discourse. (Whereby the peculiarity of critique consists in its double function:[25] to dissolve analytically, or in a critique of ideology, validity claims that cannot be discursively redeemed; but, at the same time, to release the semantic potentials of the tradition.)[26] To this extent, critique is no less a form of appropriating tradition than hermeneutics. In both cases appropriated cultural contents retain their imperative force, that is, they guarantee the continuity of a history through which individuals and groups can identify with themselves and with one another. A cultural tradition loses precisely this force as soon as it is objectivistically prepared and strategically employed. In both cases conditions for the reproduction of cultural traditions are damaged, and the tradition is undermined. This can be seen in the museum-effect of a hedonistic historicism, as well as in the wear and tear that results from the exploitation of cultural contents for administrative or market purposes. Apparently, traditions can retain legitimizing force only as long as they are not torn out of interpretive systems that guarantee continuity and identity.

The structural dissimilarity between areas of administrative action and areas of cultural tradition constitutes, then, a systematic limit to attempts to compensate for legitimation deficits through conscious manipulation. Administrative planning produces a universal pressure for legitimation in a sphere that was once distinguished precisely for its power of self-legitimation.[27] The end effect is a consciousness of the contingency, not only of the contents of tradition, but also of the techniques of tradition, that is, of socialization. Formal schooling is competing with family upbringing as early as at the pre-school age. At every level, administrative planning produces unintended unsettling and publicizing effects. These effects weaken the justification potential of traditions that have been flushed out of their nature-like course of development. Once their unquestionable character has been destroyed, the stabilization of validity claims can succeed only through discourse. The stirring up of cultural affairs that are taken for granted thus furthers the politicization of areas of life previously assigned to the private sphere. But this development signifies danger for the civil privatism that is secured informally through the structures of the public realm. Efforts at participation and the plethora of alternative models – especially in cultural spheres such as school and university, press, church, theatre, publishing, etc. – are indicators of this danger, as is the increasing number of citizens' initiatives.[28]

Demands for, and attempts at, participatory planning can also be explained in this context. Because administrative planning increasingly affects the cultural system – that is, the deep-seated representations of norms and values of those affected – and renders traditional attitudes uncertain, the threshold of acceptability changes. In order to carry through innovations in the planning process, the administration experiments with the participation of those affected. Of course, the functions of participation in governmental planning are ambivalent.[29] Gray areas arise in which it is not clear whether the need for conflict regulation is increased or decreased by participation. The more planners place themselves under the pressure of consensus-formation in the planning process, the more likely is a strain that goes back to two contrary motives: excessive demands resulting from legitimation claims that the administration cannot satisfy under conditions of an asymmetrical class compromise; and conservative resistance to planning, which contracts the horizon of planning and lowers the degree of innovation possible. Socio-psychologically viewed, both motives can be integrated into the same antagonistic interpretive pattern. Thus, analytically separable types of opposition can be represented by the same group. For this reason, laying claim to the "labour power of participation" ([F.] Naschold) is an extreme and, for the administration, risky means of meeting legitimation deficits.

These arguments lend support to the assertion that advanced-capitalist societies fall into legitimation difficulties. But are they sufficient to establish the insolubility of legitimation problems, that is, do they lead necessarily to the prediction of a legitimation crisis? Even if the state apparatus were to succeed in raising the productivity of labour and in distributing gains in productivity in such a way that an economic growth free of crises (if not disturbances) were guaranteed, growth would still be achieved in accord with priorities that take shape as a function, not of generalizable interests of the population, but of private goals of profit maximization. The patterns of priorities that Galbraith analysed from the point of view of "private wealth versus public poverty"[30] result from a class structure that is, as usual, kept latent. In the final analysis, this class structure is the source of the legitimation deficit.

We have seen now that the state cannot simply take over the cultural system, and that expansion of the areas of state planning actually makes problematic matters that were formerly culturally taken for granted. "Meaning" is a scarce resource and is becoming ever scarcer. Consequently, expectations oriented to use values – that is, expectations monitored by success – are rising in the civil public. The rising level of demand is proportional to the growing need for legitimation. The fiscally siphoned-off resource "value" must take the place of the scanty resource "meaning." Missing legitimation must be offset by rewards conforming to the system. A legitimation crisis arises as soon as the demands for such rewards rise faster than the available quantity of value, or when expectations arise that cannot be satisfied with such rewards.

But why should not the levels of demand keep within the boundaries of the operating capacity of the political–economic system? It could, after all, be that the rate of the rise in level of demand is such that it forces on the steering and maintenance systems precisely those processes of adaptation and learning possible within the limits of the existing mode of production. The obvious post-war development of advanced-capitalist societies supports the view that this has already occured.[31] As long as the welfare-state programme, in conjunction with a widespread, technocratic common consciousness (which, in case of doubt, makes inalterable system restraints responsible for bottlenecks) can maintain a sufficient degree of civil privatism, legitimation needs *do not have to* culminate in a crisis.

Offe and his collaborators question whether the form of procuring legitimation does not make it necessary for competing parties to outbid one another in their programmes and thereby raise the expectations of the population ever higher and higher. This could result in an unavoidable gap between the level of pretension and the level of success, which would lead to disappointments among the voting public.[32] The competitive democratic form of legitimation would then generate costs it could not cover. Assuming that this argument could be sufficiently verified empirically, we would still have to explain why formal democracy has to be retained at all in advanced-capitalist societies. If one considers only the functional conditions of the administrative system, it could as well be replaced by variants: a conservative–authoritarian welfare state that reduces political participation of citizens to a harmless level; or a fascist–authoritarian state that holds the population by the bit at a relatively high level of permanent mobilization without having to overdraw its account through welfare-state measures. Both variants are, in the long run, obviously less compatible with developed capitalism than the constitution of a mass democracy with government by parties, for the socio-cultural system produces demands that cannot be met in authoritarian systems.

This reflection supports my thesis that only a rigid socio-cultural system, incapable of being randomly functionalized for the needs of the administrative system, could explain a sharpening of legitimation difficulties into a legitimation crisis. A legitimation crisis can be predicted only if expectations that cannot be fulfilled either with the available quantity of value or, generally, with rewards conforming to the system systematically produced. A legitimation crisis, then, must be based on a motivation crisis – that is, a discrepancy between the need for motives declared by the state, the educational system and the occupational system on the one hand and the motivation supplied by the socio-cultural system on the other.

Notes

Translation of 1973: *Legitimation Crisis*. London: Heinemann. First published as *Legitimations-probleme im Spätkapitalismus*. Reprinted by kind permission of Blackwell Publishers, Oxford, and Beacon Press, Boston.

1 Cf. my "Vorbereitende Bemerkungen zu einer Theorie der kommunikativen Kompetenz."

2 H. Pilot attempts a similar reconstruction of "dialectic" in "Jürgen Habermas's Empirically Falsified Philosophy of History", in 1975: *The Positivist Dispute in German Sociology*. London/New York.

3 Habermas, J. 1971: *Knowledge and Human Interests*. Boston: especially p. 187ff.

4 Weber, Max 1968: The Types of Legitimate Domination, in *Economy and Society*, G. Roth and C. Wittich (eds), 3 volumes. New York.

5 Weber, M., ibid., 3: 953.

6 Lenski, G. 1966: *Power and Privilege*. New York: p. 43ff.

7 Weber, 1: 214.

8 Ibid., p. 213.

9 Ibid., 3: 953.

10 Ibid., 1: 217ff, 3: 956ff.

11 Siara, Ch. 1968: *Bürgerliches Formalecht bei Max Weber*. Frankfurt: Diplomarbeit.

12 Luhmann, N. 1970: *Soziologie des politischen Systems*, p. 167 in *Soziologische Aufklärung*. Copladen.

13   Luhmann, N. 1970: Positives Recht und Ideologie. *Soziologische Aufklärung*, Opladen, p. 180.
14   Luhmann, N. 1969: *Legitimation durch Verfahren*. Neuwied, p. 51.
15   Ibid., p. 139.
16   Ibid., p. 240.
17   "Structures reduce the extreme complexity of the world to a much narrowed and simplified domain of expectations which are presupposed as premises of behavior and normally not themselves questioned. They are always based, therefore, on *deceptions* . . . especially about the actual action-potential of men, and for this reason they must be arranged so as to take account of disappointments." Ibid., p. 233ff.
18   [Translator's note] For Weber's distinction between *zweckrational* ("purposive-rational", that is, means–ends oriented) and *wertrational* ("rationally oriented to value", that is, to the realization of certain values) see his discussion of "The Types of Social Action", in *Economy and Society*, volume 1.
19   Winckelmann, J. 1952: *Legitimität und Legalität in Max Webers Herrschaftssoziologie*. Tübingen, p. 75ff.
20   Ibid., p. 75ff.
21   Jaspers, K. 1964: *Max Weber*. (first published, Oldenburg, 1932); English translation in *Three Essays: Leonardo, Descartes, Max Weber*. Compare with W. J. Mommsen, 1959: *Max Weber und die deutsche Politik*. Tübingen, p. 418. "If Winckelmann wants to show that there are in Weber's theory of democratic authority so-called 'immanent limits to legitimation' of a value-oriented nature, then this is simply a misinterpretation."
22   Habermas and Luhmann 1971: *Theoric der Gesellschaft oder Sozialtechnologie?* Frankfurt, p. 243ff.
23   Edelmann, M. 1964: *The Symbolic Uses of Politics*; and 1971: *Politics as Symbolic Action*. Chicago.
24   Gadamer, H. G. 1969: *Wahrheit und Methode*. Tübingen.
25   Wellmer, A. 1971: *Critical Theory of Society*. New York, p. 41ff.
26   Habermas, J. 1972: Bewusstmachende ofer rettende Kritik? in *Zur Aktualitat Walter Benjamins*. Frankfurt.
27   U. Oevermann develops interesting arguments in a manuscript on the research strategy of the Institut für Bildungsforschung, Berlin 1970.
28   Bahr, H. E. (ed.) 1972: *Politisierung des Alltags*. Neuwied; Offe, Bürgerinitiativen, in *Strukturprobleme*, p. 153ff.
29   Mayntz, R. 1972: Funktionen der Beteilgung bei öffentlicher Planung. In *Demokratie und Verwaltung*. Berlin, p. 341ff.
30   On this point see H. P. Widmaier, *Machtstrukturen im Wohlfahrtsstaat*. Regensburger Diskussionsbeiträge zur Wirtschaftswissenschaft, 1973.
31   Shonfield, A. 1965: *Modern Capitalism*. London.
32   Offe, C. 1973: Krisen und Krisenmanagement in *Herrschaft und Krise*, M. Jänicke (ed.). Opladen.

3

Understanding the Roots of Publicness

BARRY BOZEMAN

"Submission to order is almost always determined by a variety of motives," Weber (1947, p. 132) tells us. Sometimes "submission," including compliance with organizational directives, is best explained by the influence of economic authority. The organization provides economic inducements for persons inside and outside the organization. While there is some dispute about the particular mechanisms of economic authority and their workings, it is easy to understand economic self-interest as a basis for action. Political compliance is not so easily understood. Do citizens, including organization members and clients, comply with political authority out of a sense of fear? Is it a "rational" response to the quality of service (Merelman, 1966) or to the coercive power of the state (Rothschild, 1977)? Is it respect for the state and its laws and recognition of the consequences of lawlessness (Friedrich, 1963)? Or is it a deep-seated sense of loyalty to shared traditions, political community, and political habits (Cochran, 1977)? And what of the motivational power of political symbols (Edelman, 1964)?

Property rights theory provides a useful and well-developed inter-pretation of the impact of economic authority on organization behavior. There is no comparable theoretical framework for explaining the impact of political authority on organizations, but instead a potpourri of assumptions and "grand theories," most of which do not directly address organization behavior.

Some of the leading controversies in the study of political authority are briefly reviewed below. A central thesis of this book is that a theory of public organizations, as distinct from a theory of government organ-izations, should be based on a publicness concept that considers the dimensional character of publicness, can cope with sector blurring, and, in principle, is applicable to any modern complex organization. A

63

concept of publicness as the level of political authority emanating from and constraining the organization meets these requirements.

Legitimacy and Political Authority

Political theorists writing about the nature of political authority have given little attention to the impact of political authority on organization behavior. Nevertheless, it is valuable to briefly review some of the leading controversies concerning legitimacy and political authority in order to place in context the organizationally relevant (but otherwise less ambitious) triadic model of political authority. Some of the questions that have drawn the attention of political theorists are pertinent to organization behavior, even if the theorists themselves have not drawn the connection. For example, political theorists have given much consideration to the question of political coercion, a topic closely related to organizational dependence and constraint. Likewise, questions about legitimacy are relevant to organizations' interactions with the public and relate to the public interest concerns of organizations.

Concepts of legitimacy

It is often argued (see Schaar, 1970; Dahl, 1956; Runciman, 1963) that the political authority of the state is unique and that its uniqueness can be traced to the legitimacy of actions taken on behalf of the state. By some conceptions (Mainzer, 1973; Lowi, 1969), the cornerstone of political authority is the state's monopoly on the legitimate use of coercion. Legitimate political authority is distinct because it takes precedence over all other authority types and over the claims of any individual or group. But one can make the case that legitimacy is chiefly psychological (Edelman, 1964), that it is embodied in the individual, and that it exists "only when someone obeys out of a belief that he ought to do so" (Lindblom, 1977, p. 19).

One does not expect consensus on the meaning and implications of the fundamental abstractions of political theory. Thus it is not surprising to find that so elemental a concept as legitimacy has taken on so many meanings and is used to serve many philosophical and instrumental purposes. Nor is it surprising that there is little agreement about how to (and even whether to) measure legitimacy (see, for example, Fraser, 1974). Yet despite the disagreement surrounding the concept, the issues upon which it turns are identifiable. One such issue is the relation of legitimacy to consent.

To Carl Friedrich (1963, p. 234), not only is consent a prerequisite of legitimacy, but it is a matter of whether "a given rulership is believed to be based on good title by most men subject to it." While such democratically oriented concepts of legitimacy are often well received, it is not clear whether they provide a firm foundation for government action. If legitimacy is dependent on individuals' contemporaneous assessments of the justness of government, legitimacy is necessarily volatile. If legitimacy is based on "good title," an explanation of the qualities of title must be supplied so that an assessment of its goodness can be made. Friedrich's concept of legitimacy is essentially Lockean and exhibits much the same problem of Locke's view of social contract. How are differences in individuals' perceptions of legitimacy resolved?

Critics of consent theory (such as McWilliams, 1971) have argued against its premises, especially against the notion that consent can be inferred. Consent cannot be inferred from receipt of state-provided benefits, because many benefits are collective goods and citizens cannot "avoid" benefit. Such political system supports as voting cannot be construed as consent unless the vote is a referendum on the state itself and not simply a choice among those who shall govern. Assuming that consent must be voluntary, one must be asked for his or her consent, there must be an opportunity for unfettered affirmation (or non-affirmation) of that consent, and consent must be communicated. Further, consent cannot be a matter of disposition or attitude but must be expressed directly. These conditions are not easily met.

Even if it were possible to meet stringent conditions for the giving of consent, the problem of intersubjective differences in perception of obligation remains. One approach to resolving this problem is to define the individual's granting of consent in terms of social compact or obligations to one's fellow citizens rather than in terms of obligation to the state (Rawls, 1971). However, as Tussman (1960) notes, there are problems with assuming that a social contract agreed on by one generation binds the next.

Some critics (such as Grafstein, 1981) charge that the chief flaw in most concepts of legitimacy, and especially in consent theory, is a focus on imputed but unknowable psychological states. It is argued that viewing legitimacy as a property of institutions is an effective means of avoiding mentalism (Martin, 1975). For legal positivist Hans Kelsen

(1949), legitimacy is a matter of the validity of the laws of the state and conformance to authorized legal process. Peter Stillman (1974) takes this view a bit further and defines legitimacy in terms of the compatibility of government actions and the value patterns of the political system. Thus, legitimacy is not so volatile as public opinion, but neither is it fixed to a Hobbesian view of virtually unlimited state prerogatives.

Most legal positivist conceptions offer some analytical convenience in that they dismiss the psychological components of legitimacy and thus skirt one of the more formidable problems of theory. However, theories that fail to come to grips with the ritualistic and symbolic elements of political authority are open to charges of unrealism (Bennet, 1975; Cobb and Elder, 1973).

Some view the contradictions of theories of legitimacy as indicative of the dialectical nature of legitimacy. Kann (1978, p. 388) resolves the paradoxes of consent theories of legitimacy in terms of the dialectic by which "the government promotes conscientiousness and reason simultaneously [and] maximizes the potential for citizens to legitimate government." Kann feels this dialectic is one that "promotes and tolerates the greatest challenge to its own authority." Morgan (1981) outlines a Madisonian view of political authority entailing a somewhat different dialectic pitting self-interest against stable institutions.

Legitimacy and public organization theory

While most works on political legitimacy are concerned with the legitimacy of the state as a whole, questions of legitimacy are important to public organization theory in at least two ways. First, one must consider the character of the state as a pervasive environmental influence on the behavior of particular organizations (Frankel, 1972; Martin, 1975). Second, it is meaningful to speak of the legitimacy of particular organizations quite apart from the legitimacy of the state (Hannigan and Kueneman, 1977; Merelman, 1966).

A government organization created by statute is imbued with the political authority of the state and, as a result, the organization's legitimacy is linked to that of the state. For many business organizations, the question of political legitimacy is relatively unimportant. Many businesses are provate agents acting independently on the basis of economic authority and the question of political legitimacy is only indirectly important insofar as it influences the legal environment of enterprise. But for many private nonprofit organizations and some businesses, the question of legitimacy is of more than passing interest. Many such organizations are endowed with political authority and thus are influenced directly by perceptions of the legitimacy not only of the state but also of the organization. For example, the American Bar Association is responsible for providing *pro bono publico* (for the public welfare) services for lawyers and for promulgating regulations that affect directly the conduct of the government system of justice. Likewise, boards of physicians are charged with similar public responsibilities for public health.

The countless advisory panels of government represent another case of private citizens and private organizations acting in a public capacity. For example, the National Science Board, a group of private individuals, is charged with significant policy-making responsibilities in science and technology. Perceptions of the legitimacy of such organizations can directly affect their ability to carry out effectively their public functions. The classic questions of legitimacy thus are pertinent to the political authority exercised by private as well as government organizations. Is the legitimacy of a physicians' review board largely a matter of legal designation, and thus is its public responsibility legally prescribed? Or is its public responsibility a matter of "good title"? If legitimacy is a matter of tolerating challenge to authority, then what does this say about the role of professionalism and technical expertise in the public arena?

While many of the classic questions of political theory are relevant to a theory of public organization behavior, it is not possible to simply direct the broader "answers" of political theory to the narrower "questions" of organization behavior. This is because political theory has been more valuable in raising the right questions about political authority than in providing answers. Many of the most basic questions of political authority remain unresolved. For example, none of the traditional rationales for legitimate political coercion is fully satisfying. Consent theory has moral appeal but is not easily translated into behavioral terms. Nor does consent theory resolve the problem of subjectivity. That is, if political authority ultimately resides with the individual, then it remains volatile. Social compact theory does not provide an adequate resolution because it is, at best, a complex mixture of consent, tradition, and habit. Legal positivism is not fully satisfying because it requires a level of agreement on procedure that is not easily guaranteed. Arguments about the supremacy of institutions in defining political legitimacy have the advantage of moving the focus away from mental states and disposition, but, in the process, they deny a role for the individual outside the framework of the institutions and thus leave one with a strong shell empty of content (Grady, 1976).

Thus, political theory, unlike property rights theory, does not provide an organizing framework for interpreting the effects of authority on organization behavior but does offer a useful point of departure. If there is any single lesson to be drawn from the diverse arguments about legitimacy and rationalization of political authority, it is that political authority is not best viewed as a unitary concept. In the discussion below, it is assumed that there are diverse sources and types of political authority, each with different implications for publicness and the behavior of organizations.

Three Types of Political Authority Endowments

Political authority can be characterized in many ways, but it is particularly useful to examine the source from which it flows and the endowments (rights, prerogatives) that result. Arguably, all political authority flows ultimately from individual citizens, but even if one takes that view it is still possible to speak of authority as mediated by institutions (Lipset, 1963). The triadic model of political authority addresses three different types of political authority. Before articulating the model, it is useful to describe each type of authority.

Primary political authority flows directly from individual citizens and is the bedrock of any political system. The ability of governments to make binding decisions is ultimately rooted in individuals' grants of legitimacy and in the commitments of individuals to both institutions and policies (Holmes, 1976). Despite the difficulties inherent in any attempt to measure or even map the flow of primary political authority, concepts of political authority based solely on institutional guarantors (see Kelsen, 1949; Stillman, 1974) are obviously incomplete. Institutions are created by individuals, commitments are made by individuals, and compliance to authority is an individual act.

As political theorists have noted, the subjectivity of individuals' judgments about the legitimacy of political acts adds an ingredient of volatility to public affairs, but one that is unavoidable and, in many respects, desirable. Historical analyses of revolution (Arendt, 1963) have demonstrated that individuals' grants of legitimacy are not immutable. Further, mass resistance to public policy (such as draft resistance during the Vietnam War and tax protest movements) is a reminder that individual grants of legitimacy are volatile.

Whereas primary political authority connects with consent theory, *secondary political authority* finds its counterparts in institutionally oriented and legal positivist theories of legitimacy. The necessity of delegating grants of authority to the polity is as much a matter of practical utility as of political philosophy. The size of the modern nation-state dictates that direct democracy is not viable for most policy initiatives and certainly not for the routine functioning of government. Secondary political authority is exercised by public officials, both elected and non-elected (including government bureaucrats and civil servants), charged with acting on behalf of the citizenry.

The grant of secondary authority is not without form and substance. In the United States, secondary authority obviously is constrained by the Constitution and accumulated statutes. But secondary political authority is not exclusively grounded in formal public policies. Indeed, it is a mistake even to define secondary authority exclusively in terms of policy. There is another element that is vitally important to an organizationally relevant concept of publicness: The term *governance structure* is used here to refer to the relatively stable patterns of political process that shape the conduct of public affairs in both the public and private sector.

Whereas primary political authority is vested in the individual citizen and secondary political authority in official institutions of government, *tertiary political authority* pertains to nongovernment organizations and private citizens. Tertiary political authority is delegated authority twice removed. Public officials are viewed as the delegates of private citizens, and these delegates sometimes endow private organizations (including business, nonprofit, and "mixed form" organizations) with political authority to act on behalf of the public. The vesting of political authority in private organizations differs from the much more common vesting of economic interests (Roy, 1981). In the latter case, the agency actively (but indirectly) represents the interest of private groups and organizations; in the former case, the private party is actually endowed with formal political authority, which is exercised directly.

Thus, some private organizations are, at the same time, constrained by secondary political authority (via government regulations, statutes, and so forth) and endowed with tertiary authority. This is a situation not unlike that in which most government organizations find themselves – endowed with secondary authority but, at the same time, subject to its constraints as dictated by government superiors. This parallel is useful in facilitating a theory of publicness based not on the legal status of organizations but on the effects of political authority.

Political Authority and Organization Behavior

Each of the three types of political authority enumerated above has implications for the behavior of individual organizations. Even primary political authority, which seems far removed from the day-to-day business of organizations, can be an important determinant of organizational actions and outcomes. Subsequently, the triadic model of political authority provides a description of the impact of political authority on organization behavior. First, however, it is useful to consider in turn how each type of political authority influences organization behavior.

Primary political authority and organization behavior

In the United States, citizens' views of the legitimacy of the state tend to be stable. Where there are major shifts in the citizenry's perceptions of the legitimacy of the state, the implications are enormous not only for organization behavior but also for general social upheaval. In such cases, organizations are affected for much the same reasons as are other social institutions, and thus these effects are not of special interest to organization behavior (but are more within the realm of social theory). But primary political authority affects organization behavior in a variety of ways, not just as a result of system changes in the legitimacy of the state.

It is convenient to view primary political authority as having effects at different orders of magnitude or at different "levels" of influence. At the most general level, primary political authority affects organization behavior as a result of shifts in the citizenry's assessment of the legitimacy of the state. At the most specific level, individual citizens' assessments of specific policies represent an influence of primary political authority.

Level I influence: assessments of the legitimacy of the state. Individual grants of legitimacy are selective, and thus the effects of primary political authority are only rarely direct. Obviously, one does not consciously consider each public policy issue that arises and evaluate it in terms of one's commitment to the legitimacy of the state. On most occasions, Level I primary political authority is on "automatic pilot." Individuals are only episodically motivated to reevaluate grants of legitimacy (Kourvetaris and Dobratz, 1982). The political system of the United States has been sufficiently stable that the only conspicuous and clear-cut example of Level I influence during the last 200 years is the Civil War. The secessionists, whether motivated by economic self-interest in slavery, loyalty to tradition and religion, or whatever, were by the act of secession declaring void the sovereignty of the United States government.

It is axiomatic that large-scale challenges to legitimacy are of sweeping consequence. But despite the United States experience, it is not the case that Level I political authority influence is either exceedingly rare or necessarily violent. As a case in point, consider the Mexican political system. In Mexico, massive changes in political systems have been frequent and, at least in some instances, nonviolent (Padgett, 1966). Of course, not every coup, whether violent or nonviolent, represents an influence of Level I political authority. Government changes based on personal power struggles are not often political system changes.

Level II influence: assessments of the role and scope of government. Somewhat more common than shifts in views of the legitimacy of government are shifts in assessments of the appropriate scope and role of state activity. Level II changes are illustrated by Franklin Roosevelt's New Deal and, perhaps, by the Reagan presidency. It is an oversimplification to say that the New Deal and the Reagan presidency can be explained entirely in terms of shifts in the citizenry's assessment of the scope and role of state activity. Public responses sometimes are better explained by perceptions of the president's personal effectiveness than by ideology (Hibbs, 1982).

The effects of Level II changes are enormous. Events such as the New Deal have far-reaching effects on the populations of organizations and on the ecology of whole classes of organizations. Kaufman (1976) has noted that federal government agencies' patterns of birth and decline are best accounted for by shifts in epochs. Similarly, students of organization life cycles (Kimberly, Miles and Associates, 1980; Kaufman, 1985) draw attention to the changes arising from such systemic effects. Primary political authority affects organization behavior through its role in determining the state's sphere of activity. In this manner, primary political authority affects not only the rise and demise of federal agencies but also the fates of business organizations. For example, the Reagan administration's emphasis on "privitization" not only has curtailed the programs and activities of federal agencies but also has shifted policy direction toward state and municipal governments (Palmer and Sawhill, 1982) and affected the range and type of activities performed by business organizations (Levine, 1986).

Level III and IV influence: assessments of policies. In some instances, public opinion is focused on general classes of policy actions – "macropolicies"; at other times, it is focused on specific policies – "micropolicies." For example, the public's views about national security and defense are often expressed in broad, unfocused terms (for example, "too much money is spent on defense"; "there is a weapons gap"). Less commonly, public opinion sometimes centers on a specific policy action (such as aid to the contras in Nicaragua). In each case, primary political authority plays a role in shaping organization behavior. A major shift in assessments of macropolicies is, for present purposes, an instance of Level III influence and, similarly, the arousal of public opinion in connection with micropolicies is an instance of Level IV influence. Note that the use of the terms *shift* and *arousal* denotes an important distinction. The macropolicies of Level III are sufficiently broad that there is a presumption of long-standing, if changeable, public opinion. Level III macropolicies are enduring. By contrast, a long-term public opinion cannot be presumed for micropolicies of Level IV, not only because the issues are more specific but also because they are shorter term.

In many cases, the effects of level III and IV exercises in primary political authority directly affect government organizations and indirectly affect other organizations. If the conviction that there should be an expanded defense establishment is acted on, the agencies of the Department of Defense (and "losers" in other budget categories) are directly affected, but the indirect effects for other organizations are substantial, especially in regions of the country where defense contractors and organizations are economically significant.

In sum, primary political authority is exercised in several ways, and for each level of activity there are strong implications for government and nongovernment organizations. Primary political authority, regardless of level, is unique in that it originates with individual citizens and their perceptions of the political environment. These perceptions are not colored by such institutions as the media, government, and political parties. Likewise, organizations and social institutions play a critical role in translating and channeling primary political authority (Hess, 1963) and in political participation. This means that it is quite difficult to trace the effects of primary political authority because it is so intertwined with other policy influences (such as elections, secondary political authority, interest group activity, and lobbying) and with perceptions of individual political actors and their roles (Weissberg, 1972; Greenstein, 1960). Nonetheless, primary political authority is as important as it is difficult to fathom.

Secondary political authority and organization behavior

When one reflects on the impact of publicness on the behavior of organizations, the examples that first come to mind are those involving the exercise of secondary political authority. Organizations are affected by statutes, administrative rules and regulations, executive orders, and judicial mandates. In many instances, these impacts are direct and easily understood. Likewise, each might be viewed as yet another instance of "government climbing on the back of industry." Or, to put it another way, secondary political authority affects not just government organizations but others as well.

To recapitulate, the souce of secondary political authority is, by definition, public officials working within the framework of formally designated government institutions. As is the case for primary political authority, the source of authority is invariate, but the type of output or influence is not. While there are a great many ways to classify the outputs of government bodies, for purposes of understanding the effects of political authority a distinction must be made among *policy constraints and benefits*, *endowments*, and *governance structures*. Roughly, these influences on organization behavior can be thought of, respectively, as public policy outputs, delegations of political authority, and structural features of policy processes. Moreover, the exercise of secondary political authority may result in influence of each type. Consider as an example the award of a defense contract. It is an endowment because, by definition, it permits the private contractor to perform activity on behalf of the government. It thereby extends the authority of the private contractor. It is a constraint in that the contract specifies obligations of the contractor and imposes performance requirements. The issue of governance structures is less clear-cut.

Governance structures are defined as the relatively stable patterns of political process that shape the conduct of public affairs. To put it simply, the effects of publicness on organization behavior accrue as often from policy process as from policy substance. To extend the example of the defense contractor, the behavior of the focal organization (the contractor) is affected not only by the specific constraints and grants of authority embodied in the DOD–contractor relationship but also by the processes that inevitably follow from interaction with a public policy agent such as the Department of Defense. In addition to any specific requirements set by the contract, the contractor is inexorably affected by government accounting and purchasing procedures, affirmative action and equal employment opportunity (EEO) hiring requirements, freedom of information provisions, and other such routine features of public processes. Since governance structures are vitally important to the understanding of the impact of political authority on organizations, some elaboration of the concept is required.

Governance structures: the publicness of process

A focus on governance structures is especially appropriate in any attempt to build public organization theory. Whereas the grants of authority and the constraints flowing from secondary public authority are highly idiosyncratic and sometimes difficult to classify, policy process effects are more stable, more easily classified, and more predictable. It is useful to distinguish between two types of governance structures. Popular discussions of the "strings" attached by government involvement often pertain to governance structures. We shall refer to these "strings" as *policy routines*. In addition to policy routines, there is another category of governance structures that is more fundamental and more stable: Governance structures such as the federal system, separation of powers, and other such rudimentary structures are referred to as *policy system elements*. Policy routines and policy system elements are often closely related such that many policy routines are shaped by policy system elements. For example, the minute specifications for General Accounting Office (GAO) audits can be understood, at least in part, as manifestations of the constitutional principle of separation of powers.

Tertiary political authority and organization behavior

Tertiary political authority is similar to the grants of authority provided by secondary political authority. But whereas secondary political authority permits the focal organization to engage in certain specified activities, tertiary authority vests policy-making power in the organization. Thus, it is a grant of authority of a peculiar type. With tertiary political authority, the organization becomes a policy actor. The effects of tertiary authority are profound because the organization's behavior is not simply affected by publicness: Its behavior *is* public. Under this peculiar endowment of authority, the focal organization is empowered to exercise secondary authority.

In the vast majority of instances, tertiary political authority is restricted to government agencies. Since the granting of tertiary authority is, in most respects, equivalent to granting governmental status, it may seem trivial to suggest that tertiary authority is restricted to government agencies. But this seemingly obvious assumption of equivalency between tertiary political status and formal governmental legal status deserves closer inspection. In the first place, there are private entities that are granted authority to act with the full backing of government and with the force of law while at the same time preserving their private status. Only a few examples come to mind, most of which are professional organizations such as physicians' review boards, American Bar Association licensing boards, and so forth. The more important – or at least more pervasive – instance of private organizations receiving grants of tertiary authority is multi-organizational entities which include some subunits that retain purely private status and some that have governmental policy-making authority. A few fully private organizations have been set up with the encourgagement and through the initiative of government. An example is Comsat (Musolf, 1983), an organization set up as a legitimate monopoly in communications. Another instance of tertiary authority flowing to a private organizational actor is the government-owned, contractor-operated [US] Department of Energy laboratories. While the political authority of the contract operator is limited to management of the government entity under its purview, this narrow policy-making responsibility is nonetheless an instance of tertiary political authority.

In addition to those cases in which legitimate political authority is formally delegated to private organizations, there is also a suggestion that most corporations are by their very nature minigovernments (Eells,

1962; Blumberg, 1971). Vogel (1975) argues that the development of the large corporation has devolved from its original limited grant of legitimacy into public operations for which it has no formal grant of authority. Vogel observes that (1) citizens make demands directly to corporations, (2) citizens behave toward corporations in a way similar to the way in which they interact with the state, and (3) citizens apply a standard of accountability to corporations similar to that applied to government. When these facts are taken together with corporations' increasing concern with social forces, the corporation is best viewed as a public organization, Vogel argues.

Tertiary political authority is an interesting question in organization theory because of the rise of new organizational forms and the rethinking of allocations of political authority. However, tertiary political authority is still much more common to governmental agencies than to other organization forms, and an understanding of tertiary political authority requires examination of the processes by which government agencies are created by other government agencies.

A Triadic Model of Political Authority

The theory presented [here] seeks to provide an alternative view of publicness relevant to the explanation of organizations' behavior. Publicness is not viewed as an absolute quality but as a dimension. The dimension is defined by the organization's mix of economic and political authority as a basis of its activity. It is argued that conventional property rights theory provides an acceptable, though not ideal, explanation of the effects of economic authority on organization behavior. Property rights theory is, in some respects, tailor-made for a public organization theory. Such is not the case with political authority. The nature of political authority is not always clear, and there is little agreement as to the causal processes by which political authority affects organization behavior.

This [section] has presented a view in which three types of political authority flow from diverse sources, with both direct and indirect influences, and entailing a variety of impacts, alternately enhancing, constraining, and legitimizing the actions of the focal organization. The effects of political authority on organization behavior are not easy to determine or to conceptualize. Conceptual difficulty is explained by a number of factors. The most important is the complexity of effects.

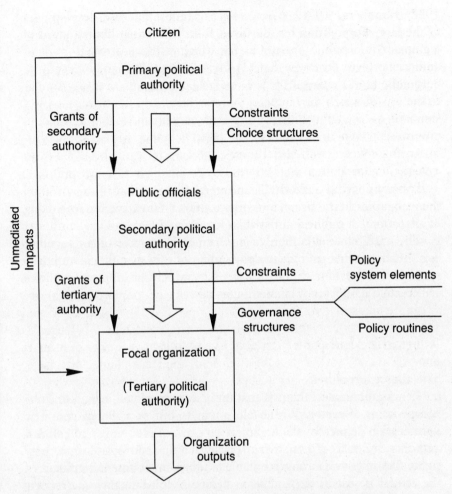

Figure 3.1 Triadic model of the effects of political authority on organization behavior

Complexity in this case arises from the breadth of impact, the simultaneous effects of diverse sources of political authority, and the difficulty of separating effects of political authority (given their breadth) from other environmental influences, especially those that are economic in origin, on organization behavior. Nevertheless, it is necessary to attempt some depiction of the impacts of political authority on organization behavior, and figure 3.1 represents a beginning attempt to sort through the complexity.

The triadic model assumes that it is useful to distinguish among the effects of three distinct types of political authority. As represented in figure 3.1, the model suggests that: (1) individuals, acting on endowments of primary authority, delegate decision authority to public officials; (2) public officials formulate laws and shape governance structures that affect organizations; (3) the behavior of organizations, both governmental and nongovernmental, is affected by endowments and constraints arising from secondary authority and, at least in some instances, primary authority; (4) the behavior of organizations is also affected by the governance structures that determine the channels for distribution of authority as well as acceptable protocol for compliance; and (5) for some organizations, tertiary authority confers on organizations the ability to perform as a public actor with governmental legitimacy.

The triadic model is highly simplified and does not seek to account for the determinants of authority; nor does it specify the range or quality of values for the terms of the model. The objectives of this abbreviated model are (1) to distinguish three types of political authority, (2) to demonstrate the flow of various types of political authority, and (3) to show in a highly general way that organization behavior is influenced by grants of tertiary political authority, constraints of primary and secondary political authority, and the channeling effects of governance structures.

The triadic model suggests that the influence of political authority is independent of sector. While one might well expect that government organizations typically would be subject to a wider range of political authority influences than would private organizations and that those influences might be stronger relative to other environmental influences, the model is just as applicable to business, third-sector, government enterprise, and mixed form organizations as it is to traditional government agencies. Property rights theory is a model of economic authority that is applicable to any organizational form, and for the purposes of symmetry it is necessary that the model of political authority developed here is likewise applicable to any organization form.

At the deepest level, political and economic cornerstones of a society are built on common cultural ground. For this reason, if for no other, one would expect significant mutual influence between political and economic authority. When we further consider that much of public policy – perhaps the majority of domestic policy – is rationalized in terms of economic goals, we can see the difficulty in separating one social instrument from another.

Political authority influences the behavior of any organization subject to the rules of a polity. In some cases, those impacts are from distant sources (such as public opinion); in other cases those impacts are proximate and direct (for instance, audits of government contracts). In some cases, the impacts flow from characteristics of policy processes, while in others they flow from the policies themselves.

The key to the publicness puzzle is the organization's mix of political and economic authority. An organization is "more public" to the extent that its ratio of political authority increases. Political authority carries with it diverse constraints, prerogatives, and even symbols (Goodsell, 1977; Pool, 1952). The organization subject to political authority may, as a result, become more or less powerful, more or less effective, and/or more or less adaptive, but it is sure to be changed.

Notes

Excerpt from chapter five of *All Organizations are Public: Bridging Public and Private Organizational Theories*. San Francisco: Jossey-Bass (1987). Reproduced by kind permission of Jossey-Bass Publishers, all rights reserved.

References

Arendt, Hannah 1963: *On Revolution*. New York: Viking Penguin.
Bennet, W. L. 1975: Political Sanctification: The Civil Religion and American Politics. *Social Science Information*, 14 (6), 79–102.
Blumberg, P. I. 1971: The Politicization of the Corporation. *Business Lawyer*, 26, 1551–87.
Cobb, R. and Elder, C. 1973: The Political Uses of Symbolism. *American Politics Quarterly*, 1, 305–38.
Cochran, C. E. 1977: Authority and Community. *American Political Science Review*, 71, 546–58.
Dahl, R. A. 1956: *A Preface to Democratic Theory*. Chicago: University of Chicago Press.
Edelman, M. 1964: *The Symbolic Uses of Politics*. Urbana: University of Illinois Press.
Eells, R. 1962: *The Government of Corporations*. New York: Free Press.
Frankel, C. 1972: Political Disobedience and the Denial of Political Authority. *Social Theory and Practice*, 2 (1), 85–98.
Fraser, J. 1974: Validating a Measure of National Political Legitimacy. *American Journal of Political Science*, 18, 117–34.
Friedrich, C. 1963: *Man and His Government*. New York: McGraw–Hill.
Goodsell, C. T. 1983: *The Case of Bureaucracy*. Chatham, NJ: Chatham House.
Grady, R. 1976: Obligation, Consent, and Locke's Right to Revolution: Who Is to Judge? *Canadian Journal of Political Science*, 9 (2), 277–92.

Grafstein, R. 1981: The Legitimacy of Political Institutions. *Polity*, 14 (1), 51–69.

Greenstein, F. 1960: The Benevolent Leader: Children's Images of Political Authority. *American Political Science Review*, 54 (4), 934–43.

Hannigan, J. A. and Kueneman, R. M. 1977: Legitimacy and Public Organization. *Canadian Journal of Sociology*, 2 (1), 125–35.

Hess, R. 1963: The Socialization of Attitudes Toward Political Authority. *International Social Science Journal*, 15 (4), 542–59.

Hibbs, D. A. 1982: Reagan Mandate from the 1980 Elections: A Shift to the Right. *American Politics Quarterly*, 10 (4), 387–420.

Holmes, R. 1976: *Legitimacy and the Politics of the Knowable*. Boston: Routledge & Kegan Paul.

Kann, M. E. 1978: The Dialectic of Consent Theory. *Journal of Politics*, 40, 386–408.

Kaufman, H. 1976: *Are Government Organizations Immortal?* Washington DC: Brookings Institution.

Kaufman, H. 1985: *Time, Chance, and Organizations*. Chatham, NJ: Chatham House.

Kelsen, H. 1949: *General Theory of Law and State*. Cambridge Mass: Harvard University Press.

Kimberly, Miles and Associates 1980: *The Organizational Life Cycle: Issues in the Creation, Transformation, and Decline of Organizations*. San Francisco: Jossey-Bass.

Kourvetaris, G. and Dobratz, B. A. 1982: Political Power and Conventional Political Participation. *Annual Review of Sociology*, 8, 289–317.

Levine, C. 1986: The Federal Government in the Year 2000: Administrative Legacies of the Reagan Administration. *Public Administration Review*, 46 (3), 195–206.

Lindblom, C. E. 1977: *Politics and Markets*. New York: Basic Books.

Lipset, S. 1963: *Political Man*. New York: Doubleday.

Lowi, T. J. 1969: *The End of Liberalism*. New York: Norton.

McWilliams, W. C. 1971: On Political Illegitimacy. *Public Policy*, 29, 440–54.

Mainzer, L. C. 1973: *Political Bureaucracy*. Glenview, Ill: Scott, Foresman.

Martin, R. 1975: Two Models for Justifying Political Authority. *Ethics*, 86 (1), 70–5.

Merelman, R. M. 1966: Learning and Legitimacy. *American Political Science Review*, 60, 548–67.

Morgan, R. J. 1981: Madison's Analysis of the Sources of Political Authority. *American Political Science Review*, 75, 613–25.

Musolf, L. 1983: *Uncle Sam's Private Profitseeking Corporations: Comsat, Fannie Mae, Amtrak, and Conrail*. Lexington, Mass: Lexington Books.

Padgett, L. 1966: *The Mexican Political System*. Boston: Houghton Mifflin.

Palmer, J. and Sawhill, I. 1982: *The Reagan Experiment*. Washington DC: Urban Institute Press.

Pool, I. 1952: *Symbols of Democracy*. Stanford CA: Stanford University Press.

Rawls, J. 1971: *A Theory of Justice*. Cambridge Mass: Harvard University Press.

Rothschild, J. 1977: Observations on Political Legitimacy in Contemporary Europe. *Political Science Quarterly*, 92, 487–501.

Roy, W. G. 1981: The Process of Bureaucratization in the United States State Department and the Vesting of Economic Interests. *Administrative Science Quarterly*, 26 (3), 419–33.

Runciman, W. G. 1963: *Social Science and Political Theory*. Cambridge UK: Cambridge University Press.

Schaar, J. H. 1970: Legitimacy in the Modern State. In P. Green and S. Levinson (eds), *Power and Community*. New York: Vintage Books.

Stillman, P. 1974: The Concept of Legitimacy. *Polity*, 7 (1), 33–56.

Tussman, J. 1960: *Obligation and the Body Politic*. New York: Oxford University Press.

Vogel, D. 1975: The Corporation as Government. *Polity*, 8, 5–37.

Weber, M. 1947: *The Theory of Economic and Social Organization*. New York: Free Press.

Weissberg, R. 1972: Adolescents' Perceptions of Political Authorities: Another Look at Virtue and Power. *Midwest Journal of Political Science*, 16 (1), 147–68.

4

Thinking about Corporate Legitimacy

Michael Gordy

Much has been said about the question of whether or not the power exercised by business corporations is legitimate, particularly in recent years when the explosion of communications and capital mobility has seemed to expand that power exponentially. This essay is meant to be a modest contribution to a necessary period of reflection on the way that the question of legitimacy is raised, particularly with respect to corporate practice in its current socio-political and historical context. My hope, somewhat less modest, is that this period of reflection will shed a bit of light on possible meanings of the concept of corporate legitimacy, by locating it in relation to other concepts that should inform managerial thinking.

Let's begin with a truism: Legitimacy has to do with the way the exercise of power is perceived. Saying this doesn't take us very far, but it sets out the terrain on which our discussion will take place. Legitimacy is a concept with certain practical political and economic implications, but it is first of all a concept, and a recognizable part of the set of ideas by which a society makes sense of itself to itself.

Of course we're interested here in the concept of legitimacy in one of its specific applications – the legitimacy of corporate power and practice – but we must make an initial detour into some fairly abstract ideas about legitimacy *per se* in order to orient our inquiry and, hopefully, avoid some of the pitfalls associated with many discussions of this type.

One possible way to begin thinking about how the exercise of power is perceived is by way of an empirical investigation. We might simply try to gather information by the use of a sort of marketing survey, asking a carefully-chosen selection of persons what they think of when and if they ever think about power, or more specifically, what they think about corporations, or even more specifically, what they think about the behavior of this or that corporation.

I use the example of a marketing survey because this is the kind of investigation a corporation might undertake in order to monitor the development of any political or social problems in its area of business. Such an approach might well give a fairly clear picture of what people are thinking at a particular moment and in a particular set of circumstances, and it might be a help in short-term managerial planning. What it will not do, however, is help anyone anticipate changes in peoples' attitudes toward corporate power, or the power of institutions in general – nor will it help anyone understand the concept of legitimacy itself.

A marketing approach to the problem would either take for granted whatever the people interrogated used as a definition of legitimacy, or else it would impose its own *ad hoc* definition on them in the way it asked the question. The first possibility would ground everything on the functional equivalent of a vote: the inquiry would necessarily remain superficial in that it would not in itself afford any insight into the meaning of the concept. The second, insofar as it imposed a definition prior to the investigation of its meaning, would short-circuit the discussion of legitimacy by using the concept it was investigating as though the investigation had already taken place.

Another approach might be to discuss the concept of legitimacy in the abstract, apart from its historical, social, political and economic context. This philosophical debate might be very useful for comparing the logical consistencies of this or that definition and for constructing an elegant definition ourselves. A problem would arise, however, as it does with so many philosophical discussions, when we tried to use the concept to understand a particular situation. Let me explain this a little further.

In the history of philosophical thought the concept of legitimacy has been closely allied with, if not derived from, questions of moral good. An action is legitimate if it is good, if it is right, if it conforms to or embodies some moral principle. If we can understand and agree upon the concept of moral good we can then derive the concept of the legitimate use of power, whether by institutions or by individuals.

The history of philosophy is replete with competing as well as complementary concepts of the moral good and the principles derived from them, and it is surely beyond the scope of this essay to rehearse that history. Nevertheless a couple of points need to be emphasized.

While there are many ethical principles espoused by philosophers, theologians, preachers of all sorts, as well as, most importantly, by countless millons of persons who do not make moral philosophy their profession, it is almost a cliché to point out that these principles do not apply themselves. Their application depends upon judgements made by human beings whose nature is formed by the social, political, cultural and economic conditions under which they live. Moreover, the very choice of *which* ethical principles to apply is made by these same human beings, a condition that engenders unending and seemingly unresolvable ethical disputes. It often seems quite impossible to understand why others take the moral positions they do; sometimes it is equally difficult to understand why we ourselves take certain positions.

Given this difficulty it is helpful to ask whether or not the very abstractness of the debate over moral principles and, concomitantly, the question of legitimacy, renders its results relatively unenlightening – albeit entertaining – within the context of concrete business practice. Do we not deflect our attention from the practical question of corporate legitimacy when we try to reproduce, perhaps badly, the history of moral philosophy in our search for a deeper understanding of the concept of legitimacy and its uses? So much that has been written about business ethics has been ignored as irrelevant by managers in their day-to-day *function* as managers that I suspect this to be the case.

It seems we've reached an impasse. Either we take a market-driven approach to the issue and elevate what may be transient opinions to the level of eternal truths, or we search abstractly for eternal truths while leaving for some future time the problem of their application.

I would like to propose the barest outline of a third approach. It appears to me that a really useful understanding of the concept of corporate legitimacy can only be obtained by investigating the historical, economic, political, cultural and social context within which it occurs. In short, I think it necessary to examine the conjuncture of social forces whose variegated dynamic gives the concept its meaning. As a preliminary step I believe it will be helpful to consider several alternative theoretical structures we might use for that examination.

What I mean by *theoretical structure* is as follows: "Information" or "facts" or "concepts" do not exist in a vacuum. The very definition of information, for instance, depends on a context of meaning within which some things are considered "facts" while others are not. Specifically, all theoretical questions, and here I use the term *theoretical* to include any ideas one has about what one is doing, are raised within a context structured by the specific interrelation of concepts used to think about the object under investigation.

Since a concept never exists in isolation, its meaning depends on its relations with other concepts in a structure that itself has a meaning. If the relationship between concepts changes, then so does the meaning of each individual concept as well as the meaning of this relation.

Consider, for example, the concept of "motion" in natural science in light of the differing theoretical structures employed in the work of Aristotle and Galileo. For Aristotle the theoretical structure used to comprehend nature depended on the central concept of *telos*, or purpose. Every physical phenomenon was described in terms of its purpose, and each individual purpose was articulated theoretically with the concept of the purpose of nature itself.

For Galileo, on the other hand, the theoretical structure of natural science did not include the concept of purpose nor was it centered around a primary concept of any sort. Rather, the concepts used, e.g., force, inertia, and so on, were decentralized. No concept was wholly reducible to any other.

The concept of motion, therefore, meant one thing within the Aristotelian structure where it was tied to the concept of *telos* and another within the structure of Galileo where it was not. There was no possible resolution of this conflict of meaning even though the name of the concept remained the same. The theoretical structures, which alone determine the meaning of the concepts within them, were too different.

Moreover, the differences in the theoretical structures of the works of Aristotle and Galileo determined what sorts of questions could or could not be raised for each thinker. To ask "What is the purpose of the growth of a tree?" is not a meaningful scientific question for Galileo, while determining the rate of acceleration of falling bodies could not really become an issue for Aristotelian theories of nature.

Recognizing this moves us beyond specific questions of fact to an examination of the context within which those questions can be asked. In terms of our present investigation it moves us into a consideration of what sort of theoretical structure might allow the question of corporate legitimacy to be meaningfully raised. We need to understand at least briefly what sort of theory of society we might best use to produce knowledge of the kind we seek, namely, knowledge of the way the concept of corporate legitimacy actually functions in the world, and knowledge of the ways it interacts with the historical forces and social structures upon which its evolution depends.

First of all we should realize that all theoretical structures have more or less intimate relations with non-theoretical practices – economic, political, legal and cultural – which constitute the social reality that any theory of society purports to know. These non-theoretical practices are the *conditions of existence* of theory insofar as the latter could not do without them: again, theory does not exist in a vacuum. But the *character* of the relation between a theoretical structure and the non-theoretical practices underlying and supporting it is crucial to whether or not the theory can produce the knowledge we want. If a theoretical structure is blindly dependent upon these non-theoretical practices it will be unable to produce knowledge of them and will give us a view of society that is malformed at best. Important elements of the social order will remain invisible, and the development of such a theory of society will reflect, completely and unconsciously, the development of these non-theoretical social forces. We shall see that the mark of such a theoretical structure is that it has a central concept whose content is taken as "given".

An example that is pertinent to our interests in this essay is the theoretical structure underlying most modern, and some not-so-modern theories of society, namely, *humanism*. This theoretical structure is organized around the concept of *Man*, or *Human Nature*. All social relations, personal histories, and history itself, are taken to be expressions of this central concept. Defined at the outset of all inquiry, that concept is not the result of any investigation based on humanism, nor is its content ever questioned: it is taken as given descriptively, directly revealed.

Moreover, humanism takes man to be the Subject of History and Society in the double sense that these are products of human action which in turn condition that action. This is indicated by the well-known humanist slogan, "Man makes history, and history is the history of man." Although the descriptions of man or of human nature may vary, they all share the feature of *purporting to be descriptions*, revelations of the "real", obvious if one would only look carefully.

But within the history of social and political theory this obviousness is not so obvious. History is, in fact, replete with a number of mutually exclusive theories of society based on different definitions or "descriptions" of human nature.

For Greek philosophers humanity was defined as basically rational and social; evidence for this was found in the existence of mathematics and in the transparency of social interdependence. "No man is self-sufficing" says Socrates at the beginning of *The Republic*, and his statement is accepted without argument. "Man is a social animal" states Aristotle in his *Politics*, taking this as a premise. The edifice of Greek theories of society was erected on this base. No wonder that the concept of society as a marketplace of free individuals is conspicuously absent.

By way of contrast, the period of early capitalism was marked by the ascendancy of the theories of Hobbes and Locke, philosophers who took a very different description of humanity for granted. Presumimg humanity to be fundamentally individual, their theories took social relations to be dependent on and secondary to the individual interests, both rational and non-rational, of each human being. No wonder that each saw society as a marketplace for competing individual interests, tending towards chaos if not for the intervention of a strong, contractually agreed-upon government.

For the Greeks, human rationality meant the ability to transcend the material conditions of life by reflecting upon the universal principles of the world, or of seeing these principles embodied in those material conditions. No doubt the existence of a large slave class made it possible for those who were not slaves to engage in this reflection. Thus the Greek definition of rationality, no matter what else it did or what other interests it served, implicitly supported and was supported by a society wherein one class of people lived by directly extracting the economic surplus produced by others without ever having to involve themselves in the nitty-gritty of material production. Moreover, since the level of technical development was basically agricultural rather than industrial, there was no intimate connection between economic life and either philosophical reflection or purportedly scientific theories of the universe, the possible exception being the relationship between mathematics and navigation. Thus the "rational nature of man" appeared to depend on the transcendence of material life.

Likewise, because the appropriation of the economic surplus took the form of direct extraction from its producers, which in turn depended upon the political system of slavery, the material interdependence of society was obvious to every member of Greek society. Hence the unquestioned definition of man as a social being.

The era of early capitalism, on the other hand, was marked by the ascendancy of market relations in the realm of economic production, and by the increasingly close relationship between scientific discovery and technical development. The definition of man as a creature of individual self-interest, whose rationality is the handmaiden of that interest, made sense in terms of the material and social conditions of the time.

Built around the buying and selling of labor power, the capitalist system of production engendered a theory of human nature appropriate to the wage relationship. That relationship presupposes the alienability of labor power, i.e., the existence of *individuals* who are free to sell their time for wages. Only if their time is considered a form of property can the exchange be made, hence the definition of man as a free individual who has "property in himself", and for whom all social relations are a matter of the contract into which he freely enters.

Because market relations dominated the forms of social and economic life, the "obviousness" of this definition of humanity remained unquestioned. The differences between the theories of Hobbes and Locke, for instance, do not revolve around the basic principles of individualism or social contract. Although these principles differ somewhat for each author, the differences do not entail any fundamental disagreement.

Important here is not the particular analysis of the social forms of material life underlying each of these theoretical constructions; in any event, I do not wish to imply that social theory is somehow *reducible* to economic practice. The point is, rather, that the concepts of humanity in each case are articulated through political and economic practice and cannot be understood apart from knowledge of those practices. But it is precisely because theories of society based on humanism take for granted the content of their particular concept of humanity, a content that is shaped by the extra-theoretical conditions we've been talking about, that they cannot produce this knowledge for us. So what can?

Let's begin by trying to conceive of a theoretical structure whose elements are arranged in a way that does not suffer from defects of the type we've been considering. Apparently the biggest problem with social theories built on humanism or like conceptions is that they revolve around a central concept and thus tend to reduce complex phenomena to a fundamental set of principles. They *interpret* social events and evolution; this is a far cry from being able to *anticipate* fundamental social change, which is what, ultimately, we want to be able to do. The most damaging aspect of this conundrum is that this type of theory takes the content of its central concept as somehow *revealed*; and what this means is that it makes no fundamental distinction between its knowledge and the reality it purports to know. Hence all its knowledge, if that is what we choose to call it, is *ex post facto*.

Now if we take another look at the differences between Galileo and Aristotle's theories of nature we can see more clearly what I'm talking about. The phenomena Galileo sought to know were not "forces" or "inertia" but falling bodies and the movements of the planets. He meant the concepts of force and inertia to be used to *produce* knowledge of something that would remain *untouched* by that knowledge. Far from testifying to revelation, he was trying to produce knowledge of reality.

Moreover, whatever knowledge he produced with these concepts did not exhaust the possibilities for further investigation. In principle it is always possible to learn more about falling bodies and the movements of the planets by building on existing knowledge, using and modifying the concepts Galileo invented. In short, Galileo's theoretical framework *opened up* the road to scientific experimentation and discovery.

The contrast with Aristotle is enlightening. By organizing their conceptions of nature around the central, given concept of *telos*, Aristotelian philosophers of nature (the scientists of the time) found purpose expressed anywhere and everywhere. Each natural phenomenon was for them an expression of the teleological character of the universe, and each was considered to have been fully "explained" once its relation to this teleology was revealed. *Telos* found its concrete embodiment in natural phenomena, while those phenomena were fully understood in terms of *telos*.

Rather than troubling to argue against the Aristotelian theoretical structure, Galileo simply broke with it by developing concepts whose arrangement was independent of teleology or any other central concept. This freed him from any need to reduce his discoveries to mere expressions of a pre-given idea. In practice, therefore, he was distinguishing his theory from the reality he was investigating. This left open the possibility for other scientists to modify his theories, the better to produce knowledge of that reality without having to abandon the theoretical framework he created. Science as we now think of it was born precisely in this break with the practice of *interpreting* reality.

Science does not reduce its knowledge to a mere expression of reality. Its theoretical tools are just that: tools, modified by their use. Just as a knife is shaped over time by the things it cuts, so scientific theory is altered by the discoveries it makes, discoveries made possible by the openness of its theoretical structure, but discoveries that in turn require modification of that theoretical structure in order to be accommodated by it. Science is "scientific" *precisely because* it can profoundly transform its theoretical structure, and this it can do because in its practice it distinguishes between the knowledge it produces and the reality it seeks to know.

Consider the fact that the meaning of Galileo's concept of "force" was very different for him than the highly technical meaning it has in physics today. There is nevertheless a profound continuity between the two meanings. From its use throughout the history of post-Galilean science, the concept of force has made possible discoveries that have in turn ramified and modified the determinations of its own meaning: determinations that have become increasingly complex. Yet in all this its theoretical function has remained intact; its meaning has never been taken as "given", nor has it evolved into a concept to which other concepts in its theoretical context are reduced. Because of this it can never be captured once and for all in a single definition; it remains open to further knowledge of the reality which stands beyond it.

If we are to produce knowledge of society so that we can understand the concept of corporate legitimacy in relation to the social and historical forces that shape its content, we must try to find tools that will help us produce that knowledge in ways analogous with (but not reducible to) the practice of post-Galilean natural science. What this means is that we must choose concepts whose content is not taken as given, that we must not conflate the knowledge we produce with the reality we seek to know, that we must arrange our concepts in such a way that they can be modified in light of what we might discover, and that we must keep in mind that one of the major purposes of this whole exercise is to be able to anticipate changes in the meaning of the concept of corporate legitimacy. This will allow us to glimpse the way it affects the business environment as a whole, as well as the context within which particular businesses operate, and in so doing unblock the path to practical application.

Let's begin by thinking of society as made up of a variety of different *practices*: political, cultural, economic, ideological, social, and so on. These practices are unified in some way or another because together they comprise what we might call the "social whole". Yet they are also different from one another or we wouldn't be calling them different names. It is easy enough to accept that cultural practice is different from economic practice is different from political practice is different from . . . etc. The problem we must now address is how to express theoretically this unity-in-diversity without falling into the trap of seeing the various social practices as expressions of a central concept.

No society can exist without dealing with the basic economic needs of its population, and every society organizes itself around economic practice first of all. Subsistence societies are called that precisely because virtually all the energies of the members of that kind of society are taken up in the struggle with material scarcity. Economic practice did not produce the surplus necessary for freeing up time for other activities in any organized way.

Over the many millenia of human existence these societies found, by trial and error, ways to organize their material production so that a surplus evolved. The discovery and development of agriculture was the first, most important step. With this the cultural activities that had been inextricably bound up with economic practice could gradually be separated out from material production and established as really distinct practices, often associated with persons or groups of persons whose primary task was to oversee these newly-distinguished activities. Like-wise, the existence of a material surplus made possible struggles over its disposition, and with these struggles came new ways of organizing society politically. Without belaboring the point, human material evolution made possible the development of separate social practices that were not *inherent* in economic production, but which were nonetheless dependent upon it.

Given this rather sketchy analysis it is reasonable to conclude that economic practice dominates any social whole, but not in the sense that the other practices of which society is constituted are reducible to economic practice. Rather, the practices that comprise any society are arranged in a hierarchy dominated by the economy, but within which hierarchy each practice has a certain *relative* autonomy. We must now consider what this means.

Because the conception of society we are looking at explicitly excludes the notion of some central, unifying essence to which all social practices can be reduced as expressions, it follows that the social whole must be seen to be essentially complex and "de-centered". Causal relationships do not occur from some centre outwards; the effectivity of social practices displays a mutuality through which any one of them might have a determining influence on any other. Each social practice is therefore characterized by an autonomous existence with respect both to what it is in itself and to the ways in which it interacts with other practices in society.

Indicative of this is the role of the state in late capitalist society. It is pretty obvious that state action often delimits the process of capital accumulation insofar as regulation, fiscal and monetary policy, market protection and, finally, military intervention, have made possible certain fundamental economic developments while inhibiting others. The de-regulation of many forms of market transactions during the Reagan administration and the effect of this on the flourishing of junk bonds, leveraged buy-outs and other speculative activities are only some recent examples.

Here the state, the dominant institution of political practice, reacts decisively on economic practice, while on the other hand changes in the economy can either restrict or enhance the state's access to resources and thereby shape its activities.

If we left it at this we'd have no real conception of the unity of the social whole; we'd have no social *whole* at all. While I've been stressing the independence of the various social practices in order to emphasize the essential complexity of the social whole, I now have to elaborate their simultaneous dependence.

The social whole I'm trying to articulate is a structure of mutually-effective social practices arranged in a hierarchy. This hierarchy does not determine the specific *content* of any of the practices, only their *locus of effectivity*: it defines the cross-relations of dominance and sub-ordination, of cause and effect, between them. The various practices within a society are therefore related to each other not through the mediation of a mutually-expressed central essence but through their positions in a hierarchy of effectivity. This hierarchy itself is articulated at any moment in time by the conjoint operation of two factors, one structural and the other conjunctural.

The structural factor is economic practice. We have seen that every society must first of all organize itself to meet its economic needs, but that this economic practice does not determine the content of the other social practices that depend upon it. Yet economic practice dominates. A specific form of political practice, for instance, has its effect on the practices and institutions of religion and vice-versa; politics and religion have their effect on the style and content of cultural production – art, literature, music, philosophy – and are in turn influenced by these products; and all the elements affect and in turn are affected by economic practice. But the domination of economic practice means that whatever might be the form and consequence of a particular practice at a specific moment in time, the ultimate tendency of every practice is to support and reinforce the economic relations specific to that society. If this were not so, then the structure of the social whole would be fundamentally transformed.

From this perspective it would appear that developments in the economy set out fairly strictly the hierarchy of mutual effectivity of all the practices in the social whole. This would be true except for what I called earlier the "conjunctural factor".

If the social whole is essentially complex, then each social practice has a certain autonomy, even though the dominance of the economy makes that autonomy relative. This means that the developments in each practice can be said to have their own histories; developments in one practice cannot be reduced to developments in another. As we have seen, the structural dominance of the economy means that the relations between the various practices are set out by the history, rhythm and tempo of economic practice. Nonetheless each practice is characterized by its own particular history. The conjuncture of the histories of the various practices depends, therefore, not only on the hierarchical relations between them but also on the particular histories of each practice. Thus the structural and conjunctural factors are complementary but not reducible to one or the other. On this view, then, developments within one practice are seen to be affected by developments in others, the specific intensity of these effects being determined by developments in the economy.

This is what I meant when I said that the specific practices that comprise a social whole display a "relative autonomy": relative because the complex interaction and mutual effectivity of the various practices is *dominated* by economic practice, and *autonomous* because the economy's domination does not imply that the dominated practices are absorbed. It is possible to think, therefore, of cases where political, cultural and ideological developments have had a decisive effect on economic practice without losing sight of the fact that developments in the economy left the space for these non-economic developments to occur. We'll look more closely at this later on.

Keep in mind that in all this I am proposing concepts that are explicitly not descriptive; they are meant to be tools for the production of knowledge of society. I cannot overemphasize the necessity for maintaining the position that the knowledge we seek to produce is not the same thing as the reality of which it is knowledge. Without holding onto this principle, a principle informing all natural science since Galileo, we should fall into the trap of mere *ex post facto* interpretation and reductionism as indicated earlier.

By this time you may be wondering how this increasingly abstract theoretical discussion could ever produce the kind of insights into the question of corporate legitimacy that might be helpful to managerial planning and decision-making. It is probably the moment to bring our discussion back to a less abstract level in order to demonstrate the usefulness of this theoretical foray, and also show that the trip was really necessary.

Every society, and every member of society, has a set of ideas that make sense of the way that society functions and of the way people live within it. These ideas, whether they be religious, cultural, moral, or whatever, tend to be embodied in institutions that codify and transmit them. Institutions of this sort, whether they be formal or informal, we might call ideological practice, for want of a more precise term.

The reason any society needs ideological practice is that mere instinct is not enough to reproduce the social relations that characterize the society itself. Without a set of social ideas, people wouldn't know what was expected of them in their social roles; moreover, they'd have no conception of who they were. It would be impossible to speak of society at all. And since language is a social construct, there being no such thing as a "private language", we'd be hard put to explain how we could be having this discussion.

So let's assume here that any society needs an ideological practice.

The social ideas I'm talking about are ideas about the concrete social experience members of society have. People act in certain specific ways in different societies and they have different ideas about what they're doing depending on the way their particular society is constituted; the way its economy is set up, its political life is structured, its cultural life proceeds, and so forth. It is almost a truism that the dominant social ideas support the notion that the way one's society is arranged is somehow natural, that calling the basis of those arrangements into question borders on the absurd. People then find that the reproduction of those social arrangements is almost inevitable; it appears to occur automatically.

Without going too much further into this, let me say that ideological practice, supported as it is by the other practices of society, reinforces those other practices in turn. In general this support is generated by the overwhelming belief that the arrangement of the individual practices, and of the social whole they constitute, is *legitimate*. In this sense the concept of the overall legitimacy of social arrangements serves as a standard for judging the legitimacy of the various institutions that embody different aspects of the practices comprising society.

I'm not using the concept of legitimacy here in any specific sense; in each society the meaning of that concept will reflect the historical development of the ideological practices of that society, which will in turn reflect the developments of other practices with which ideological practice intersects. And in the last instance, the interaction of these various developments will reflect developments in the economic life of the society, for it is, after all, economic practice that sets out the framework within which other social developments can take place. But whatever the particular content a specific society gives to the idea of legitimacy, it is certain that legitimacy serves as a means whereby people accept the social arrangements under which they live.

If those social arrangements are generally accepted as legitimate, then the legitimacy of particular institutions is judged in terms of whether or not a specific institution conforms to what is expected of society as a whole. In other words, if a society is seen to be legitimate for certain reasons, then its institutions, i.e., the institutions that embody the different practices that make it up, will be judged by the same or at least similar criteria. And if the particular institution in question is, at a particular moment in history, a pivotal element in society, then the judgement of its legitimacy will have a profound impact on the sense of whether or not the general structure of society is legitimate. Briefly, if an institution has become so powerful that its behavior shapes the overall character of a society, then the question of its legitimacy may, at times, overshadow the question of the legitimacy of the society of which it is a part.

This is, of course, pertinent to the question of corporate legitimacy, and here we'll have a look at the case of the United States. The rise of corporations to their current level of economic power (and I'd have to include financial institutions under the heading of corporations) is a fairly recent phenomenon, even in the history of capitalism. The tendency for the control of capital to concentrate and centralize, and this at an accelerating rate, necessitated the formation of organizational structures that would both codify the division of labour within the firm, and de-personalize the ownership of capital from a legal point of view. Moreover, the freedom of capital to move from one sector of enterprise to another resulted in the *de facto* separation of management from ownership. The corporate entity developed largely in response to these developments and needs.

As long as corporations were perceived to be functioning for the good of the society in which they were based, their legitimacy was not fundamentally in question. Corporate organization, albeit undemocratic, was nevertheless perceived to be under the control of a democratically-elected government. If the state was generally accepted as legitimate, then the institutions under its control were considered legitimate as well. Any particular misdemeanors on the part of a specific corporation could be addressed as individual problems rather than problems with the institution of corporate business as a whole. The statement "What is good for General Motors is good for the country," while the butt of many jokes, nonetheless embodied the widely-accepted view that the health of the corporate community was essential to the well-being of American society.

While corporations produced primarily within the US and only exported their products, this view was easy enough to support. But the need to maintain a stable or even increasing rate of profit, plus the increasing dependence of production on raw materials available only abroad, made it reasonable for corporations to export capital and eventually set up production facilities in other countries. There was the added advantage that taxation could be minimized by the movement of capital in this way. Likewise, pressure could be increased on union wage demands by the threat of moving factories abroad. Since the purpose of a corporation is first and foremost to make money for its shareholders, any other considerations necessarily took a back seat.

As I said, corporate interest in profit-making was considered legitimate insofar as it was seen to be subject to control by the state for the good of society as a whole. But once it became evident that certain large corporations could escape that control by becoming truly multinational, and as evidence accrued that in a number of instances corporate behavior worked in direct opposition to stated governmental goals (Gulf Oil's behavior during the Angolan civil war is one example), corporate legitimacy could no longer be taken for granted.

The perception, then, that corporations were somehow able to escape all governmental control undermined the belief that they were working for the "common good" nationally defined. A part of the government's legitimacy comes from the belief that it is governing for the good of all; by escaping from nationally-imposed laws, and by having that fact become apparent to the public, corporations lost a lot of the acceptance that comes from being perceived as subordinate to the state.

Let's take a look at the recent past. One of the enduring legacies of the Reagan administration is the deregulation of the financial markets. There were numerous political reasons for this, but the background for the various decisions taken in this regard was that speculative investment had become, over time, more profitable than investment in production.

Everyone knows that production takes time: building factories, developing new products, organizing sales forces, etc., all require that money invested stay in place for awhile. Anyone investing in new or expanded production must necessarily take a longer view of his return than someone investing in trading existing production facilities.

With the end of the 1960s came the beginning of a long-term decline in the profitability of new production. This occurred for various reasons, but by the end of the 1970s it was clear that more money was to be made, and faster, by investing in speculative areas like real estate and financing rather than in industry. But because the government in the 1930s had erected barriers to untrammeled trading in equities and bonds, and because banking laws were generally enforced, the incentive for speculation was dampened.

Reagan was elected on the promise, among others, that he would bring back expanding prosperity to the average middle-class American and provide opportunity for entrepreneurship. The image of what he projected centered on increasing freedom, and one of his administration's top priorities was to increase the freedom of speculators. By forcing deregulation of the money markets while fueling an upper-middle class feeding frenzy with tax reductions and a hugely-expanded military budget, the Reaganites were able to construct a formidable pillar to their continued electoral success. People with disposable income were able to invest in undertakings the likes of which would never have been approved before the Reagan years, and money traders jumped at the opportunity to make profits off the ensuing expansion of corporate, personal, and especially governmental debt.

Building on a cultural mix of xenophobia, individualism and belief in a fuzzily-defined concept of "freedom", the Reagan Administration was able to present military spending and financial deregulation in a package wrapped in the image of hyperpatriotism and megaconsumption – using to great effect the fact that television had become the cornerstone of shared consciousness amongst an increasingly atomized and manipulable population.

The various effects of this period are the subject for many books. For our purposes it is sufficient to note that while the extremely negative long-term economic effects of these developments are only now becoming evident to a majority of economic thinkers, the short-term effects on the financial markets created a boom mentality that effectively covered up the dangers of speculation. Investors would have felt foolish if they had refused to partake in the feast of superprofits because the ubiquitous cultural and political message was that prosperity was here to stay. Elaborate rationalizations were invented for leveraged buyouts and other financial bonanzas while the retail boom at the upper end of the market fostered the illusion of increased economic strength. The fact that the Gross National Product (GNP) does not distinguish between productive and speculative economic activity masked the degradation of the productive infrastructure.

Meanwhile, inflation was exported via an over-valued dollar that was supported by high interest rates, interest rates which fueled a massive inflow of foreign capital to US financial markets. Public debt increased exponentially while the marketing of debt itself via the deregulated bond market became one of the chief growth sectors of the entire economy.

Here we have a situation where trends in the economy created space for the decisive intervention of cultural and political developments into economic practice, which intervention rebounded to effect further change in the cultural and political spheres. Our theoretical framework allows us to see this interaction by tracking the differing histories of the social practices without reducing them to each other, nor to a pre-given concept. Thus we can begin to clarify a very complex situation without reducing it to simplifications.

But if we accept this overall framework, how can we understand the actions of a single firm in a specific set of circumstances? To answer this question we must now turn to a brief examination of a fictitious case study.

Let's say that a certain multinational corporation, X, is threatened by a hostile takeover attempt. X is a highly diversified multinational whose original product base was a set of household products whose usefulness was generally recognized and appreciated. In recent years X diversified into financial services, real estate investment and tourism, while maintaining its predominance in the manufacture and marketing of its original line of products.

Based in the US, X nonetheless did the largest share of its manufacturing abroad. X had built a modern, efficient plant in France that was the flagship of its production operations, combining the latest in technology with innovative and imaginative employee relations to achieve a level of productivity and profitability that was the envy of its competitors. In fact, the high motivation and excellent training of its workforce made this factory a model for other industries as well.

Located in a small town, the factory provided employment to almost a thousand people and accounted, directly and indirectly, for over half of the community's economic activity. As a result, loyalty to the company extended far beyond the actual workforce. The town identified its well-being with the well-being of the firm.

With the deregulation of speculative stock activities in the US, X became a prime candidate for takeover. Relative to the value of its assets and goodwill, X was undervalued on the stock exchange, and because of its diversity it could be unbundled and sold relatively easily. Moreover, even though its manufacturing plant in France was highly profitable, X's overall balance sheet did not ensure the fidelity of its shareholders. A raider would have a fairly easy time of it.

X's management, sensing the threat, tried to find ways to defend against it. Unable to secure sufficient financing to buy back X's stock, they set about making the corporation less attractive to the raider. They decided to close their French plant.

From the point of view of X's management this was an unavoidable action. For them, a company has a legitimate obligation to survive, and it was clear from their perspective that if X was bought out it would have been dismembered. The fact that their own position as managers was under attack only lent poignancy to their principled point of view. Their action was legitimate because, according to their lights, they would be promoting the greatest good for the greatest number of people, i.e., themselves, the stockholders, and the employees in the diverse elements of X's empire.

The perspective of the fired employees, and those who depended on them for their own livelihood, was understandably different. Above and beyond their own personal plight they could not understand why a profitable, efficient and harmoniously-running plant should be closed. Why should they be punished for their success? Why, when the perceived purpose of the company was to create wealth and well-being, should those very qualities be the reason for its demise? Why, when their loyalty had been built on the foundation of shared benefits and mutual interdependence, should a decision be taken thousands of miles away without their position and viewpoint being taken into account? Moreover, how is it legitimate from society's point of view that commercial logic require the destruction of efficient production facilities?

From the managers' perspective they had the right to do what they wanted with the resources under their control; that was the meaning of freedom to them. They also considered that they had no choice, given that the threat of a hostile takeover had put them in this position. What they did not consider was the fact that as a group they had supported lobbying efforts to deregulate the financial markets in order to enhance X's ability to expand its own speculative activities. In any event, "then was then and now is now", and there was nothing for them to do in the event other than what they did. Or so it seemed to them. The laws of the market economy forced their hand.

Even though this account is sketchy almost to the point of caricature, I believe we can see from it the interplay of social forces that conjoined to create this conflict in the perception of the use of corporate power. Both the management of X and the plant employees perceived the plant closing within what we might call "local" structures, using categories shaped by the interaction of economic, social, political and ideological practices that constituted the environment in which they worked. Crudely put, the first difference in their outlooks was the difference between laboring in a small town in France and overseeing the disposition of resources throughout a highly diversified corporate institution from an office in New York.

But this was not all. For the workers in France, freedom was conjoined with a sense of personal responsibility which enhanced the overall discipline and efficiency of the workforce, while for X's management the term was linked with the free movement of capital. From the point of view of the employees, management had a choice: it could have sold the plant rather than closing it. Their personal vulnerability as managers may not have been diminished, since the cash made available by the sale would have made X even more attractive to a raider, but the production facilities and the workers' jobs would have been saved. For the managers, of course, there was no choice given the climate of speculation encouraged by deregulation. They believed that they were obliged, in their function as managers, to do whatever they could to save the company from dismemberment.

In neither case was it possible to see beyond a basic conflict of interest to try and understand how it came about. But by taking a larger, less "local" historical perspective, we can begin to clarify the situation. Having laid out briefly an account of the political and economic environment of the late 1980s in the US, I indicated how the interaction between economic, political and ideological trends set the stage for the kind of speculative activity that made the conflict of perception at X inevitable.

The conflict of perception, as we can see, was not simply a reflection of a conflict in economic interest, although that conflict of interest was certainly real. The conflict in perception of the legitimacy of X's behavior resulted from the fact that the ideology of "the good of the whole" means different things when conjoined with different non-ideological developments. Corporate legitimacy cannot be abstracted from its context, from its interrelationships with politics, economic developments, cultural milieu, etc. Moreover, the differing perceptions of corporate legitimacy in specific instances can only be understood in reference to a wider theater of social interaction. This wider perspective, in turn, leaves open the possibility for anticipating conflicts about legitimacy without having recourse to abstract, universal formulations.

There is no "final point" to be made here. What I have tried to do is indicate a general frame of reference and theoretical apparatus that I believe could be helpful in clarifying the concept of corporate legitimacy and its uses. If the exposition of this perspective seems open-ended, it is meant to be. I believe that the work of understanding these issues has just begun, and I see this essay as a small contribution to that work.

Part II

Management *v.* Owners:
Who Should Control?

5

Traditional Theory and the New Concept of the Corporation

ADOLF A. BERLE AND GARDINER C. MEANS

When such divergent results are obtained by the application of the logic of two major social disciplines to a new fact situation, we must push our inquiry still further back into the assumptions and concepts of those disciplines.

Underlying the thinking of economists, lawyers and business men during the last century and a half has been the picture of economic life so skillfully painted by Adam Smith. Within his treatise on the "Wealth of Nations" are contained the fundamental concepts which run through most modern thought. Though adjustments in his picture have been made by later writers to account for new conditions, the whole has been painted in the colors which he supplied. Private property, private enterprise, individual initiative, the profit motive, wealth, competition – these are the concepts which he employed in describing the economy of his time and by means of which he sought to show that the pecuniary self-interest of each individual, if given free play, would lead to the optimum satisfaction of human wants. Most writers of the nineteenth century built on these logical foundations, and current economic literature is, in large measure, cast in such terms.

Yet these terms have ceased to be accurate, and therefore tend to mislead in describing modern enterprise as carried on by the great corporations. Though both the terms and the concepts remain, they are inapplicable to a dominant area in American economic organization. New terms, connoting changed relationships, become necessary.

When Adam Smith talked of "enterprise" he had in mind as the typical unit the small individual business in which the owner, perhaps with the aid of a few apprentices or workers, labored to produce goods for market or to carry on commerce. Very emphatically he repudiated the stock corporation as a business mechanism, holding that dispersed ownership made efficient operation impossible. "The directors of such companies," he pointed out, "being the managers rather of other people's money than their own, it cannot well be expected that they should watch over it with the same anxious vigilance with which the partners in a private copartnery frequently watch over their own. Like the stewards of a rich man, they are apt to consider attention to small matters as not for their master's honour, and very easily give themselves a dispensation from having it. Negligence and profusion, therefore, must always prevail, more or less, in the management of the affairs of such a company. It is upon this account that joint stock companies for foreign trade [at the time he was writing the only important manifestation of the corporation outside banks, insurance companies, and water or canal companies] have seldom been able to maintain the competition against private adventurers. They have, accordingly, very seldom succeeded without an exclusive privilege, and frequently have not succeeded with one. Without an exclusive privilege they have commonly mismanaged the trade. With an exclusive privilege they have both mismanaged and confined it."[1]

Yet when we speak of business enterprise today, we must have in mind primarily these very units which seemed to Adam Smith not to fit into the principles which he was laying down for the conduct of economic activity. How then can we apply the concepts of Adam Smith in discussing our modern economy?

Let us consider each of these concepts in turn.

Private Property

To Adam Smith and to his followers, private property was a unity involving possession. He assumed that ownership and control were combined. Today, in the modern corporation, this unity has been broken. *Passive property*, – specifically, shares of stock or bonds, – gives its possessors an interest in an enterprise but gives them practically no control over it, and involves no responsibility. *Active property*, – plant, good will, organization, and so forth which make up the actual enterprise, – is controlled by individuals who, almost invariably, have only minor ownership interest in it. In terms of relationships, the present situation can be described as including: (1) "passive property," consisting of a set of relationships between an individual and an enterprise, involving rights of the individual toward the enterprise but almost no effective powers over it; and (2) "active property," consisting of a set of relationships under which an individual or set of individuals hold powers over an enterprise but have almost no duties in respect to it which can be effectively enforced. When active and passive property relationships attach to the same individual or group, we have private property as conceived by the older economists. When they attach to different individuals, private property in the instruments of production disappears. Private property in the share of stock still continues, since the owner possesses the share and has power to dispose of it, but his share of stock is only a token representing a bundle of ill-protected rights and expectations. It is the possession of this token which can be transferred, a transfer which has little if any influence on the instruments of production. Whether possession of active property – power of control over an enterprise, apart from ownership – will ever be looked upon as private property which can belong to and be disposed of by its possessor is a problem of the future, and no prediction can be made with respect to it.[2] Whatever the answer, it is clear that in dealing with the modern corporation we are not dealing with the old type of private property. Our description of modern economy, in so far as it deals with the quasi-public corporation, must be in terms of the two forms of property, active and passive, which for the most part lie in different hands.

Wealth

In a similar way, the concept "wealth" has been changed and divided. To Adam Smith, wealth was composed of tangible things – wheat and land and buildings, ships and merchandise – and for most people wealth is still thought of in physical terms. Yet in connection with the modern corporation, two essentially different types of wealth exist. To the holder of private property, the stockholder, wealth consists, not of tangible goods – factories, railroad stations, machinery – but of a bundle of expectations which have a market value and which, if held, may bring him income and, if sold in the market, may give him power to obtain some other form of wealth. To the possessor of active property – the "control" – wealth means a great enterprise which he dominates, an enterprise whose value is for the most part composed of the organized relationship of tangible properties, the existence of a functioning organization of workers and the existence of a functioning body of consumers.[3] Instead of having control over a body of tangible wealth with an easily ascertainable market value, the group in control of a large modern corporation is astride an organism which has little value except as it continues to function, and for which there is no ready market. Thus, side by side, these two forms of wealth exist: – on the one hand passive wealth, liquid, impersonal and involving no responsibility, passing from hand to hand and constantly appraised in the market place; and on the other hand, active wealth – great, functioning organisms dependent for their lives on their security holders, their workers and consumers, but most of all on their mainspring – "control." The two forms of wealth are not different aspects of the same thing, but are essentially and functionally distinct.

Private Enterprise

Again, to Adam Smith, private enterprise meant an individual or few partners actively engaged and relying in large part on their own labor or their immediate direction. Today, we have tens and hundreds of thousands of owners, of workers and of consumers combined in single enterprises. These great associations are so different from the small, privately owned enterprises of the past as to make the concept of private enterprise an ineffective instrument of analysis. It must be replaced with the concept of corporate enterprise, enterprise which is the organized activity of vast bodies of individuals, workers, consumers and suppliers of capital, under the leadership of the dictators of industry, "control."

Individual Initiative

As private enterprise disappears with increasing size, so also does individual initiative. The idea that an army operates on the basis of "rugged individualism" would be ludicrous. Equally so is the same idea with respect to the modern corporation. Group activity, the coordinating of the different steps in production, the extreme division of labor in large scale enterprise necessarily imply not individualism but cooperation and the acceptance of authority almost to the point of autocracy. Only to the extent that any worker seeks advancement within an organization is there room for individual initiative – an initiative which can be exercised only within the narrow range of function he is called on to perform. At the very pinnacle of the hierarchy of organization in a great corporation, there alone, can individual initiative have a measure of free play. Yet even there a limit is set by the willingness and ability of subordinates to carry out the will of their superiors. In modern industry, individual liberty is necessarily curbed.

The Profit Motive

Even the motivation of individual activity has changed its aspect. For Adam Smith and his followers, it was possible to abstract one motive, the desire for personal profit, from all the motives driving men to action and to make this the key to man's economic activity. They could conclude that, where true private enterprise existed, personal profit was an effective and socially beneficent motivating force. Yet we have already seen how the profit motive has become distorted in the modern corporation. To the extent that profits induce the risking of capital by investors, they play their customary role. But if the courts, following the traditional logic of property, seek to insure that all profits reach or be held for the security owners, they prevent profits from reaching the very group of men whose action is most important to the efficient conduct of enterprise. Only as profits are diverted into the pockets of control do they, in a measure, perform their second function.

Nor is it clear that even if surplus profits were held out as an incentive to control they would be as effective an instrument as the logic of profits assumes. Presumably the motivating influence of any such huge surplus profits as a modern corporation might be made to produce would be subject to diminishing returns. Certainly it is doubtful if the prospect of a second million dollars of income (and the surplus profits might often amount to much larger sums) would induce activity equal to that induced by the prospect of the first million or even the first hundred thousand. Profits in such terms bear little relation to those envisaged by earlier writers.

Just what motives are effective today, in so far as control is concerned, must be a matter of conjecture. But it is probable that more could be learned regarding them by studying the motives of an Alexander the Great, seeking new worlds to conquer, than by considering the motives of a petty tradesman of the days of Adam Smith.

Competition

Finally, when Adam Smith championed competition as the great regulator of industry, he had in mind units so small that fixed capital and overhead costs played a role so insignificant that costs were in large measure determinate and so numerous that no single unit held an important position in the market. Today competition in markets dominated by a few great enterprises has come to be more often either cut-throat and destructive or so inactive as to make monopoly or duopoly conditions prevail. Competition between a small number of units each involving an organization so complex that costs have become indeterminate does not satisfy the condition assumed by earlier economists, nor does it appear likely to be as effective a regulator of industry and of profits as they had assumed.

In each of the situations to which these fundamental concepts refer, the Modern Corporation has wrought such a change as to make the concepts inapplicable.[4] New concepts must be forged and a new picture of economic relationships created. It is with this in mind that at the opening of this volume the modern corporation was posed as a major social institution; and its development was envisaged in terms of revolution.

The New Concept of the Corporation

Most fundamental to the new picture of economic life must be a new concept of business enterprise as concentrated in the corporate organization. In some measure a concept is already emerging. Over a decade ago, Walter Rathenau wrote concerning the German counterpart of our great corporation:

"No one is a permanent owner. The composition of the thousandfold complex which functions as lord of the undertaking is in a state of flux ... This condition of things signifies that ownership has been depersonalized ... The depersonalization of ownership simultaneously implies the objectification of the thing owned. The claims to ownership are subdivided in such a fashion, and are so mobile, that the enterprise assumes an independent life, as if it belonged to no one; it takes an objective existence, such as in earlier days was embodied only in state and church, in a municipal corporation, in the life of a guild or a religious order ... The depersonalization of ownership, the objectification of enterprise, the detachment of property from the possessor, leads to a point where the enterprise becomes transformed into an institution which resembles the state in character."[5]

The institution here envisaged calls for analysis, not in terms of business enterprise but in terms of social organization. On the one hand, it involves a concentration of power in the economic field comparable to the concentration of religious power in the mediaeval church or of political power in the national state. On the other hand, it involves the interrelation of a wide diversity of economic interests, – those of the "owners" who supply capital, those of the workers who "create," those of the consumers who give value to the products of enterprise, and above all those of the control who wield power.

Such a great concentration of power and such a diversity of interest raise the long-fought issue of power and its regulation – of interest and its protection. A constant warfare has existed between the individuals wielding power, in whatever form, and the subjects of that power. Just as there is a continuous desire for power, so also there is a continuous desire to make that power the servant of the bulk of the individuals it affects. The long struggles for the reform of the Catholic Church and for the development of constitutional law in the states are phases of this phenomenon. Absolute power is useful in building the organization. More slow, but equally sure is the development of social pressure demanding that the power shall be used for the benefit of all concerned. This pressure, constant in ecclesiastical and political history, is already making its appearance in many guises in the economic field.

Observable throughout the world, and in varying degrees of intensity, is this insistence that power in economic organization shall be subjected to the same tests of public benefit which have been applied in their turn to power otherwise located. In its most extreme aspect this is exhibited in the communist movement, which in its purest form is an insistence that *all* of the powers and privileges of property, shall be used only in the common interest. In less extreme forms of socialist dogma, transfer of economic powers to the state for public service is demanded. In the strictly capitalist countries, and particularly in time of depression, demands are constantly put forward that the men controlling the great economic organisms be made to accept responsibility for the well-being of those who are subject to the organization, whether workers, investors, or consumers. In a sense the difference in all of these demands lies only in degree. In proportion as an economic organism grows in strength and its power is concentrated in a few hands, the possessor of power is more easily located, and the demand for responsible power becomes increasingly direct.

How will this demand be made effective? To answer this question would be to forsee the history of the next century. We can here only consider and appraise certain of the more important lines of possible development.

By tradition, the corporation "belongs" to its shareholders, or, in a wider sense, to its security holders, and theirs is the only interest to be recognized as the object of corporate activity. Following this tradition, and without regard for the changed character of ownership, it would be possible to apply in the interests of the *passive* property owner the doctrine of strict property rights, the analysis of which has been presented previously. By the application of this doctrine, the group in control of a corporation would be placed in a position of trusteeship in which it would be called on to operate or arrange for the operation of the corporation for the *sole* benefit of the security owners despite the fact that the latter have ceased to have power over or to accept responsibility for the *active* property in which they have an interest. Were this course followed, the bulk of American industry might soon be operated by trustees for the sole benefit of inactive and irresponsible security owners.

In direct opposition to the above doctrine of strict property rights is the view, apparently held by the great corporation lawyers and by certain students of the field, that corporate development has created a new set of relationships, giving to the groups in control powers which are absolute and not limited by any implied obligation with respect to their use. This logic leads to drastic conclusions. For instance, if, by reason of these new relationships, the men in control of a corporation can operate it in their own interests, and can divert a portion of the asset fund of income stream to their own uses, such is their privilege. Under this view, since the new powers have been acquired on a quasi-contractual basis, the security holders have agreed in advance to any losses which they may suffer by reason of such use. The result is, briefly, that the existence of the legal and economic relationships giving rise to these powers must be frankly recognized as a modification of the principle of private property.

If these were the only alternatives, the former would appear to be the lesser of two evils. Changed corporate relationships have unquestionably involved an essential alteration in the character of property. But such modifications have hitherto been brought about largely on the principle that might makes right. Choice between strengthening the rights of passive property owners, or leaving a set of uncurbed powers in the hands of control therefore resolves itself into a purely realistic evaluation of different results. We might elect the relative certainty and safety of a trust relationship in favor of a particular group within the corporation, accompanied by a possible diminution of enterprise. Or we may grant the controlling group free rein, with the corresponding danger of a corporate oligarchy coupled with the probability of an era of corporate plundering.

A third possibility exists, however. On the one hand, the owners of passive property, by surrendering control and responsibility over the active property, have surrendered the right that the corporation should be operated in their sole interest – they have released the community from the obligation to protect them to the full extent implied in the doctrine of strict property rights. At the same time, the controlling groups, by means of the extension of corporate powers, have in their own interest broken the bars of tradition which require that the corporation be operated solely for the benefit of the owners of passive property. Eliminating the sole interest of the passive owner, however, does not necessarily lay a basis for the alternative claim that the new powers should be used in the interest of the controlling groups. The latter have not presented, in acts or words, any acceptable defense of the proposition that these powers should be so used. No tradition supports that proposition. The control groups have, rather, cleared the way for the claims of a group far wider than either the owners or the control. They have placed the community in a position to demand that the modern corporation serve not alone the owners or the control but all of society.

This third alternative offers a wholly new concept of corporate activity. Neither the claims of ownership nor those of control can stand against the paramount interest of the community. The present claims of both contending parties now in the field have been weakened by the developments described in this book. It remains only for the claims of the community to be put forward with clarity and force. Rigid enforcement of property rights as a temporary protection against plundering by control would not stand in the way of the modification of these rights in the interest of other groups. When a convincing system of community obligations is worked out and is generally accepted, in that moment the passive property right of today must yield before the larger interests of society. Should the corporate leaders, for example, set forth a program comprising fair wages, security to employees, reasonable service to their public, and stabilization of business, all of which would divert a portion of the profits from the owners of passive property, and should the community generally accept such a scheme as a logical and human solution of industrial difficulties, the interests of passive property owners would have to give way. Courts would almost of necessity be forced to recognize the result, justifying it by whatever of the many legal theories they might choose. It is conceivable – indeed it seems almost essential if the corporate system is to survive – that the "control" of the great corporations should develop into a purely neutral technocracy, balancing a variety of claims by various groups in the community and assigning to each a portion of the income stream on the basis of public policy rather than private cupidity.

* * * * *

In still larger view, the modern corporation may be regarded not simply as one form of social organization but potentially (if not actually) as the dominant institution of the modern world. In every age, the major concentration of power has been based upon the dominant interest of that age. The strong man has, in his time, striven to be cardinal or pope, prince or cabinet minister, bank president or partner in the House of Morgan. During the Middle Ages, the Church, exercising spiritual power, dominated Europe and gave to it a unity at a time when both political and economic power were diffused. With the rise of the modern state, political power, concentrated into a few large units, challenged the spiritual interest as the strongest bond of human society. Out of the long struggle between church and state which followed, the state emerged victorious; nationalist politics superseded religion as the basis of the major unifying organization of the western world. Economic power still remained diffused.

The rise of the modern corporation has brought a concentration of economic power which can compete on equal terms with the modern state – economic power versus political power, each strong in its own field. The state seeks in some aspects to regulate the corporation, while the corporation, steadily becoming more powerful, makes every effort to avoid such regulation. Where its own interests are concerned, it even attempts to dominate the state. The future may see the economic organism, now typified by the corporation, not only on an equal plane with the state, but possibly even superseding it as the dominant form of social organization. The law of corporations, accordingly, might well be considered as a potential constitutional law for the new economic state, while business practice is increasingly assuming the aspect of economic statesmanship.

Notes

Excerpt from *The Modern Corporation and Private Property*, by Adolf A. Berle and Gardiner C. Means, first published by Macmillan in 1933. This reprint possible by kind permission of W. S. Hein, Buffalo, New York, all rights reserved.
1 Adam Smith, The Wealth of Nations. Everyman's Library edition, volume 2, p. 229.
2 Such would be the case, for instance, if by custom the position of director became hereditary and this custom were given legal sanction.
3 The concept of the consumer as a functioning part of a great enterprise is one which may at first be difficult to grasp. Yet, just as a body of members is essential to the continued existence of a club, so a body of consumers is essential to the continued existence of an enterprise. In each case the members or consumers are an integral part of the association or enterprise. In each case membership is obtained at a cost and for the purpose of obtaining the benefits.
4 It is frequently suggested that economic activity has become vastly more complex under modern conditions. Yet it is strange that the concentration of the bulk of industry into a few large units has not simplified rather than complicated the economic process. It is worth suggesting that the apparent complexity may arise in part from the effort to analyze the process in terms of concepts which no longer apply.
5 *Von Kommenden Dingen* [In Days to Come], translated by E. and C. Paul, Berlin 1918/London 1921, pp. 120–1.

6

Ideology and Managerial Control

JAMES BURNHAM

It is even harder than in the case of political institutions to generalize about the belief patterns of capitalist society. For our purpose, however, it is not necessary to be at all complete. It is enough if we choose a few prominent beliefs – the prominence can be tested by their appearance in great public documents such as constitutions, or declarations of independence or of the rights of man – which nearly everyone will recognize as typical of capitalist society and which both differ from typical feudal beliefs and are sharply at issue in the present period of social transition.

The beliefs with which we are concerned are often called "ideologies", and we should be clear what we mean by "ideology". An "ideology" is similar in the social sphere to what is sometimes called "rationalization" in the sphere of individual psychology. An ideology is *not* a scientific theory, but is non-scientific and often anti-scientific. It is the expression of hopes, wishes, fears, ideals, not a hypothesis about events – though ideologies are often thought by those who hold them to be scientific theories. Thus the theory of evolution or of relativity or of the electronic composition of matter are scientific theories; whereas the doctrines of the preambles to the Declaration of Independence or the Constitution of the United States, the Nazi racial doctrines, Marxian dialectical materialism, St Anselm's doctrine of the meaning of world history, are ideologies.

Ideologies capable of influencing and winning the acceptance of great masses of people are an indispensable verbal cement holding the fabric of any given type of society together. Analysis of ideologies in terms of their practical effects shows us that they ordinarily work to serve and advance the interests of some particular social group or class, and we may therefore speak of a given ideology as being *of* the group or class in question. However, it is even more important to observe that no major ideology is content to profess openly that it speaks only for the group whose interests it in fact expresses. Each group insists that its ideologies are universal in validity and express the interests of humanity as a whole; and each group tries to win universal acceptance for its ideologies. This is true of all the ideologies mentioned in the preceding paragraph.

The significance of ideologies will be further elaborated in connexion with the managerial revolution.

1 Among the elements entering into the ideologies typical of capitalist society, there must be prominently included, though it is not so easy to define what we mean by it, *individualism*. Capitalist thought, whether reflected in theology or art or legal, economic, and political theory, or philosophy or morality, has exhibited a steady concentration on the idea of the "individual". We find the "individual" everywhere we turn: in Luther's appeal to "private interpretation" of the Bible as the test of religious truth; in the exaggerated place of "conscience" in Puritanism; in the economic notion of the economic process's consisting of millions of separated individuals each pursuing his own highest profit, or the correlated moral notion of morality's consisting in each individual's pursuing his own greatest personal pleasure; in the individualistic heroes of the Renaissance and modern art or the individualistic heroes of modern literature (the fascination that Hamlet has had for capitalist society is well deserved); in the very conception of the heart of democracy's lying in the private individual's privately setting forth his will by marking a private ballot . . .

Now the individualist idea of the individual is not an ultimate any more than any other idea. It has its special and distinguishing features, differing from those possessed by the idea of the individual found in other types of society. According to the prevailing capitalist idea, the fundamental unit of politics, psychology, sociology, morality, theology, economics was thought of as the single human individual. This individual was understood as complete "in himself", in his own nature, and as having only *external* relations to other persons and things. Though Hegel and his followers notoriously reject this conception, it is unquestionably typical, and is implicit where not explicit in most of the influential doctrines and the public documents of the fields just mentioned. The Church, the state, the ideal Utopia, are not realities in themselves, but only numerical sums of the individuals who compose them.

2 In keeping with the general ideology of individualism was the stress placed by the capitalist society on the notion of "private initiative". Private initiative, supposed, in the chief instance, to provide the mainspring of the economic process, was discovered also at the root of psychological motivation and moral activity.

3   The status of the capitalist individual was further defined with the help of doctrines of "natural rights" ("free contract", the standard civil rights, "life, liberty, and the pursuit of happiness", etc.) which are held to belong in some necessary and eternal sense to each individual. There is no complete agreement on just what these rights are, but lists of them are given in such documents as the Declaration of Independence, the preamble and Bill of Rights of the Constitution of the United States, or the French Declaration of the Rights of Man.

4   Finally, in capitalist society, the theological and supernatural interpretation of the meaning of world history was replaced by the idea of progress, first appearing in the writers of the Renaissance and being given definite formulation during the eighteenth century. There were two factors in the idea of progress: first, that mankind was advancing steadily and inevitably to better and better things; and, second, the definition of the goal toward which the advance is taking place in naturalistic terms, in terms we might say of an earthly instead of a heavenly paradise.

It should not be supposed that there was any systematically worked-out ideology which can be considered the ideology of capitalism. Many variants are possible. Dozens of differing ideologies were elaborated by philosophers, political theorists, and other intellectuals. Their concepts, slogans, and phrases filtered down, became the commonplaces of mass thinking. But all, or almost all, the ideologies, and mass thinking, were, we might say, variations on related themes. They had a common focus in a commonly held set of words and ideas and assumptions, among which were prominently to be found those that I have listed.

In developed capitalist society it is evident that the position of greatest social power and privilege was occupied by the capitalists, the *bourgeoisie*. The instruments of economic production are, simply, the means whereby men live. In any society, the group of persons controlling these means is by that very fact socially dominant. The bourgeoisie, therefore, may be called in capitalist society the *ruling class*. The idea of a "ruling class", as well as the notion of a "struggle for power" among classes, raises issues . . . closely related to the central problem of this [work].

*   *   *   *   *

The general field of the science of politics is the struggle for social power among organized groups of men. It is advisable, before proceeding with the positive elaboration of the theory of the managerial revolution, to try to reach a certain clarity about the meaning of the "struggle for power".

The words which we use in talking about social groups are, many of them, taken over directly from use in connexion with the activities of individuals. We speak of a group "mind" or group "will" or "decision"; of a war of "defence"; and similarly of a "struggle" among groups. We know, roughly at least, what we mean when we apply these words to individuals and their actions; but a moment's reflection should convince us that groups do not have minds or wills to make decisions in the same sense that applies to individuals. "Defence" for an individual usually means preventing some other individual from hitting him; "struggle" means literal and direct physical encounter, and we can easily observe who wins such a struggle. But "defence" and "struggle" in the case of social groups – classes or nations or races or whatever the groups may be – are far more complicated matters.

Such words are, when applied to groups, *metaphors*. This does not mean, as we are told by our popularizing semanticists, who do not understand what semantics teaches, that we ought not to use such words. It means only that we must be careful, that we must not take the metaphor as expressing a full identity, that we must relate our words to what actually happens.

In all but the most primitive types of organized society, the instruments by which many of the goods (almost all of them nowadays) which are necessary for the maintenance and adornment of life are produced are *technically* social in character. That is, no individual produces, by himself, everything that he uses; in our society most people produce, by themselves, hardly anything. The production is a social process.

In most types of society that we know about, and in all complex societies so far, there is a particular, and relatively small, group of men that *controls* the chief instruments of production (a control which is summed up legally in the concept of "property right", though it is not the legal concept but the *fact* of control which concerns us). This control (property right) is never absolute; it is always subject to certain limitations or restrictions (as, for instance, against using the objects controlled to murder others at will) which vary in kind and degree. The crucial phases of this control seem to be two: first, the ability, either through personal strength, or as in complex societies, with the backing – threatened or actual – of the state power acting through the police, courts, and armed forces to prevent access by others to the object controlled (owned), and, second, to preferential treatment in the distribution of the products of the objects controlled (owned).

Where there is such a controlling group in society, a group which, as against the rest of society, has a greater measure of control over the access to the instruments of production and a preferential treatment in the distribution of the products of those instruments, we may speak of this group as the socially dominant or ruling class in that society. It is hard, indeed, to see what else could be meant by "dominant" or "ruling" class. Such a group has the power and privilege and wealth in the society, as against the remainder of society. It will be noted that this definition of a ruling class does not presuppose any particular kind of government or any particular legal form of property right; it rests upon the facts of control of access and preferential treatment, and can be investigated empirically.

It may also be observed that the two chief factors in control (control of access and preferential treatment in distribution) are closely related in practice. Over any period of time, those who control access not unnaturally grant themselves preferential treatment in distribution; and contending groups trying to alter the relations of distribution can accomplish this only by getting control of access. In fact, since differences in distribution (income) are much easier to study than relations of control, those differences are usually the plainest evidence we have for discovering the relations of control. Put more simply: the easiest way to discover what the ruling group is in any society is usually to see what group gets the biggest incomes. Everyone knows this, but it is still necessary to make the analysis because of the fact that control of access is not *the same thing* as preferential treatment in income distribution. The group that has the one also, normally, has the other: that is the general historical law. But for brief periods this need not invariably be the case, and we shall see later how significant the distinction is at the present time.

In feudal society by far the major instrument of production was the land – feudal economy was overwhelmingly agricultural. *De facto* control of the land (with important restrictions) and preferential treatment in the distribution of its products were in the hands of the feudal lords (including the lords of the Church), not of course as capitalist landlords but through the peculiar instruments of feudal property rights. These lords therefore constituted the ruling class in feudal society. So long as agriculture remained the chief sector of economy and so long as society upheld the feudal property rights, the lords remained the ruling class. The ruling class remained the same in structure, even though the individuals composing it might, and necessarily did (through marriage, ennoblement, and so on) change.

Since the coercive institutions of the state (armed forces, courts, etc.) in feudal society enforced these rights, we may properly speak of the medieval state as a *feudal* state.

To an ever-increasing extent in post-medieval society, the decisive sectors of economy are not agricultural but mercantile, industrial, and financial. In modern society, the persons who control access to, and receive preferential treatment in, the distribution of the products of the instruments of production in these fields – and to a varying extent in the land also – are those whom we call "capitalists"; they constitute the class of the "bourgeoisie". Their control is exercised in terms of the typical property rights recognized by modern society, with which we are all familiar. By our definition, the *bourgeoisie* or capitalists are the ruling class in modern society. Since the society recognizes these rights, we may properly speak of it as bourgeois or capitalist society. Since these rights have been enforced by the political institutions of modern society, by the state, we may speak similarly of the bourgeois or capitalist state.

Once again, the existence of the bourgeois *class* does not depend upon the existence of any particular individuals; the individual members change. The existence of the class means only that there is in society a group exercising, in terms of these recognized bourgeois property institutions, a special degree of control over the access to the instruments of production, and receiving as a group preferential treatment in the distribution of the products of these instruments.

What, let us ask, would be the situation in a *classless* society, a society organized along socialist lines? For society to be "classless" would mean that within society there would be no group (with the exception, perhaps, of temporary delegate bodies, freely elected by the community and subject always to recall) which would exercise, as a group, preferential treatment in distribution. Somewhat more strictly on the latter point: there would be no group receiving by virtue of special economic or social relations preferential treatment in distribution; preferential treatment might be given to certain individuals on the basis of some non-economic factor – for example, ill persons might receive more medical aid than healthy persons, men doing heavy physical work more food than children or those with sedentary occupations – without violating economic classlessness.

A new class rule in society would, in contrast, mean that society would become organized in such a way that a new group, defined in terms of economic or social relations differing from both feudal relations and bourgeois relations, would, as a group, in relation to the rest of the community, exercise a special degree of control over access to the instruments of production and receive preferential treatment in the distribution of the products of those instruments.

The Theory of the Managerial Revolution

We are now in a position to state in a preliminary way the theory of the managerial revolution, the theory which provides the answer to our central problem.

The theory holds, to begin with, that we are now in a period of social transition in the sense which has been explained, a period characterized, that is, by an unusually rapid rate of change of the most important economic, social, political, and cultural institutions of society. This transition is *from* the type of society which we have called capitalist or bourgeois *to* a type of society which we shall call *managerial*.

This transition period may be expected to be short compared with the transition from feudal to capitalist society. It may be dated, somewhat arbitrarily, from the First World War, and may be expected to close, with the consolidation of the new type of society, by approximately fifty years from then, perhaps sooner.

I shall now use the language of the "struggle for power" to outline the remaining key assertions of the theory:

What is occurring in this transition is a drive for social dominance, for power and privilege, for the position of ruling class, by the social group or class of the *managers* (as I shall call them, reserving for the moment an explanation of whom this class includes). This drive will be successful. At the conclusion of the transition period the managers will, in fact, have achieved social dominance, will be the ruling class in society. This drive, moreover, is world-wide in extent, already well advanced in all nations, though at different levels of development in different nations.

The economic framework in which this social dominance of the managers will be assured is based upon the state ownership of the major instruments of production. Within this framework there will be no direct property rights in the major instruments of production vested in individuals as individuals.

How, then, it will be at once asked (and this is the key to the whole problem), if that is the economic framework, will the existence of a ruling class be possible? A ruling class, we have seen, means a group of persons who, by virtue of special social-economic relations, exercises a special degree of control over access to the instruments of production and receives preferential treatment in the distribution of the product of these instruments. Capitalists were such a group precisely because they, as individuals, held property rights in the instruments of production. If, in managerial society, no individuals are to hold comparable property rights, how can any group of individuals constitute a ruling class?

The answer is comparatively simple and, as already noted, not without historical analogues. The managers will exercise their control over the instruments of production and gain preference in the distribution of the products, not directly, through property rights vested in them as individuals, but indirectly, through their control of the state which in turn will own and control the instruments of production. The state – that is, the institutions which comprise the state – will, if we wish to put it that way, be the property of the managers. And that will be quite enough to put them in the position of ruling class.

The control of the state by the managers will be suitably guaranteed by appropriate political institutions, analogous to the guarantee of bourgeois dominance under capitalism by the bourgeois political institutions.

The ideologies expressing the social role and interests and aspirations of the managers (like the great ideologies of the past an indispensable part of the struggle for power) have not yet been fully worked out, any more than were the bourgeois ideologies in the period of transition to capitalism. They are already approximated, however, from several different but similar directions, by, for example: Leninism–Stalinism; fascism–Nazism; and, at a more primitive level, by New Dealism and such less influenced American ideologies as "technocracy".

This, then, is the skeleton of the theory, expressed in the language of the struggle for power. It will be observed that the separate assertions are designed to cover the central phases involved in a social "transition" and in the characterization of a "type of society" [discussed previously].

But we must remember that the language of the struggle for power is metaphorical. No more than in the case of the capitalists, have the "managers" or their representatives ever got together to decide, deliberately and explicitly, that they were going to make a bid for world power. Nor will the bulk of those who have done, and will do, the fighting in the struggle be recruited from the ranks of the managers themselves; most of the fighters will be workers and youths who will doubtless, many of them, believe that they are fighting for ends of their own. Nor have the managers themselves been constructing and propagating their own ideologies; this has been, and is being done for the most part by intellectuals, writers, philosophers. Most of these intellectuals are not in the least aware that the net social effect of the ideologies which they elaborate contributes to the power and privilege of managers and to the building of a new structure of class rule in society. As in the past, the intellectuals believe that they are speaking in the name of truth and for the interests of all humanity.

In short, the question whether the managers are conscious and critical, whether they, or some of them, set before themselves the goal of social dominance and take deliberate steps to reach that goal, this question, in spite of what seems to be implied by the language of the "struggle for power" is not really at issue.

In simplest terms, the theory of the managerial revolution asserts merely the following: Modern society has been organized through a certain set of major economic, social, and political institutions which we call capitalist, and has exhibited certain major social beliefs or ideologies. Within this social structure we find that a particular group or class of persons – the capitalists or bourgeoisie – is the dominant ruling class in the sense which has been defined. At the present time these institutions and beliefs are undergoing a process of rapid transformation. The conclusion of this period of transformation, to be expected in the comparatively near future, will find society organized through a quite different set of major economic, social, and political institutions and exhibiting quite different major social beliefs or ideologies. Within the new social structure a different social group or class – the managers – will be the dominant or ruling class.

If we put the theory in this latter way, we avoid the possible ambiguities of the over-picturesque language of the "struggle for power" metaphor. Nevertheless, just as in the case of the bourgeois revolution against feudalism, human beings are concerned in the social transformation; and, in particular, the role of the ruling-class-to-be is by no means passive. Just what part, and how deliberate a part they play, as well as the part of other persons and classes (bourgeois, proletarian, farmer and the like) is a matter for specific inquiry. What they *intend* and *want* to do does not necessarily correspond with the actual effects of what they *do* say and do; though we are primarily concerned with the actual effects – which will constitute the transformation of society to a managerial structure – we are also interested in what various groups say and do.

These remarks are necessary if we are to avoid common misunderstandings. Human beings, as individuals and in groups, try to achieve various goals – food, power, comfort, peace, privilege, security, freedom, and so on. They take steps which, as they see them, will aid in reaching the goal in question. Experience teaches us not merely that the goals are often not reached, but that the effect of the steps taken is frequently toward a very different result from the goal which was originally held in mind and which motivated the taking of the steps in the first place. As Machiavelli pointed out in his *History of Florence*, the poor, enduring oppressive conditions, were always ready to answer the call for a fight for freedom; but the net result of each new revolt was merely to establish a new tyranny.

Many of the early capitalists sincerely fought for the freedom of individual conscience in relation to God; what they got as a result of the fighting was often a harsh and barren fundamentalism in theology, but at the same time political power and economic privilege for themselves. So, today: we want to know what various persons and groups are thinking and doing; what they are thinking and doing has its effects on historical processes; but there is no obvious correspondence between the thoughts and effects; and our central problem is to discover what the effects, in terms of social structure, will be.

It should be noted, and it will be seen in some detail, that the theory of the managerial revolution is not merely predicting what may happen in a hypothetical future. The theory is, to begin with, an interpretation of what already has happened and is now happening. Its prediction is simply that the process which has started and which has already gone a very great distance will continue and reach completion. The managerial revolution is not just around the corner, that corner which seems never quite to be reached. The corner of the managerial revolution was turned some while ago. The revolution itself is not something we or our children have to wait for; we may if we wish, observe its stages before our eyes. Just as we seldom realize we are growing old until we are already old, so do the contemporary actors in a major social change seldom realize that society is changing until the change has already come. The old words and beliefs persist long after the social reality that gave them life has dried up. Our wisdom in social questions is almost always retrospective only. This is, or ought to be, a humiliating experience for human beings; if justice is beyond us, we would like at least to claim knowledge.

The so-called "separation of ownership and control", paralleling the growth of the great corporations of modern times, has, of course, been a widely recognized phenomenon. A decade ago it was the principal subject of the widely-read book, *The Modern Corporation and Private Property*, by Berle and Means. In this book, the authors showed that the economy of the United States was dominated by the two hundred largest non-banking corporations (they did not discuss the relations of these to financial houses); and, second, that the majority of these corporations were no longer, in practice, controlled by their nominal legal owners (that is, stockholders holding in their names a majority of the shares of stock).

They divided these corporations according to "types of control". In a few, control was exercised by a single individual (more often, single family) who was legal owner of all or a majority of the stock; in others, by individuals or groups which owned not a majority but a substantial percentage of the stock. Most, however (in 1929, 65 percent of these 200 corporations with 80 percent of the total assets), they decided were what they called, significantly enough, "management-controlled". By "management-controlled", as they explained, they meant that the management (executives) of these companies, though owning only minor percentages of the shares of their corporations, were in actuality self-perpetuating in control of the policies and the boards of directors of the companies, and able to manipulate at will, through proxies, majority votes of the nominal owners, the shareholders. The American Telephone and Telegraph Corporation is the classic example of "management-control".

Though briefly, Berle and Means also took up the extremely important point that in the nature of the case there were sources of frequent conflict between the interests of the "control group" (most often, the management) and the legal owners. This is apparent enough to anyone who recalls the economic events of the past generation. Many books have been written about the difficulties of the run-of-the-mine common stockholders, often as a result of the policies of the "control group" of "their own" company. Wealth, power, and even other possible interests (such as maximum industrial efficiency) of the control group quite naturally do not often coincide with maximum dividends and security for the common stockholders.

The analysis by Berle and Means is most suggestive and indirectly a powerful confirmation of the theory of the managerial revolution, but as it stands it is not carried far enough for our purposes. In their concept of "management-control" they do not distinguish between management in the sense of actual direction of the process of production and management in terms of profit, selling, financing, and so on. Indeed, their use of "management", as is usually the case, is closer to the latter than the former, which results really from the fact that in most big corporations today the chief and best-known officials are of the second executive, not of the first or manager, type. Moreover, Berle and Means do not include any study of the way in which their supposedly self-perpetuating and autonomous managements are in actuality often controlled by big banks or groups of financiers.

One result of such a refinement and amplification of the Berle and Means analysis would be to show that the sources of possible and actual conflict among the groups are far more numerous and more acute than they indicate. Among these sources, three should be stressed:

1   It is a historical law, with no apparent exceptions so far known, that all social or economic groups of any size strive to improve their relative position with respect to power and position in society. This law certainly applies to the groups into which we have divided those who stand in some sort of relationship of ownership, management, or control toward the instruments of production. Each of these groups seeks to improve its position of power and privilege. But, in practice, an improvement in the position of one of them is not only not necessarily an improvement for the others; often it means a worsening of the position of one or all of the others.

In periods of great prosperity and expansion, this is not very irritating, since all four can advance relatively as against the rest of society; but, as we have already seen, such periods have ended for capitalism.

Even more apparently, the relations of control over the operations of the instruments of production raise conflicts, since the sort of operation most favorable to one group (expanding or contracting production, for example) very often is not that most favorable to another. And, in general, there is a source of permanent conflict: the managers proper receive far less reward (money) than the executives and especially the finance-capitalists, who get by far the greatest benefits. From the point of view of the manager group, especially as economic conditions progressively decay, the reward allotted to the finance-capitalists seems inordinate and unjustified, all the more so because, as the managers see it more and more clearly, the finance-capitalists are not performing any function necessary to the process of production.

2 All ... of these groups, to one or another degree, are powerful and privileged as against the great masses of the population, who have no interest of ownership, management, or control in the instruments of production and no special preferential treatment in the distribution of their products. Consequently, the masses have a tendency to strive for a greater share of power and privilege as against all ... of these groups. The result of this situation might be expected to be a merging of the conflicts among the groups and a common front against the pressure of the masses. This has indeed been often the case. Nevertheless, the conflicts among the groups are real and cannot be eliminated even in the face of a common danger. In fact, the presence of the common danger is itself a source of new conflicts. This follows because the groups, from the very status they occupy and the functions they fulfill, favour different methods of meeting the danger and of maintaining privileges as against the masses. The differences become sharpened under the crisis conditions of contemporary capitalism.

3 A third source of conflict is found in what we might call "occupational bias". The different things which these different groups do promote in their respective members different attitudes, habits of thought, ideals, ways and methods of solving problems. To put it crudely: the managers tend to think of solving social and political problems as they coordinate and organize the actual process of production; the non-managerial executives think of society as a price-governed profit-making animal; the finance-capitalists think of problems in terms of what happens in banks and stock exchanges and security flotations; the little stockholders think of the economy as a mysterious god who, if placated properly, will hand out free gifts to the deserving.

But there is a more basic deficiency in the analysis of Berle and Means or any similar analysis. The truth is that, whatever its legal merits, the concept of the "separation of ownership and control" has no sociological or historical meaning. Ownership *means* control; if there is no control, there is no ownership. The central aspects of the control which is ownership are, as we have seen, control over access to the object in question and preferential treatment in the distribution of its products. If ownership and control are in reality separated, then ownership has changed hands to the "control" and the separated ownership is a meaningless fiction.

This is perfectly obvious as soon as we think about it. If I own a house, let us say, that means that – at least under normal circumstances – I can prevent others from entering it. In developed societies with political institutions, it means also that the state (the police in this instance, backed by the courts) will, if necessary, enforce this control of mine over access to the house. If I cannot, when I wish to, prevent others from entering the house, if anyone else or everyone has the same rights of entry as I, then neither I nor anyone would say that I am the "owner" of the house. (I can, of course, alienate my control, either temporarily – through a lease – or permanently – through sale or gift – but these and similar acts do not alter the fundamental point.) Moreover, in so far as there are products of the house (warmth, shelter, privacy might be so considered, as well as rent) I, as owner, am, by the very fact of control over access in this case entitled to preferential treatment in receiving these products.

Where the object owned takes the form of instruments of production (factories, machines, mines, railroads . . .) the situation is the same, only more complicated. For sociological and practical purposes, the owner (or owners) of the instruments of production is the one (or group) that in *fact* – whether or not in theory and words – controls access to those instruments and controls preferential treatment in the distribution of their products.

These two rights (control of access and preferential treatment in distribution) are fundamental in ownership and, as we have noted, determine the dominant or ruling class in society – which consists simply of the group that has those rights, or has them, at least, in greater measure than the rest of society, with respect to the chief instruments of production.

Moreover, historical experience shows (as would be obvious without much experience) that these two rights are inter-related and that the first (control of access) is determinative of the second. That is to say: the group or groups which have control over access to the instruments of production will, as a matter of experienced fact, also receive preference in the distribution of the products of those instruments. Or in other words: the most powerful (in terms of economic relations) will also be the wealthiest. This does not apply to every separate individual concerned; and there may be a temporary dislocation in the relationship; but to groups, and over any period of time beyond a comparatively few years, it seems to apply always. Social groups and classes are, we might say, "selfish"; they use their control to benefit primarily (not necessarily exclusively) themselves.

Berle and Means are therefore inconsistent, or at least incomplete, when they speak of "the separation of ownership and control". Those who control *are* the owners. The fact is that all four groups we have dealt with share at least to some degree in *control*; at the least they all control perferential treatment in the distribution of the products of the instruments of production, which is enough to constitute them owners; though in the case of the bulk of stockholders, who have this control to a minor extent and none of the more decisive control over access, the ownership is of a very subordinate kind.

But if we re-interpret the phrase "separation of ownership and control" to mean "separation of control over access from control over preferential treatment in distribution" – and this is partly what lies behind the Berle and Means analysis – then we are confronted with a fact of primary importance. It is true that a partial separation of this kind has been taking place during recent decades. Income and power have become unbalanced. Those who receive the most preferential treatment in distribution (get the biggest relative share of the national income) have, in differing degrees in different nations and different sections of the economy, been losing control over access. Others, who do not receive such a measure of preferential treatment in distribution, have been gaining in the measure of control over access which they exercise. Historical experience tells us that such a lack of correlation between the two kinds of control (the two basic rights of property) cannot long endure. Control over access is decisive, and, when consolidated, will carry control over preferential treatment in distribution with it; that is, will shift ownership unambiguously to the new controlling, a new dominant class. Here we see, from a new viewpoint, the mechanism of the managerial revolution.

It could not be otherwise. Somebody is going to do the actual managing; and, the way things have happened, as the big capitalists do less of it, the managers have been doing more. Of course, as the situation still is in the United States, the power of the managers is still far from absolute, is still in the last analysis subordinate to that of the big capitalists. The big capitalists and the institutional framework of capitalism continue to provide a framework within which the managers must work: for example, in determining the raising or lowering of production output, the large-scale financial operations, the connexions between different units of industry, and so on. The big capitalists intervene at occasional key moments that affect the broad direction of major policies. They keep, as a rule, a kind of veto right which can be enforced when necessary by, for example, getting rid of any rebellious managers. The managers remain in considerable measure delegates ("servants") of the big capitalists.

Such a delegation of power and control is, however, highly unstable. It has always happened that servants who discover themselves to be solidly enough established gradually turn on their masters, especially if they wake up to the fact that their masters are no longer necessary to them. Under the Merovingian kings of France in the Dark Ages, the Mayor of the Palace was originally the mere vulgar chief of the court servants. Gradually the actual control of administration got into the hands of the Mayors of the Palace. But, for several generations thereafter, the Merovingians, becoming more and more mere puppets, were kept as kings and lived with all the outward signs of kingship. The final act of doing away with them, which took place when the Mayor who was the father of Charlemagne proclaimed himself king, simply put in a formal way what had already happened in sociological reality.

The instruments of production are the seat of social domination; who controls them, in fact not in name, controls society, for they are the means whereby society lives. The fact today is that the control of the big capitalists, the control based upon capitalist private property rights, over the instruments of production and their operation is, though still real, growing tenuous, indirect, intermittent. More and more of the time, over more and more phases of the productive process, no capitalist intervention appears. In another transitional age, feudal lords, on harsh enough terms, leased out towns or lands to capitalists, who conducted capitalist operations with them in place of the feudal operations which the lords had before them directed. The lords remained lords and lived like lords; they had, seemingly, controlling rights, could throw out the capitalists at will and bleed them for even more returns than the contracts called for. But, somehow, after a while, it was the capitalists who had the town and the land and the industry, and the lord who was left with a long ancestry and noble titles – and an empty purse and vanished power.

Throughout industry, *de facto* control by the managers over the actual processes of production is rapidly growing in terms both of the aspects of production to which it extends and the times in which it is exercised. In some sections of the economy the managerial control is already fairly thorough, even though always limited indirectly by big capitalist control of the banks and finance. Though the Berle and Means conception of "management-controlled" corporations fails, as we have seen, to clarify what is meant by management and how management is related to finance, yet there are many corporations, and these from among the greatest, not the secondary, where the managers in our sense are quite firmly entrenched, where owners, in the legal and historical capitalist meaning, have scarcely anything to do with the corporations beyond drawing dividends when the managers grant them.

But it might be asked: assuming that this development is taking place, does it not mean simply that the old big bourgeois families are on their way out of the front rank and new persons are about to take their places? This has happened many times before during the history of capitalism. The survival of capitalism, as we have seen, does not depend upon the survival of any given individual capitalists, but of a ruling capitalist class, upon the fact that the social place of any individual capitalists who are eliminated is taken by other capitalists. This was what happened before, and outstandingly in the United States. If the old and wealthiest capitalists are slipping, then, it would seem, the newer managers will utilize their growing power to become the new members of the big *bourgeoisie*.

However, in spite of the fact that many of the managers doubtless have such an aim as their personal motivation, it will not happen. In the first place, with the rarest exceptions, it is no longer possible for the managers to realize such an aim, even if they have it. The chance to build up vast aggregates of wealth of the kind held by the big bourgeois families no longer exists under the conditions of contemporary capitalism. Lundberg shows that since the end of the First World War there has been only a single change in the listing of the first Sixty Families in this country [the US]; only a single new-comer has penetrated that stratum (and this closing of the doors to the top rank occurred much later in the United States than in the other great capitalist nations). The inability of a ruling class to assimilate fresh and vigorous new blood into its ranks is correctly recognized by many sociologists as an important symptom of the decadence of that class and its approaching downfall.

In addition, however, because of the structural changes within society, the future road toward social domination and control no longer lies in the massing of personally held capitalist property rights. Not merely is getting these rights on a big scale nearly impossible for new-comers, but also, if the aim is greater social domination and privilege, there are now and for the future more effective means for achieving the aim. With capitalism extending and ascendant, individual capitalists together making up the ruling class are, when they disappear, replaced by other individual capitalists. With capitalism collapsing and on its way out, the ruling capitalist class as a whole is being replaced by a new ruling class.

The Managerial Ideologies

All organized societies are cemented together, not merely by force and the threat of force, and by established patterns of institutional behaviour, but also by accepted ways of feeling and thinking and talking and looking at the world, by ideologies. No one today will deny the crucial social function of ideologies, though we are always more critical about others' ideologies than about our own. Indeed, many of us like to feel ourselves free from the influence of any ideology, though we are seldom prepared to grant such enlightenment to anyone else. A society cannot hold together unless there is a fairly general acceptance on the part of most of its members, not necessarily of the same ideology, but, at any rate, of ideologies which develop out of similar root concepts as starting points.

Scientific theories are always controlled by the facts: they must be able to explain the relevant evidence already at hand, and on their basis it must be possible to make verifiable predictions about the future. Ideologies are not controlled by facts, even though they may incorporate some scientific elements and are ordinarily considered scientific by those who believe in them. The primary function of ideologies – whether moral or religious or metaphysical or social – is to express human interests, needs, desires, hopes, fears, not to cover the facts. A dispute about scientific theories can always be settled, sooner or later, by experiment and observation. A dispute between rival ideologies can never be thus settled. Arguments about ideologies can, and do, continue as long as the interests embodied by them are felt to be of any significance.

After that they become curiosities to be studied by philosophers or anthropologists. There can never be, as there are in the case of scientific theories, satisfactory tests for the "truth" of ideologies, since in reality the notions of truth and falsity are irrelevant to ideologies. The problem with an ideology is not, when properly understood, whether it is true, but: what interests does it express, and how adequately and persuasively does it express them?

However, though ideologies are not controlled by facts, they are nevertheless subject to controls. In particular, the major ideologies of a class society must be able to perform two tasks: (1) They must actually express, at least roughly, the social interests of the ruling class in question, and must aid in creating a pattern of thought and feeling favorable to the maintenance of the key institutions and relations of the given social structure; (2) They must at the same time be so expressed as to be capable of appealing to the sentiments of the masses. An ideology embodying the interests of a given ruling class would not be of the slightest use as social cement if it openly expressed its function of keeping the ruling class in power over the rest of society. The ideology must ostensibly speak in the name of "humanity", "the people", "the race", "the future", "God", "destiny", and so on. Furthermore, in spite of the opinion of many present-day cynics, not just any ideology is capable of appealing to the sentiments of the masses. It is more than a problem of skilfull propaganda technique. A successful ideology has got to seem to the masses, in however confused a way, actually to express some of their own interests.

In a period of social transition, the ideologies of the old society are under attack by the rising ideologies of the society-to-be, just as the institutions of the old society and the economic and political power of the old ruling class are under attack. The rising ideologies naturally devote much of their attention to the negative task of undermining mass acceptance of the old ideologies.

The major ideologies of capitalist society, as we noted briefly earlier, were variants on the themes of: *individualism*; opportunity; "natural rights", especially the rights of property; freedom, especially "freedom of contract"; private enterprise; private initiative; and so on. These ideologies conformed well to the two requirements stated above. Under the interpretations given them, they expressed and served the interests of the capitalists. They justified profit and interest. They showed why the owner of the instruments of production was entitled to the full product of those instruments and why the worker had no claim on the owner except for the contracted wages. They preserved the supremacy of the field of private enterprise. They kept the state to its limited role. They protected the employers' rights of hiring and firing. They explained why an owner could work his factory full time or shut it down at his discretion. They assured the full rights of owners to set up factories or to buy and sell wherever they might choose, to keep money in a bank or in cash or in bonds or in active capital as seemed most expedient. So long as ideologies developed from such conceptions as these were not seriously and widely questioned, the structure of capitalist society was reasonably secure.

At the same time, these ideologies were able to gain the acceptance and often enthusiasm of the masses. Men who were not capitalists were willing to swear and die by slogans issuing out of these ideologies. And, as a matter of fact, the way of life embodied in these ideologies was for some while beneficial to large sections of the masses, though never to the extent advertised or in any way comparable to what it was for the capitalists.

The capitalist ideologies are today in a very different position from that which they held even a generation ago. The differences are plainly written on the surface of events.

Once these ideologies provided the slogans for what nearly everyone would call the most "progressive" groups in society – among them the English and French and American revolutionists – and in later times for groups which in any case were not the most conservative. Today the same slogans, proceeding from the same ideological bases, are found most often and most naturally among the words of what everyone recognizes to be the most conservative, or even reactionary, groups in society.

The claim of the Tories to these slogans and these ideologies is one hundred percent legitimate. These are the slogans and ideologies of capitalism, and the Tories are the bona fide representatives of capitalism. The slogans mean for them what they have always meant in practice for capitalism; it the world, not they and their ideas, that has changed. If these slogans are now associated, and correctly associated, with the most conservative (that is, backward-looking) sections of society, that is because the old structure of society, once healthy, is now breaking up and a new structure is being built; an old class is on its way out and a new class marching in.

But, second and even more revealing, the capitalist ideologies have largely lost their power to appeal to the masses. This is not in the least a subjective and personal opinion; it may be perfectly well established by impersonal observation.

When old ideologies wear out, new ones come in to take their place. The capitalist ideologies are now wearing out, along with the capitalist society of which they are the ideologies; and many new ideologies are contending for the jobs left vacant. Most of the new ideologies don't get very far, because they do not fulfill the requirements for great social ideologies. The new "agrarianism", medievalism, regionalism, religious primitivism pick up a few recruits and may have a few months of notoriety, but they remain the preoccupation of small sects. At the present time, the ideologies that can have a powerful impact, that can make real headway, are, naturally, the *managerial* ideologies, since it is these alone that correspond with the actual direction of events.

The general basis of the managerial ideologies is clear enough from an understanding of the general character of managerial society. In place of capitalist concepts, there are concepts suited to the structure of managerial society and the rule of the managers. In place of the "individual", the stress turns to the "state", the people, the folk, the race. In place of gold, labor and work. In place of private enterprise, "socialism" or "collectivism". In place of "freedom" and "free initiative", planning. Less talk about "right" and "natural right"; more about "duties" and "order" and "discipline". In addition, in these early decades of managerial society, more of the positive elements that were once part of capitalist ideology in its rising youth, but have left it in old age: destiny, the future, sacrifice, power.... Of course, some of the words of the capitalist ideologies are taken over: such words as "freedom" are found in many ideologies since they are popular and, as we have seen, can be interpreted in any manner whatever.

These concepts, and others like them, help break down what remains of capitalism and clear the road for managers and managerial society. They prepare the psychic atmosphere for the demolition of capitalist property rights, the acceptance of state economy and the rule of a new kind of state, the rejection of the "natural right" of capitalism (that is, the rights of the capitalists in the private market place), and the approval of managerial war. When enough people begin thinking through these instead of the capitalist categories, the consolidation of the managerial structure of society is assured.

Notes

Excerpted from *The Managerial Revolution* by James Burnham. Middlesex UK: Penguin Books, 1962 edition; first published 1941. Reprinted by kind permission from Harper Collins Books, all rights reserved.

7

The Problem of Legitimacy in the Modern Corporation

Edward S. Mason

Everyone talks about the corporation, but, in the words of Mark Twain, no one does anything about it. And for this there are some pretty good reasons. In the first place, something very like the modern corporation is the inevitable product of an industrializing society, whether that society follows a capitalist or a socialist trend of development. Lawyers love to describe the corporation as a creature of the law, but law in a major manifestation is simply a device for facilitating and registering the obvious and the inevitable. Given the technologically determined need for a large stock of capital, the managerial requirements set by the problem of administering the efforts of many men, and the area of discretion demanded for the effective conduct of an entrepreneurial function, the corporation, or a reasonable facsimile thereof, is the only answer.

In the second place the business corporation is so much our most important economic institution and it is so thoroughly integrated into our business culture that to suggest a drastic change in the scope or character of corporate activity is to suggest a drastic alteration in the structure of society. If and when this comes about, it will take place not by radical changes in public policy toward the corporation but by radical changes much broader in scope. We are now a nation of wage and salaried employees and, in the main, we work for corporations. The days of Jeffersonian democracy are over and nothing can be done to resurrect them. We look to the corporation for the technical improvements that spark our economic growth. The corporation recruits our youth from college and provides them with pensions in their old age. It is the present support of community chests and other local charities and the future hope of institutions of higher learning. All this is to suggest not that the corporation cannot be touched but that to touch the corporation deeply is to touch much else.

In the third place, though many people have ideas on what to do about the corporation, there is little evidence of consensus. The "viewers with alarm" are approximately balanced by the "pointers with pride." On the one hand, we hear much talk of "a new feudalism," of "self-perpetuating oligarchies," of "irresponsible private power," and of "the euthanasia of the capitalist owner." But on the other, we are told of "the twentieth-century revolution," the "professionalization of management," the various "public" whose interests are sedulously cared for, and the beneficence of the "corporate conscience." It is not to be wondered that, to date, this cacophony of voices has not produced a very firm view on what to think or what to do about the corporation either in the general public or in the minds of legislators.

The problem of what to think and what to do becomes the more difficult when one considers that, despite the fact that the United States has, over the last century, undergone a revolutionary change in which the rise of the corporation has played a dominant role, the rate of economic growth and the shares in which our increasing product has been distributed to the various recipients have remained remarkably stable. Under corporate dispensation the large economic classes in the community seem, over time, to be faring not much better and not much worse than they did before. Yet no one can doubt that the structure of our economy and our society has been profoundly altered. The mid-nineteenth-century nation of farmers, shopkeepers, and small manufacturers has become a highly industrialized economy dominated by organized groups. The percentage of the population in urban areas has continually increased and, despite the fact that it now approaches 60 percent, the end is not yet in sight. Innovation at the hands of the small-scale inventor and individual enterpriser has given way to organized research. The role of government in the economy persistently increases. The rugged individualist has been supplanted by smoothly efficient corporate executives participating in the group decision. The equity owner is joining the bond holder as a functionless *rentier*.

If these changes had markedly accelerated or markedly diminished the rate of growth of which the economy seems capable or if they had profoundly changed the distribution between property and labor income, the popular attitude toward the corporation and all its works might be less ambivalent. But this has not happened. To be sure, employment under the combined influence of public policy and the policies of corporations and trade unions seems to be substantially more stable, a stability that may or may not turn out to have been purchased at the expense of persistent inflation. Furthermore, there is no doubt that the class conflicts and acerbities of business conduct of an earlier age have been substantially softened. But, so far as the essential rates and percentages that describe the performance of our economy are concerned, the key word is stability. What seems to have happened in our corporate society is that the prime movers of economic growth, the rate of capital formation, and the rate of technological improvement have become institutionally determined. And the political and economic balance among forces in society seems sufficiently resistant to change to prevent any marked redistribution of the fruits of its growth. The stock of capital continues to grow at about twice the rate of growth of the labor force. The average yield per unit of capital falls slightly or not at all. The per capita real earnings of labor increase at about 2 percent a year and the shares of property and labor in the division of the product change with a glacial slowness. *Plus ça change plus c'est la même chose.*

But if the inevitability of something like the corporate form, the degree of its integration with our culture, and the absence of any markedly adverse influence of the "corporate revolution" on the overall performance of the economy help to explain the lack of a generally accepted bill of indictment against the corporation, this does not prove that all is well. Even A. A. Berle, who has done more than most to justify corporate man to his society – and incidentally, has thrown more light than any other man on [these] questions – admits that he is afraid.[1] What Mr Berle and the rest of us are afraid of is that this powerful corporate machine, which so successfully grinds out the goods we want, seems to be running without any discernible controls. The young lad mastering the technique of his bicycle may legitimately shout with pride, "Look, Ma, no hands," but is this the appropriate motto for a corporate society?

Almost everyone now agrees that in the large corporation, the owner is, in general, a passive recipient; that, typically, control is in the hands of management; and that management normally selects its own replacements. It is, furthermore, generally recognized that, in the United States, the large corporation undertakes a substantial part of total economic activity, however measured; that the power of corporations to act is by no means so thoroughly circumscribed by the market as was generally thought to be true of nineteenth-century enterprise; and that, in addition to market power, the large corporation exercises a considerable degree of control over nonmarket activities of various sorts. What all this seems to add up to is the existence of important centers of private power in the hands of men whose authority is real but whose responsibilities are vague. At this point a confused medley of voices breaks in to assert the claims of various corporate "publics" – labor, owners, suppliers, customers, creditors, and so on – to whom management is *really* responsible; to point to the ever-widening scope of government jurisdiction and authority which managements must "take into account," and to extoll the emergence of a code of behavior generally recognized by professional managements, serving for the moment as a "corporate conscience," but in process of becoming a "rule of law."

All this is very interesting but very unsatisfactory, particularly to the intellectual who is bothered by apparent missing links in the chain of authority and by a seeming equilibrium of forces that by every right should be disequilibrating. The nineteenth century produced a social doctrine that not only explained but justified. But the functioning of the corporate system has not to date been adequately explained, or, if certain explanations are accepted as adequate, it seems difficult to justify. The man of action may be content with a system that works. But one who reflects on the properties or characteristics of this system cannot help asking why it works and whether it will continue to work. I shall attempt a brief statement of some of the principal questions that the rise of this modern leviathan are putting to us.

I.   The Problem of Legitimacy

The one-hundred-and-thirty-odd largest manufacturing corporations account for half of manufacturing output in the United States. The five hundred largest business corporations in this country embrace nearly two thirds of all nonagricultural economic activity. These or similar figures are reiterated with such frequency that they tend to bounce off our heads rather than to penetrate. But by now we are all aware that we live not only in a corporate society but a society of large corporations. The management – that is, the control – of these corporations is in the hands of, at most, a few thousand men. Who selected these men, if not to rule over us, at least to exercise vast authority, and to whom are they responsible? The answer to the first question is quite clearly: they selected themselves. The answer to the second is, at best, nebulous. This, in a nutshell, constitutes the problem of legitimacy.

In the mid-nineteenth-century economy, corporate management was nothing if not legitimate. The generalizing of the privilege of incorporation was an aspect of a liberal movement that sought to give to all men equal opportunity under law. And the elimination of restrictions on the duration, size, purposes, and powers of the corporation represented an attempt to convert the corporation from a special agency of the state into just another form of business enterprise. And indeed in the early stages of manufacturing development the corporation was just another form of enterprise, enjoying, it is true, limited liability, but functioning in essential respects like an individual proprietorship. The owner, if not the manager himself, selected the management, and the management was responsible to the owners. The traditional justification not only of private enterprise but of private property rested on that assumption. But those days are gone forever, and not even the assiduous efforts of the SEC can put ownership back in the saddle.

The phrase "self-perpetuating oligarchy" rings harshly in our democratic ears. But it must be recognized that some of our best people are oligarchs. The Harvard Corporation is self-perpetuating, and no one would deny – at least no one in my position – that this is an able and estimable body of men. The fact of the matter is that in some of the most effective and longest-lived organizations known to man, the management, in effect, is self-selected. So why not in the business corporation?

The answer, I would suppose, depends in part on how effective is self-selection as a method of assuring that the "best people" will continue to be chosen. But it also depends in part on whether good government, if assured, is an adequate substitute for self-government. A lot of people around the world have recently decided that it is not, and are now in process of discovering that self-government is not always an adequate substitute for good government. It would be nice to have both, but it may be necessary to give up a little of the one in order to secure an appropriate measure of the other.

The meaning of self-government within the context of corporate organization depends on who are considered to be "citizens." Some would say they are the salaried and wage employees and would devise plans of "industrial democracy" that lead straight toward syndicalism. But syndicalism has never had much appeal to the Anglo-Saxon mentality. Others consider the citizens to be members of the various corporate "publics" – owners, employees, customers, suppliers, and creditors – and managerial spokesmen assert the responsibility of management to these "publics" without making it clear, however, how divergent interests are to be reconciled. This also is a quasi-syndicalist solution to the problem of legitimacy and one that inevitably assigns different weights to the "votes" of various constituencies. The consumer public, because of lack of organization, is obviously low man on the totem pole.

Legitimacy can ultimately be conferred only by the sovereign, and in the American tradition only the people are sovereign. But the sovereign acts through duly constituted representatives, and this opens the possibility for alternative routes to legitimacy. One possible route leads through court decisions to a rule of law designed to make equitable and tolerable the actions of inevitable private power. Another envisages an extended federalism, with corporations recognized as quasi-political entities properly legitimated. Still other routes move in the direction of public ownership or an expansion of the public-utility concept.

II. The Problem of Power

Legitimacy is a problem mainly because of the existence of private power. And private power now concerns us because that vision echoing Adam Smith, of an atomistic society, no longer seems quite relevant to a corporate universe. In that society managerial control was made legitimate by ownership, and ownership was justified in part because of limitations on the power of ownership imposed by the competitive market.

Power, however, is a tricky concept, and it is even trickier to measure. There is a useful distinction between power to do (that is, a capability) and power over, which is anathema. Unfortunately, in any group or society there is little power to do without some power over. This is the dilemma of the philosophical anarchist. He cannot practice his faith, which is concerned with eliminating man's power over man, without becoming in fact a nihilist: one who is against all doing.

Faced with these and other difficulties, the search is directed toward ways of limiting or governing power that may be used against the interests of others while keeping as much as possible of the ability to act in his own or his organization's interest. Economists have been inclined to think of market power which they conceive, and sometimes try to measure, in terms of a departure from its opposite, an impersonal, and hence powerless, purely competitive market. But all markets that have ever existed inevitably contain certain buyers and sellers with some degree of market power. Consequently the search is for that degree of market power which is necessary to an efficient conduct of business but beyond which there is an inevitable divergence between the particular and the general interest. Some call this nirvana "workable competition," others prefer the term "effective competition," and still others draw a distinction between "reasonable" and "unreasonable" market power. Whatever the nomenclature, this concept embraces two ideas worth pondering. The first is that technological and organizational influences inevitably bring about, in a large sector of the economy, markets served by the few rather than the many and that not very much, really, can be done about it. The second is that in a dynamic economy, characterized by product changes, process innovation, advertising, and growth, competition among the few may not be so bad after all. This may be whistling in the dark, but the whistling is going to go on in any case.

But what if technological and organization considerations decree a size and a fewness – a type of competition – that not even a business economist would call workable? Under these circumstances, some would say, break them up even at the cost of some loss of efficiency. Others would turn to public ownership or regulation. And still others, I suspect, despairing of the first and dubious of the second, might prefer the known evil to the unknown consequences of action.

Even if competition among the few is "workable," the problem of private power is not exorcised. Industrializing economies inevitably move away from market relations among firms and toward administrative relations within the firm. Contractual relations between legal equals give way to relations between employer and employee within a bureaucratic hierarchy. This is an aspect of the "power over" that, in our industrialized society, seems inseparably connected with the "power to do." Furthermore, this exercise of power by management and the accompanying loss of freedom by the managed is independent of who does the managing. As Clark Kerr puts it,

Some loss of freedom . . . is inevitable in an effective industrial system. It will occur, more or less, whether the system is run by the employers alone, by the State alone, or even by unions alone. Industrial society requires many rules and reasonable conformity to those rules. There must be a wage structure, a work schedule, and so forth, no matter who operates the system. This loss of freedom is one of the prices paid by man for the many benefits in income and leisure that can flow from industrial society.[2]

Labor has met this problem in part by the organization of trade unions, whose most important function, undoubtedly, has been to assure labor a voice in determining those rules and regulations that affect working conditions. There remains, however, the question: how responsive are union leaders to the wishes of their constituents? Economic bureaucracy is not limited to the corporation. For the salaried employee there are all those pressures and subtle influences on the organization man – and his wife – so graphically depicted by W. H. Whyte.

Market power and managerial power reinforce each other in complex ways. In a vertically integrated enterprise economic processes are subject to managerial control from raw material to finished product, but with market power waxing and waning at different stages, depending on the vigor of competition. A large unintegrated firm buying from many small producers sometimes obtains what amounts to managerial control over these enterprises through the leverage of its market position.

Nor do managerial and market aspects exhaust the content of private power in the economy and the society. Large firms and large trade unions exert an influence on wages and prices outside the jurisdictions of their own managers and markets. Key wage and price bargains are made that affect the general level of wages and prices and wage-price relationships. If we are in for "creeping inflation," large corporations and trade unions are the principal creepers.

One is led on from this point to speculations concerning the political influence of large firms and other organized groups. Here we are offered a broad spectrum of choice ranging from "Business as a System of Power"[3] to the iniquities of a "laboristic economy." Does corporate size bring with it political influence or political vulnerability? Probably the first in some contexts and in others the second. Perhaps the safest thing that can be said is that politics inevitably reflects the structure of society and in a society characterized by large organizations, politics will be pressure-group politics.

III. The Managerial Revolution

Managerial direction is, of course, an aspect of bureaucracy, and its characteristic methods and attitudes have been with us for a long time.

Before the rapid technological changes which we call the industrial revolution had confronted business enterprise with the need for complex administrative organization, the state, large municipalities, armies, the church, universities, and indeed all institutions bringing together the efforts of a sizable group of men had developed bureaucracies. Business bureaucracies as we know them, however, date from the industrial revolution, and the first area in which they significantly flowered was railway transportation. As late as 1900, three quarters of American corporations large enough to have their securities listed on the New York Stock Exchange were railways. But from the Civil War on, this form of organization made progress in other sectors of the economy.

People who talk about a "managerial revolution" usually have in mind, on the one hand, the increasing importance of large corporations on the American scene and, on the other, changes in administrative techniques that have continually increased the size of the enterprise that can be effectively managed. Those who doubt the significance of this "revolution" point to figures on economic concentration, and indeed it is possible to show that, during the last fifty years, there has been no significant increase, however measured, in the share of economic activity controlled by the largest corporations. The largest corporations have grown mightily, but so has the economy. This, in my view, does not dispose of the matter. In the first place, conclusions on the trend of concentration depend heavily on the date from which one measures the trend. If the date chosen is before the great merger movement of 1887–1903, it can be shown that concentration has, in fact, increased. In the second place, the phenomena we are concerned with are more a product of absolute size than of relative share. And about absolute size, however measured, there is no shadow of doubt. In the third place, there is probably a substantial lag between changes in the size of enterprises and changes in managerial techniques adapted to the new sizes. For these and other reasons, I conclude that, despite the lack of evidence of increased concentration during the last half century, there may well have occurred a profound change in the way industrial enterprises are managed. It goes without saying that in other broad sectors of the economy small-scale enterprise, managed in a traditional fashion, not only is holding its own but will continue to do so.

These changes in management are commonly grouped under the heading of bureaucracy. And bureaucracy, as the political scientists tell us, is characterized by a hierarchy of function and authority, professionalization of management, formal procedures for recruitment and promotion, and a proliferation of written rules, orders, and record keeping. All of this is true of business administration in large corporations, but corporate bureaucracies also exhibit certain differences from typical government bureaucracies that are worth emphasizing. In the first place, corporate managements enjoy a much greater freedom from external influence than do the managements of government bureaucracies. As we have seen, management has pretty much escaped from ownership control, but though private ownership may no longer carry with it control, it does guarantee corporate management against most of the political, ministerial, and legislative interference that commonly besets public management. Perhaps in a corporate society this is becoming one of the primary contributions of private property. Needless to say, this independence of corporate management from any well-defined responsibility to anyone also carries with it the possibilities of abuse we have noted above in our discussion of legitimacy.

In the second place, corporate managements have traditionally been considered to have as their single-minded objective, in contrast to most government bureaucracies, maximization of business profits. And traditionally the incentives connected with profit maximization have been thought to constitute an essential part of the justification of a private-enterprise system. Now managerial voices are raised to deny this exclusive preoccupation with profits and to assert that corporate managements are really concerned with equitable sharing of corporate gains among owners, workers, suppliers, and customers. If equity rather than profits is the corporate objective, one of the traditional distinctions between the private and public sectors disappears. If equity is the primary desideratum, it may well be asked why duly constituted public authority is not as good an instrument for dispensing equity as self-perpetuating corporate managements? Then there are those, including the editors of Fortune, who seek the best of both worlds by equating long-run profit maximization with equitable treatment of all parties at issue.[4] But to date no one has succeeded in working out the logic of this modern rehabilitation of the medieval "just price."

Finally, since corporate managements work exclusively in the business area, which government bureaucracies ordinarily do not, it can be said that the possibility of monetary measurement in the former permits a closer adjustment of rewards to performance, and hence a closer observance of the causes of efficiency than is possible in the latter. This is true, and it is important, but the distinction is not between public and private efficiency but between the efficiency of operations susceptible to the measuring rod of money and the efficiency of those that are not. Furthermore, if equity rather than profits is the desideratum, even this advantage is lost. If equity rather than productivity is to determine the reward, what happens to the canons of efficiency?

One of the leading characteristics of well-ordered bureaucracies both public and private – a characteristic justly extolled by the devotees of managerialism – is the increasing professionalization of management. This means, among other things, selection and promotion on the basis of merit rather than family connections or social status, the development of a "scientific" attitude towards the problems of the organization, and an expectation of reward in terms of relatively stable salary and professional prestige rather than in fluctuating profits. This professionalization of management has, of course, been characteristic of well-ordered public bureaucracies for a long time. It helps to explain why able young Indians, for example, have in general preferred to cast their lot with a civil service selecting and promoting on the basis of merit rather than with the highly nepotistic business firms of the subcontinent. But it is a relatively new phenomenon in American business and one of increasing importance.

The degree of freedom enjoyed by corporate managements, in contrast to their governmental counterparts, has affected personnel as well as other policies. And no one who has observed at first hand the red-tape inefficiencies of the United States Civil Service can fail to be aware of the superiority of corporate practice. This relative freedom from hampering restrictions on selection plus a high level of monetary rewards has brought the cream of American professional management into business corporations. No one doubts the superiority of American business management. Unwitting testimony, if testimony is needed, is supplied by the care with which Soviet planners examine American management practices.

But the process of managerial self-selection common in large corporations does raise certain questions worth pondering. Granting that we have been vouchsafed good corporate government, is the process of selection likely to assure us continued good government? Is good government enough or shouldn't we be permitted a modicum of self-government? Has corporate government, in fact, been as good as all that: aren't certain limitations in this process of recruitment already becoming visible?

If the truth be known, no very coherent account of how corporate executives are in fact chosen is available. This is one of those situations in which those who know don't tell, and those who tell don't know. C. Wright Mills, who, so far as I am aware, has had no experience in choosing corporate executives, asserts that advancement is "definitely mixed up in a 'political' world of corporate cliques."[5] This sounds very much like the process of promotion in a university department. Chester I. Barnard, who has had experience, strongly emphasizes the importance of "compatibility of personnel." Those are chosen who fit and fitness includes "education, experience, sex, personal distinctions, prestige, race, nationality, faith, politics, sectional antecedents," and "manners, speech, personal appearance."[6] This is a comprehensive list of qualifications and it recalls an alleged selection to a post at All Souls, Oxford, where the varied capacities of the two rival candidates were so evenly matched that the choice finally depended on the relative neatness with which each disposed of his artichoke.

Drawing on experience in other contexts, one would suppose that an able group of men in choosing successors would emphasize ability but that various considerations making for "togetherness" would strongly impinge. In the process of university selection, excessive concern for the old school tie is apt to be discouraged by the possibility of intervention from above and even more by active competition from rival institutions. University professors can and do move. So do corporate executives on occasion, but the increasing drag of pension rights and other endowments which ordinarily cannot be transferred seriously handicap movement. Nor is the process of executive selection subject to higher review. Since the managerial elite in our large corporations consist of a few thousand at most and since this elite has an influence that far transcends the immediate corporate jurisdiction, it is highly important that the process of selection be kept as competitive as possible even if this requires, as suggested by Brewster, some degree of government intervention.[7]

IV. The Changing Character of Private Property

Berle draws a distinction between "individual possessory holdings" and "power systems" and imaginitively sketches a cyclical development from feudal power systems to the seventeenth – and eighteenth – century emphasis on private property and from that into the modern corporate power system.[8] Certainly ownership of a local grist mill has a different economic significance than the ownership of 100 shares of United States Steel. And issues other than economic are involved.

To a Jeffersonian society of small and relatively equal property owners, the "rights of property" was a phrase fraught with social significance. In a nation of wage and salaried employees, even though many are participants in stock ownership plans, the accent is apt to be on "privilege" rather than "right." Schumpeter contrasts the "full-blooded" capitalist owner of the nineteenth century, ready to fight for his property, with the stock-and-bond owner of the twentieth who has only the vaguest idea where "his property" is or of what it consists. The eighteenth-century philosophers considered property ownership as essential to the full development of personality, to the maintenance of individual freedom from the encroachment of those power systems represented by church and state, and to the formation of a citizenry capable of self-government. Corporate ownership is not usually defended in those terms today.

When questions are raised concerning a contemporary justification of private property, the ownership of one's house, its furnishings, and other consumers goods is not an issue. No one except for a few communal crackpots ... is concerned with this type of property ownership. The problem arises approximately where "individual pos-sessory holdings" give way to "systems of power" – that is, at the point at which corporate size divorces control from ownership and converts owners essentially into rentiers. In Berle's terms, "The capital is there, and so is capitalism. The waning figure is the capitalist."

The fact that private property of this sort presents a "problem" does not mean that it is devoid of justification. But it does mean that the doctrines of Locke and Jefferson are no longer quite relevant. And it probably means that the content of the "rights" and "privileges" that may be justified will differ substantially from their eighteenth-century content. After all, it is a little difficult to see in the ownership of corporate securities the source of that invigorating moral, social, and political development that Jefferson saw in private property. And certainly the eighteenth-century economic justifications of private property based on the assumption that ownership carries with it control lack relevance to the corporate universe.

V.   The Corporation and the State

The economies of Western Europe and, increasingly, that of the United States are frequently described as "mixed" economies. This phrase is commonly interpreted to indicate a situation in which the role of government as owner and regulator has become sufficiently large to cast doubt on the validity of "capitalist" and "free enterprise" as appropriate adjectives but not sufficiently large to justify the appelation "socialist." Government ownership and regulation are important ingredients, but they inadequately characterize the "mixture" of public and private that the rise of the large corporation has produced. The growth of the modern corporation has been accompanied by an increasing similarity of public and private business with respect to forms of organization, techniques of management, and the motivations and attitudes of managers. Government has sought increasingly to use the private corporation for the performance of what are essentially public functions. Private corporations in turn, particularly in their foreign operations, continually make decisions which impinge on the public – particularly foreign – policy of government. And government, in pursuit of its current objectives in underdeveloped areas, seeks to use techniques and talents that only the business corporation can provide. Decidedly a *"verwickelte Verwandschaft,"* as our German friends might say. Under these circumstances the classic arguments of the socialism-versus-free-enterprise debate seem a bit sterile, to say the least.

The increasing similarity of public and private enterprise has impressed both liberals and conservatives, though the conclusions drawn therefrom have tended to differ. In an early recognition of this trend, Keynes described it as a "tendency of big enterprise to socialize itself." A point is reached in the growth of big enterprises, he says, at which "the stockholders are almost entirely dissociated from the management, with the result that the direct personal interest of the latter in the making of great profit becomes quite secondary."[9] American managerial spokesmen supplement this thought by emphasizing management's responsibility to customers, workers, suppliers, and others, though they would hardly describe living up to this responsibility – as Keynes probably would – as behaving like Civil Servants. These and similar considerations have led elements in the British Labour Party to the conclusion that the form of ownership of large enterprise is irrelevant. "The basic fact is the large corporation, facing fundamental similar problems, acts in fundamentally the same way, whether publicly or privately owned."[10]

While large private corporations have been forced by their sheer size, power, and "visibility" to behave with a circumspection unknown to the untrammeled nineteenth century, government, on the other hand, has attempted to give its "business-like" activities a sphere of independence approaching that of the private corporation. Experience with the public corporation in the United States has, it is true, somewhat dampened an earlier enthusiasm for this type of organization. And even Britain, which has sought much longer and harder than we for a workable compromise between independence and accountability in its publicly managed enterprises, has not yet found a satisfactory solution. Nevertheless, it remains true that managerial practices and attitudes in the public and private sectors of most Western economies tend to become more similar.

Private ownership in the United States, however, still confers an immunity from detailed government supervision that a public corporation does not enjoy. And government takes advantage of the independence and flexibility of the private corporation to contract out the performance of what are essentially public services. Private firms become official inspectors of aircraft; various types of military "operations analysis" are undertaken by Rand and other privately organized corporations, and substantially more than half of public research and development expenditures go to private rather than public organizations. In commenting on these phenomena, Don Price observes, "If the question (of public versus private) is seen in realistic terms, we shall have to devise some way of calculating whether a particular function can be performed best in the public interest as a completely governmental operation at the one extreme, or by some mixture of the nearly infinite possibilities of elements of ownership regulation and management that our variety of precedents suggests . . ."[11]

If private corporations perform in certain areas services essentially public in character at the request of government, in other areas they perform services essentially public without being asked. It is probably true to say that not since the seventeenth century, when the Levant Company conducted Britain's foreign policy in the Near East as an adjunct to its business operations and the East India Company acquired India for the Empire "in a moment of inadvertence," have the activities of business corporations impinged so closely on foreign policy. Of course, the classic example is that of the oil companies in the Middle East, but in almost every overseas area in which large American corporations operate, their business activities either impede or advance the foreign policy of the United States. This is not because these corporations behave in a manner different from the way they would have behaved in the nineteenth century – although indeed they do – but rather because the foreign policy of the United States has become so comprehensive that it is touched by almost any sizable business activity. This picture of oil companies "making foreign policy" for the United States raises hackles in some quarters and stimulates demands for the bringing of private business activities under public control. But, in the first place, these are not "private business activities" in the nineteenth-century sense of the term, nor are they conducted as if they were. And second, although private and public relations in this area are probably in need of rethinking, further thought is unlikely to lead to a nineteenth-century type of solution in which authority was either private or public, with little or no commingling of the two.

This lack of a clear-cut separation of public and private authority and responsibility offends some people. And, indeed, the eighteenth-century political philsophers and political economists provided for their epoch a much more satisfactory intellectual framework than any vouchsafed for us today. The fact seems to be that the rise of the large corporation and attending circumstances have confronted us with a long series of questions concerning rights and duties, privileges and immunities, responsibility and authority, that political and legal philosophy have not yet assimilated. What we need among other things is a twentieth-century Hobbes or Locke to bring some order into our thinking about the corporation and its role in society.

Notes

Extract taken from Introduction to Edward S. Mason (ed.) 1959: *The Corporation in Modern Society*. Cambridge Mass: Harvard University Press. Reproduced by kind permission of Harvard University Press.

1 Berle, A. A. Jr. 1957: *Economic Power and the Free Society*. New York, p. 15.
2 Kerr, Clark 1957: *Unions and Union Leaders of Their Own Choosing*. New York.
3 Cf. Brady, Robert 1943: *Business as a System of Power*. New York.
4 Editors of *Fortune*, with the collaboration of Russell W. Davenport, 1954: *USA: The Permanent Revolution*. New York.
5 Mills, C. Wright 1956: *The Power Elite*. New York, p. 133.
6 Barnard, Chester I. 1938: *The Functions of the Executive*. New York, p. 224.
7 Cf. Brewster, Kingman Jr., The Corporation and Economic Federalism.
8 Berle, A. A., *Economic Power and the Free Society*, p. 3.
9 Keynes, J. M. 1926: The End of Laissez-Faire. Republished in *Essays in Persuasion*, London 1931, pp. 314–15.
10 Crosland, C. A. R. 1957: *The Future of Socialism*. London, p. 480.
11 Price, Don K.: Creativity in the Public Service. Harvard Graduate School of Public Administration, *Public Policy*, Volume IX.

8

A Question of Managerial Legitimacy

Marion S. McNulty

The concept of authority involves the power of decision makers to implement their decisions through subordinates. Acceptance of these directives by subordinates involves a perception of the superior's "right" to give orders, i.e., managerial legitimacy. Management's right to be obeyed traditionally has rested on an autocratic basis. Its acceptability in a democratic environment was based on three factors: (a) property rights, (b) the corporate charter, and (c) the competitive market. It will be argued here that managerial prerogatives are subject to question because (a) the concept of property has shifted, (b) responsibilities implied in the charter have been ignored, and (c) the market has ceased to unilaterally maximize consumer sovereignty. Additionally, the divorce of ownership from control has diverted individual self-interest from the communal interest of the larger society and has left management a free hand to determine the public interest unaccountable to any effective constituency.

Thus, corporate management, alone of all American institutional arrangements, exists outside a contractual network which prescribes the acceptable texture of American life. Could it be that some part of the growing edge of alienation found among even managerial and professional employees, as well as the rank and file, reflects a failure to extend contractual reciprocity to the corporation? It is suggested that the restorative powers of legitimacy be sought in a reconsideration of a neglected aspect of Locke's definition of property – the right to property found in the application of expertise, the human factor of production. Decision makers thus become the integrative element in the productive process; indeed, this is their special expertise, their *raison d'être*. It is argued that organizational goals and strategies, and their implementation, no longer are the exclusive property of management, but rather become subject to some sort of accountability to all employees, those who

153

possess rights derived from human input – regardless of variation in
the degree of expertise. As such, management becomes an elite whose
authority rests on the consent of the governed.

The Bases of Managerial Legitimacy

"What constitutes 'legitimacy' is a question that must be answered in
terms of a given society and its given political beliefs," comments Peter
Drucker. He adds, "Power is legitimate when it is justified by an
ethical or metaphysical principle that has been accepted by society." In
most areas of American life, authority rests on the consent of the
governed. In the political sphere, the ferment which culminated in
1776 with the Declaration of Independence gave rise to a political
system based on "inalienable rights" that were effectuated through a
check and balance governmental structure which operated on the
principles of pluralism and constitutionalism. These inalienable rights
were reluctantly delegated to the governing elite only to insure the
survival of the community and then only on terms which vested its
legitimacy, through the rule of law, in the people. These concepts were
based on ideas regarding the social contract, the history of which can
be traced to the beginning of Western Civilization and whose most
prestigious manifestation was the Mayflower Compact. Essentially, the
social contract vested the source of authority in the people themselves,
who delegated to an elected minority the determination of goals and
strategies and the tasks of governance. The circularity of feedback
within the system, essential to the formulation of a "general will," was
further assured through the freedom guaranteed to the fourth estate
and the pluralism generated by voluntary associations. In the flexibility
of these arrangements lies its success in meeting not only political but
social, economic, and technical challenges.

    The economic sphere, on the other hand, was dominated by voluntary
associations whose goal was functional, i.e., the production of goods
and services. These voluntary associations were thought to be outside
governmental perusal, assuming their activities were legal, since the
competitive market system guaranteed consumer sovereignty. The
Smithian concept of consumer sovereignty resulted from competitive
markets, which in turn generated allocative and productive efficiency
by allowing free reign to acquisitive instincts via the profit motive.
Consumer market behavior as a directive agent for resource allocation

and the acquisitive instinct as a force for profit maximization guaranteed to the economy a mechanism to effectuate both the private good and the public interest. Thus it is assumed that the individual is in the best position to know where his best interests lie, given the options at his disposal. The similarity between consumer sovereignty in the economic sphere and the "general will" in the political sphere is readily apparent. The meritocracy so envisioned in the economic sphere parallels the liberty and freedom goals in the political sphere.

Behind the success of the corporate form of business organization lies its mandate for entrepreneurial activity, given by the people themselves, interceded only through the political sphere, i.e., government and the courts. This mandate derives from three important sources: (a) the emphasis placed on property rights by society, (b) the nature of the corporation as determined by the legal system, and (c) the acceptance by society of the market system, whose competitiveness theoretically guarantees the public interest.

Property rights

The importance of property, as a bundle of rights and powers defined by law, lies imbedded in the conceptualizations of the Enlightenment, which reached fruition in Jeffersonian democracy. The inalienable rights of the Declaration of Independence – life, liberty, and the pursuit of happiness – were grounded in the Lockean rights of life, liberty, and estate, of which the greatest was estate. Randall notes that the term "property" included all natural rights since material possessions were the most important and controlling. However, all of these rights and freedoms were contractual in nature, i.e., they were conceptualized in terms of the social contract. In Lockean terms, man entrusted to government protection of life, liberty, and property and thus forfeited individual rights of self-defense and self-aggrandizement through force. In so doing, he voluntarily gave up these "inalienable" rights for the benefit of an open system, whose circularity of information and policy formation granted him some degree of control over the governing elite that was entrusted to promulgate the general will. Although Locke emphasized property even to the extent of encompassing life and liberty into it, it is evident that the individual's command over the material goods of life is prerequisite not only to physical survival but also to the creation of choice in decision making on which liberty must depend. A. H. Maslow's hierarchy of needs, constructed with the intent of exploring questions of motivation, reemphasizes the importance of higher level needs in man's search for freedom. The question centers, then, not so much on the prerequisite nature of property in relation to life and liberty but on the relationship between "command over resources" and the kind of property ownership recognized by society. The corporation's right to own property, as distinct from that of individual stockholders, gave it such advantages as immortality and a capacity for growth unequalled by other forms of business organization. The governance of the corporation, i.e., the exercise of entrepreneurial authority, implies not only the right to direct and lead, but also to control. As long as stock ownership was closely held, managerial authority was virtually synonymous with property ownership.

Legal nature of the corporation

A second source of managerial prerogatives lies in the inherent nature of the corporation itself, i.e., the basis on which the state and the corporation coexist. Historically, the corporation is based, rather ambiguously, on two streams of thought: (a) the source of legitimacy of its precursor, the European joint-stock company, which owed its existence to royal procreation, and (b) the sanctity of contractual obligations between two or more natural persons involving an exchange of property. In the United States, the corporation was defined by Chief Justice Marshall in *Dartmouth College v. Woodward* as "an artificial being, invisible, intangible, and existing only in the contemplation of law." Its powers, he defined as "being the mere creature of law, it possesses only those properties which the charter of its creation confers upon it, either expressly or as incidental to its very existence." Both concepts of corporate legitimacy imply a relationship of the organization to the larger society which lies within the framework of the social contract. Responsibility for the general will or public interest, in more modern terms, is delegated by the government, which is representative of the electorate, to a voluntary association formed to fill a need within a specified area, namely, the production of goods and services. Chief Justice Marshall, in the same decision, goes on to note that "the objects for which a corporation is created are universally such as the government wishes to promote. They are deemed beneficial to the country; and this benefit constitutes the consideration, and in most cases, the sole consideration of the grant."

Essentially, then, in return for the right to profits accrued in the conduct of business, i.e., in the performance of the entrepreneurial function, the artificial person, the corporation, agrees to accept the responsibility for the general will in its decision making which was delegated to it by the government. The entrepreneurial function here refers to the "ultimate management of the responsibility for the enterprise." Thus the corporation agrees to miniaturize the body politic into the confines of its operational area, with, one might add, due recognition to system ramifications and repercussions outside its technical jurisdiction. An arrangement therefore developed between the first order system and a subsystem characterized by a complex set of interrelationships which are reciprocal in nature, a social contract which promised power and wealth in return for economic services compatible with the public interest. Indeed, in the A. P. Smith case the New Jersey court declared:

> It seems to us that just as the conditions prevailing when corporations were originally created required that they serve public as well as private interests, modern conditions require corporations acknowledge and discharge social as well as private responsibilities as members of the communities in which they operate.

In discharging these social responsibilities it would seem that the underlying values of the larger system become subsumed by the corporation. The conditional basis on which the "grant" was made, plus the dependency of the corporation on the pervasiveness of democratic values for its survival, appear to place it entirely within the contractual network on which American society is based. Thus, both the responsibility to society implied by the chartering process and the functional property rights support the legitimacy of managerial prerogatives.

Societal acceptance of the market mechanism

Public reliance on the competitive market system was the third factor endorsing equity rights to entrepreneurial authority. Considering the reality in which the ideas of the Enlightenment were spun, it perhaps was justifiable to assume the adequacy of the competitive market to produce an acceptable approximation of the public interest at that time. The industrial revolution introduced such monopolistic elements as economies of scale, technological innovations, and marketing ingenuities, as well as the motivation and the means to reduce the rigors of competition by businessmen themselves. As a result, justification of laissez-faire capitalism came more and more to rely on the arguments of national growth and affluence. A high growth rate rapidly made visible even to the poor the promise of greater affluence through the miracles of technology and rational business organization. Needless to say, such costs as pollution, industrial accidents and illness, consumer fraud, and defective merchandise went unnoticed until fairly recently.

The growth of big business, especially the escalation of corporate size and concentration, introduced structural and operational complexities which obscured from the average worker formal managerial legitimacy, i.e., Barnard's objective authority. As identification of managerial authority with stockholder property rights became difficult, greater attention was paid to subjective authority. Even the rewards and deprivations of coercive power were found to be malleable under pressure from subjective authority. As a result, in a society in which a President could announce that "the business of America is business," enthusiasm for managerial authority which rested exclusively on an ownership basis was, at best, restricted to a few. Eells and Walton note that:

> In the historical development of American business (wherein business leaders have rather regularly asserted that free enterprise is as essential to democracy as free elections) a curious paradox still persists. What was noted at the turn of the century still persisted in 1961, and may be found to persist in 1970. It is this: despite the widely held view that the United States is a business society, the majority of wage earners did not regard themselves as businessmen or pro-business.

To the evolving complexities of the business world, especially after the turn of the century, must be added the divorce of ownership from management and the professionalization of management itself. Berle and Means in their landmark study noted that:

> In the development of the corporation, constantly widening powers over the management of the enterprise have been delegated to groups within the corporation. . . . Within the separation of ownership and control, these powers developed to a stage permitting those in control of a corporation to use them against the interests of ownership. Since powers of control and management were created by law, in some measure this appeared to legalize the diversion of profit into the hands of the controlling group.

This development, therefore, removed the connecting link in the chain delegating both (a) the entrepreneurial function and (b) the "general will" responsibility from ownership to management. The result was a veritable no-man's-land, a grey area, in which the legitimacy of managerial authority was highly questionable although it remained unchallenged in reality. Eells and Walton in their three volume collection of readings on the ideas and concepts of the business system summarize this phenomenon very succinctly.

> The meaning of executive authority in the contemporary business organization involves reappraisal of the concepts of authority and power in an industrial setting whose separation of control from ownership is the commonly recognized fact. If authority no longer rests on possession of property, is not the legitimization thereof (and the legitimacy of managerial authority is a perennial issue for current debate) to be sought on other grounds? Historically the effective performance of a function deemed necessary to assure community prosperity was sufficient justification for authority. Is the current criticism of the executive power based on contined application of an anachronistic criterion, namely, the loss of ownership over property?

A Reconstruction of Managerial Legitimacy

One avenue of investigation is to reexamine the basis of the contractual society; those ideas of the Enlightenment which not only engineered the complex government structure but laid the foundation for the emphasis on property, however complex its evolution became in response to industrialized pressure. These concepts convolute around the central idea of the social contract. "The idea of a social contract seems like such nonsense at first that one is tempted to throw the whole notion in the wastebasket," says Kenneth E. Boulding in a review of John Rawls, *A Theory of Justice*. "Nevertheless," he continues, "as a myth the social contract should perhaps be fished out of the wastebasket. In some respects, human society does operate as if there is an implicit social contract; we are most aware of it when we feel outrage at its being violated."

The social contract is alive and well. One example of an "implicit social contract" which is apparently operative between management and labor involves a sense of equity beyond a mere "fair day's pay for a fair day's work." One of the more sophisticated theories is that of J.

Stacey Adams, who builds on such precedents as Festinger's theory of cognitive dissonance and Homans' distributive justice. Adams' "input" and "outcome" approximate Homans' concept of "investment" and "profit," respectively. Adams is concerned with the relationship between employee inputs and outcomes relative to other's inputs and incomes, where inputs are defined as the employee's perception of his contribution to the job, e.g., effort, skill, training, experience, intelligence, etc., and outcomes as "pay, rewards intrinsic to the job, seniority benefits, fringe benefits, job status and status symbols and a variety of formally and informally sanctioned prerequisites" as perceived by the employee.

> Inequity exists ... whenever his perceived job inputs and/or outcomes stand psychologically in an adverse relation to what he perceives are the inputs and/or outcomes of other [reference group].

If inequity is felt and if the employee's efforts in terms of manipulation and a weighting of inputs fails to reduce this adverse relationship, he "may 'leave the field'. ... This may take the form of quitting his job or obtaining a transfer or reassignment or of absenteeism." The process of being "turned off," i.e., alienated, may well be an additional effect if other alternatives, such as quitting, are perceived as being unavailable or involving too high a risk.

The injustice perceived by the individual when his contributions to the organization are not appropriately recognized and rewarded normally might be reflected in a homeostatic process whereby inputs become curtailed to restore the balance. The phenomenon of "they won't work" has received much attention lately. Is it not conceivable that the process of balancing rewards with input is not so much a labor market phenomenon as a reflection of a larger societal value which implicitly recognizes the ambiguous position of managerial legitimacy and furnishes living proof of the contractual, rather than authoritarian nature, of the corporate system? It is suggested here that there exists a parallel with the political sphere in that the underlying basis of these theories and their manifestations in the business world rests on the extension of the contractualism within the traditionally autocratic bureacracy of the corporation.

The divorce of ownership from control destroyed the mandate for authority based on equity interest. On what, then, does management base its legitimacy? A second look at Locke's social contract reintroduces a conception of property perhaps more relevant to modern industrialism – property rights vested in the personal contribution of employees to the organization.

Locke, who subsumed life and liberty under the concept of property, defined property as:

> Every man has a "property" in his own "person." This nobody has any right to but himself. The "labour" of his body and the "work" of his hands we may say, are properly his. Whatsoever he removes out of the state that Nature hath provided and left it in, he hath mixed his labour with it, and joined to it something that is his own, and thereby makes it his property.

Although Locke needed his explanation to avoid defining the distribution of wealth in terms of some antecedent contract, it was evident that the idea of man's imprint on nature as a fountainhead of value tapped deep well-springs of response not only in his time but throughout preceding and succeeding periods. The labor theory of value has persisted through a singularly long period of time. In addition, Locke's use of the exchange mechanism, with reference to a money economy, to justify a certain inevitability and "goodness" in an income distribution inequality did not depend on defining property in terms of a man's ability "to remove it from a state of nature," i.e., a labor theory of value. It is suggested that this might be indicative of a responsiveness to demands for human dignity based on inputs to society and on the justice implicit in a reward system based on perceived contribution.

The shift from power vested first in the ownership of physical things, e.g., land, factories, capital equipment, etc., to that of ownership of claims to physical things was extended even further to profits yet to be earned. Similarly, claims on job methods, even jobs themselves, have achieved a quasi-property status in situations where distributive bargaining has been sufficiently strong. Economic complexity gave rise to yet another type of property, that based on specialized knowledge – scientific, technical, etc., which gave access to wealth and, thereby, power.

> more and more of our wealth takes the form of rights or status rather than of tangible goods. An individual's profession or occupation is a prime example.... A profession or a job is frequently far more valuable than a house or a bank account, for a new house can be bought and a new bank account created, once a profession or job is secure. (Reich, 1964)

As Eells and Walton point out, "In the economic sphere, rights are now more clearly attached to men rather than to things – something that has always been true in the political sphere. The result is that, from an economic point of view, society has passed from a private property system to a corporate power system."

In this paraproprietal society, to use the Harbrecht and Berle term, the definition of property has broadened to include not only the expertise of the managerial hierarchy but also the skills and contractual rights of the rank and file. The effect is to shift the question of legitimacy from stockholder to employees, whose contribution to organization goals is essential. It is then a step to recognize their ultimate basis of authority. Finally, it seems appropriate to quote from Mary Parker Follett, who, handicapped by the lack of a vocabulary not yet invented, suggested that a "right and proper" decision, i.e., an authoritative decision, must always be based on the "law of the situation."

> The moral right of an authority . . . which is not an expression of capacity is an empty ethic. . . . We have always to study in a plant how far the authority of the management is real, how far it comes from fulfilling function, from knowledge and ability, and how far it is a nominal or arbitrary authority. . . . We shall always be seeking an external, and arbitrary authority . . . until we [learn] to direct our efforts toward seeking – the law of the situation.

Summary

It appears that the convention of the social contract essentially is an expression of the inherent reciprocity in interpersonal and group relationships. L. T. Hobhouse calls it "the vital principle of society" and a key contributor to the stability of social systems. The application of the social contract to the governance of a political entity serves to make the elite responsible for the public good by basing the legitimacy of their sovereignty on the governed. Similarly, its application to the governance of corporations, a subsystem concerned with economic production, lies exposed when an ineffective competitive market system abrogates the goals of consumer sovereignty and allocative and corporate efficiency, and divorces the equity-control functions. Only when equity interests and the competitive market mechanism supersede the basic compact between individual and organization on the basis of guaranteeing human rights and public interest can managerial authority be justified in terms of property – narrowly defined.

A theory of managerial legitimacy based on employee citizenship which designates some of their own (a managerial elite) to protect and further organization goals not only recognizes the ultimate harmony of labor-management interests but also the essential integrity of the political and economic systems. It also recognizes the legitimate interest of all employees in formulating corporate goals in terms analogous to Rousseau's general will, which in all likelihood would augment the ability to improve intersystem collaboration and minimize suboptimization.

Notes

First printed in McNulty, Marion 1975: A Question of Managerial Legitimacy. *Academy of Management Journal*, 18 (7). Reprinted by kind permission of The Academy of Management.

References

Adams, J. Stacey 1963: Towards an Understanding of Inequity. *Journal of Abnormal and Social Psychology*, 67, 422–34.

Adams, J. Stacey 1963: Wage Inequities, Productivity, and Worker Quality. *Industrial Relations*, 3, 9–16.

Adams, J. Stacey and Rosenbaum, W. E. 1962: The Relationship of Worker Productivity to Cognitive Dissonance about Wage Inequities. *Journal of Applied Psychology*, 46, 161–4.

Barnard, Chester L. 1938: *The Functions of the Executive*. Cambridge Mass: Harvard University Press.

Berle, Adolf A. and Means, Gardiner C. 1932: *The Modern Corporation and Private Property*. New York: Macmillan.

Boulding, Kenneth E. 1973: Review of John Rawls' *A Theory of Justice. Journal of Economic Issues*, 7 (4).

Chicago, Milwaukee and St. Paul Railway Co. v. Minnesota, 134 US 418, 1890.

Cooke, J. W. 1973: Jefferson on Liberty. *Journal of the History of Ideas*, 34 (4), 563–76.

Drucker, Peter 1942: *The Future of Industrial Man*. New York: John Day.

Eells, Richard and Walton, Clarence 1974: *The Conceptual Foundations of Business*, 3rd edn. Homewood IL: Irwin.

Festinger, Leon 1957: *A Theory of Cognitive Dissonance*. Stanford, CA: Stanford University Press.

Follett, Mary Parker: Power. In Henry C. Metcalf and L. Urwick (eds), *Dynamic*

Administration, The Collected Papers of Mary Parker Follett. New York: Harper and Row.

French, Wendell 1974: *The Personnel Management Process*, 3rd edn. Boston: Houghton Mifflin.

Harbrecht, Paul B. and Berle, Adolf Jr. 1959–60: *Toward the Paraproprietal Society.* New York: The Twentieth Century Fund.

Hobhouse, L. T. 1951: *Morals in Evolution: A Study of Comparative Ethics.* London: Chapman and Hall.

Homans, George C. 1961: *Social Behavior: Its Elementary Forms.* New York: Harcourt Brace and World.

Kuhn, James W. 1968: Business Unionism in a Laboristic Society. In Ivar Berg (ed.), *The Business of America.* New York: Harcourt Brace and World.

Locke, John 1943: *Of Civil Government.* Ernest Hays (ed.), Everyman Library. London: J. M. Dent and Sons.

Locke, John B. 1960: *Two Treatises on Government.* Peter Laslett (ed.). Cambridge: Cambridge University Press. Maslow, A. H. 1954: *Motivation and Personality.* New York: Harper and Row.

Mason, E. S. 1959: *The Corporation in Modern Society.* Cambridge Mass: Harvard University Press.

Pritchard, Robert, Dunnettee, Marvin D., and Jorgenson, Dale O. 1972: Effects of Perception of Equity and Inequity on Worker Performance and Satisfaction. *Journal of Applied Psychology*, Monograph 56, 75–94.

Randall, John H. Jr. 1963: *The Career of Philosophy.* New York: Columbia University Press.

Reich, Charles A. 1964: The New Property. *Yale Law Journal*, 73.

Riley, Patrick 1973: How Coherent is the Social Contract Tradition? *Journal of the History of Ideas*, 34 (4), 542–62.

Rousseau, Jean-Jacques 1954: *The Social Contract.* William Kendall (trans.). Chicago: Henry Regnery.

A. P. Smith Manufacturing Company v. Barlow et al 1953: 26 N.J. Super. 106; affirmed, 98 Atl. (2nd) 581; appeal to US Supreme Court dismissed, 346, US 861.

The Trustees of Dartmouth College v. Woodward 1819: 4 Wheaton 518.

Walton, Clarence, and Eells, Richard 1967: *The Business System: Readings in Ideas and Concepts.* New York: Macmillan.

9

Growing Corporate Governance: From George III to George Bush

ROBERT A. G. MONKS

In this complicated world, we delegate authority to make many critical decisions about our lives and society. Increasingly, we are delegating those decisions to private entities, now eclipsing government in reach and power. Traditionally, countries have been able to assure that private power was exercised in the public interest through law. As private enterprises become preponderantly multinational in character, any one country's capacity to affect the impact of commerce on its citizens through laws is vastly diminished. This has been the pattern in the United States with the interplay between state and federal laws, and this is what I see in Europe with the emergence of the European Community corporate laws.

Experience in the US has shown that the current governance system is no governance system at all. This is despite clear evidence, as demonstrated by the Honeywell example, that good governance is good value, and the incentives that should provide for participation in governance. My conclusion is that we must have an effective multinational organization of institutional owners and that the NAPF [National Association of Pension Funds], as the premier national institution of this kind in the world today, is in the best position to begin.

I. World dynamics: the evolution from political and military to economic and business

Our grandchildren will find that their affiliation with an industrial group is far more important than their citizenship in a particular country.

While the post-World War II international system really could be

165

modeled as a two party game, this is clearly no longer the case. First, economic developments have diminished the relative power of the US and USSR within their respective blocs. The soaring wealth of Japan and the economic integration of the EC has created two more superpowers of sorts. Second, the very rationale for the existence of two superpowers has been thrown into question by the Gorbachev initiatives and the eagerness with which they are being embraced by the West.

In some ways, World War II is ending at last. We must be very sensitive to the kinds of changes that brings. First, the dominant mode of expression of power in the world will be decreasingly political and increasingly economic, less military and more corporate. Second, an escalating percentage of corporate activity will be conducted by companies having operations across national boundaries. Third, the effective combination of culture, public opinion and law that, in the past, has assured the compatibility of corporate power to the public interest will be insufficient for that purpose in the future. Fourth, restraints on corporate power based on the law of their domicile will follow the pattern in the US of a "race to the bottom" and will have little impact. Fifth, we must therefore ensure a structure adequate to compel accountability of those in charge of corporations to some source outside of their organizations – and we have to accept that it cannot be left to individual country's political systems. Sixth, in law, tradition, and common sense, the best place to start is with owners.

Attempting to predict who the players will be in this new game forces us to confront the perhaps most important reason to expect heightened instability in the future; the likelihood that the typical "player" will consist of nations and/or organizations lacking any aligned set of public policy objectives. Indeed, it is almost a certainty that the nations comprising each bloc will have differing economic and security concerns. For example, we would hardly expect the concerns of the British to parallel those of a reunified Germany. This lack of internally cohesive objectives within a geopolitical block reflects a deeper problem, namely the reduced importance of classical territorial imperatives and the increased significance of technology-based economic imperatives. These have little to do with geographical boundaries of any kind.

For example, what if the US, Canada and Mexico decided to form a North American Alliance, and erect protectionist tariffs? Will the existence of this trading bloc be good news for the Boeing Corporation? Will Boeing use its considerable political clout to champion barriers to trade with Japan – potentially its largest customer? Boeing would not, but the National Semi-Conductor Company might. And yet, its suppliers probably would not. And so on. In such an environment, can we really expect anyone to have a clear idea of national priorities? Most probably not, because there won't be any.

II. The increased need for a system of effective governance of corporations, particularly in light of 1992

Corporations appear to be a straightforward proposition. They are artificial creatures of the state, authorized to permit the most efficient combination of capital, labor and management. Governments should have the capacity to make sure that they act in the public interest. But we have been shown in the most compelling terms that they do not. Factors other than law – national culture (as in Japan), concentrated stock ownership (Germany), national ownership (Italy) have been moderately successful in assuring corporate "good citizenship." In the US, where these factors do not exist, we do not even have that. But the failure by any government to assure effective corporate governance, already a problem, seems certain to get worse, as a result of two emerging trends: multinational enterprises who are virtually free to charter and to operate their business from any national base(s) and the creation in Europe of a new legal authority having jurisdiction over the entire community.

It is in this climate that we must look at the questions of corporate governance. Corporations will be able to formulate and promote their self-interest more confidently than nations can. There are two reasons: first, the issues tend to be one-dimensional; and, second, corporations are free to walk away from both internal and external liabilities. If companies are then not going to be accountable to citizens through the power of the laws enacted by governments, we must determine what power will be able to hold them accountable. After all, it is only accountability that legitimizes the exercise of any power; because it is the only way to ensure that the power which has been delegated is not abused – that any conflicts of interest that arise between those who delegate the power and those who exercise it are properly resolved.

The American legal system developed at a time when the greatest threat to individual freedom was the power of the state; this system has proven to be inadequate now that the threat is from private, largely corporate, power. Restraint through enactment of laws has been less and less successful. Keep in mind that in the United States, state, in contrast to federal, law has primary authority over corporate chartering and functioning. The result has been called the "race to the bottom" – states (both legislatures and courts) design their laws to be as inviting as possible to corporate management, so that they may have the benefit of the tax revenues. And why not? They are not the ones who pay the price. As the supra-national European Community takes shape, I hope it will avoid the problems caused by our melange of state and federal authority.

III. American governance in 1989: the difference between what is right and what is legal (MBOs, GAF, UAL, Time/Warner and Loral)

The *Wall Street Journal*, in an editorial comparing the takeover battles of Time in America and BAT in Britain concluded: "It's better to be a shareholder in Britain. It's better to be a lawyer in America."[1]

Corporate governance in the United States is largely a tale of the difference between what is legal and what is right. Sam Heyman, whose MBO at GAF stands as an example, showed how little value really matters when he revised his bid, following the 1987 stock market crash. Heyman originally offered $66.50 for each share of GAF common stock in September 1987. That offer was rejected by a special committee of GAF's independent directors, then withdrawn by Heyman himself after the October stock market crash. Some months later, he offered bids of $48.50 and $51.00, which were also rejected by the special committee. The final bid of $53.00 – $46.00 in cash and subordinated debt with a face value of $7.00 – was ultimately accepted by the committee. To operating management, a company's asset value does not change with a sudden drop in the entire stock market, yet to the management trying to purchase those assets, it does.

How can management possibly mediate fairly between its shareholders' interest in the highest price and its own interests in the lowest price? It cannot. Inevitably, the interests of management, which controls the information and timing – and the board – will prevail. This is why the law of trusts inveterately and unchangingly does not permit a trustee to profit personally from dealings with the trust estate. Yet a corporate manager or director, in a similar position as a fiduciary, has no such strictures.

It is almost tautological that recent MBOs have served, first and foremost, the personal pocket book interest of management. Consider the massive sums management awards itself: Stephen Wolf, CEO of UAL, proposed personal profit approximating $75 million in the failed UAL MBO. This actually pales in comparison to the deals made in the management-led Time-Warner merger. Steve Ross of Warner acquired a salary/compensation/bonus package worth an estimated 300 million dollars. And the CEO of Loral, Bernard L. Schwartz, sold himself two divisions of his own company, despite a higher bid from Banner Industries, and billed himself about $4,000 an hour to run them, still drawing full salary from Loral.

The UAL transaction in particular represents a crescendo of many unsavory themes in management-led buyouts. The company – make that the shareholders – are now paying more than $58 million in legal and financing fees for the deal which did not go through. The attempted MBO was designed to protect management from a takeover. If it had been successful, management would have been rewarded on a scale beyond opulence. Why should shareholders bear the downside risk and pay the costs for a venture so blatantly in the principal interests of management?

IV. The ascent of directors – the corruption of "pre-emptive rights" and the business judgment rule

I follow with great respect (and, I hope, politely concealed envy) the effectiveness that NAPF and sister organizations have had in the area of preemptive rights. Arising out of the chaos of our multiple state jurisidiction over hostile takeovers, management's latest means for protecting itself is the creation of a new class of stock with particularly attractive characteristics, to be issued to a friendly "white squire." (There can be, however, a bit of a problem when a squire gets less friendly, as with Lawrence Tisch, who decided that he wanted the CBS throne for himself.)

Let me describe a recent example. In its struggle with Roy Disney, Polaroid developed two vehicles. The first, a so-called ESOP (Employee Stock Ownership Plan) was created by the Board literally while Mr Disney was in the air coming to Boston from California to talk with

Polaroid's management. The ESOP contained fifteen percent of the total outstanding shares, a determinative amount under the friendly law of Delaware, where Polaroid, like most large American companies, is incorporated. The Delaware Court, always aware of the importance of chartering revenue to that state (20% of total tax receipts), upheld the validity of the directors' action. Not satisfied with this standoff, the Polaroid corporation proceeded to issue to an affiliate of Lazard Freres a new class of security with a guaranteed minimum rate of return over ten years, board representation and voting rights over some twenty percent of the total. At no point was the approval of the shareholders sought or received, notwithstanding the existence of at least one alternative offer – and notwithstanding the fact that the obligation to the holders of the new shares put the old shareholders in a significantly poorer position. This began a significant new trend; the most recent example is the deal Warren Buffett made with Champion International.

V.   Corporate management – the "new philosopher king" – Pennsylvania bill #1310

Another deal that left shareholders in a significantly poorer position was the Time–Warner merger. The Delaware Court upheld the Time directors' decision to sell, despite uncontradicted evidence that (1) Paramount was offering more money, (2) the transaction, designed over a two-year period as an equity deal, was restructured in a few days as a debt deal, just to take the decision away from the shareholders. The court held that the Board's consideration of the merger for two years was entitled to deference, despite the fact that the deal that went through was not the one they had planned. Indeed, during that two-year period, it had been explicitly considered and rejected. The court held that Time was not for sale, despite the fact that sixty percent of the stock was changing hands.

This gives some indication of the Through the Looking Glass aspect of Delaware law; like Humpty Dumpty, they decide what they want the words to mean. The courts and state legislatures have bent so far backwards to defer to the "business judgment" of directors – some have even gone so far as to eliminate liability not just for acts committed in good faith, but for negligent acts as well.

A recent proposal to amend Pennsylvania law, designed to give corporate officers and directors the maximum protection from any accountability to shareholders, goes further than anything I have seen in granting sovereign power to establish public policy to the corporation. The proposed amendments provide:

> In discharging the duties of their ... respective positions, the board of directors ... may, in considering the best interests of the corporation, consider the effects of any actions upon employees, upon suppliers and customers of the corporation and *all other pertinent factors*. ... The consideration of those factors shall not constitute a violation of subsection (b) (emphasis added).

Subsection (b) sets forth the standards for director liability. The effect of this language is that directors may consider any factor they chose to, without any risk of liability for breach of their duty as fiduciaries. Directors *can not* be held liable, without direct self-dealing or fraud. It should be kept in mind that in the United States, the theoretical legal liability of management for breaches of duty to ownership is the instrument through which governance is enforced. Accountability is thus eliminated under the proposed Pennsylvania statute.

It is not hyperbole to say that this is corpocracy. Our current system is based on Adam Smith's theory that the pursuit of profit would provide the best assurance that what corporations did was in fact congenial to the citizens' interests. Pennsylvania SB 1310 would permit decisions to be made on another basis, based on their own evaluation of the trade-offs, and therefore grants to corporations the power to establish public policy. By doing so, it repudiates the entire basis for corporate legitimacy. All power is delegated in exchange for some accountability, whether in the political context or the corporate context. By delegating additional authority to corporations, just as accountability is being diminished, this proposal undermines both political and private systems.

VI. No set of laws can ensure an adequate system of corporate governance, without a supporting culture and institutional structure. The informed and active involvement by owners is essential

The solution may be found within the structure of the corporation itself. Owners are increasingly institutional, with little need for day-today liquidity and with a long-term interest in value enhancement that is compatible with those of the enterprise and its management, as well as with the overall society and the world economy. Both shareholders and management must realize that the tension in their relationship provides checks and balances that are creative, constructive, and cooperative. This brings corporate power almost back to where it began, before the stress on instant liquidity sundered the common interest of manager and owner.

To quote Sir John Hicks: "There is something to be said for the system which seems to be evolving under the pressure of taxation, in which the shares of large companies are held, in large blocks, by institutions – banks, pension funds, and so on – which have a sufficient stake in the company to have an incentive to keep in close touch with its affairs, just as the holder of a non-transferable share has an incentive to do. Such a system could indeed be regarded as that of the private company writ large. It would indeed lose something, perhaps much, in flexibility; but it could offer gains in other ways."[2]

The conventional wisdom is that corporate management is accountable to ownership, that the directors and officers work for the shareholders and that this accountability sufficiently limits corporate power so as to make it tolerable in a free society. During the last several decades, it has been convenient for all parties to maintain lip service to this fiction, for government, because of a wish to avoid confrontation from which it was uncertain to emerge successful; for management, because of the convenience of actually being accountable to no one while having an absolute defense against charges of excessive power; for shareholders, because of the excuse from expending resources with only vague possibility of returns. There should be no doubt, however, that accountability to ownership in the United States is only a polite fiction.

VII. *"Rational ignorance" and "rational involvement" by shareholders – Honeywell*

Commentors have used the oxymoronic term "rational ignorance" to explain one of the reasons for this fiction. The problem is one of collective choice, often called the "prisoner's dilemma." Any shareholder, even a large institutional shareholder, who wants to take action to hold management accountable must pay all of the costs, for only a pro rata share of the returns, if there are any. A fiduciary shareholder can barely justify the costs of educating himself about governance, much less participating in it.

But last year gave us an example of "rational involvement," of collective action that was not only prudent, it was one of the best investments of the year. It was the first ever full-scale proxy fight[3] that was not about control of the corporation; it was also the first time that shareholders defeated a management proposal, without a contest for control to provide the fuel.

The company was Honeywell.

Late 1980s: Honeywell's poor performance was a source of concern to shareholders. A major restructuring was announced in 1986, which helped to improve performance in the company's control division, but did not help improve performance in the defense division. In February 1987, restructuring costs resulted in the company's first loss, of $500 million. Honeywell's 1986 acquisition of the Sperry group from Unisys resulted in more major losses. Honeywell eventually sued Unisys for misrepresentation. Stock analysts, however, placed the blame with Honeywell, saying it had not studied the acquisition adequately. The company entered into fixed-price contracts with the Defense Department, and major cost overruns led to more losses. In late 1988, the company's chief financial officer resigned, shortly before the announcement of another $500 million fourth quarter loss. Throughout this period, Honeywell stock languished.

Spring 1989: ISS (of which I was then president) learned that at Honeywell's upcoming annual meeting, the company intended to propose to eliminate the annual election of directors and to classify its board, and to eliminate the shareholders' ability to act by written consent. We thought this was an inappropriate response from a management team plagued with problems; it appeared to be an entrenching strategy, rather than a constructive response to its problems. Around the same time, ISS was contacted by Edward S. Lampert of North American Partners, LP, owner of 4.4 percent of Honeywell common, and his colleague Richard Rainwater, former financial advisor to the Bass brothers. Lampert and Rainwater shared our views, and we agreed that some concentrated shareholder initiative might convince the company that its shareholders were dissatisfied, which would encourage the company to take positive steps to improve share value. A stockholder group was formed that included the California Public Employees' Retirement System and the Pennsylvania Public School Employees' Retirement System, as well as the North American Partners and ISS. The group retained Georgeson & Co. as its proxy solicitor.

While our explicit purpose was to defeat the two proposals, we were much more interested in presenting to management hard evidence that the majority of its shareholders were unhappy with management's performance and expected something better; defeating the proposals would be the best evidence available.

April 1989: The stockholder group notified Honeywell management of its concerns and expressed its desire to meet to discuss ways to improve share value. Management declined to pursue discussions, and the stockholder group filed its preliminary proxy material with the SEC.

Thursday, April 27: We were informed that the SEC would clear our proxy material the next day, and Georgeson started its "search card calls." These were calls to stockbrokers, custodian banks and the Independent Election Corporation of America (IECA), to inform them that a counter-solicitation was about to begin, and that they should notify their clients. Since our proxy material had not yet been cleared, we were not allowed to indicate the subject matter of the solicitation, or to say who was behind it. Trading volume was high that day, but at the time nobody knew what was behind it.

Friday, April 28: Our proxy material was cleared, and we immediately distributed our news release to the press, and, even more important, to the wire services. Within minutes, every analyst knew what we were doing. Trading volume in Honeywell was over 500,000 shares, double Honeywell's "normal" daily trading volume of 250,000 shares. Honeywell commonly closed that day at $72.50, up 2.3 percent from Thursday's close. Trading volume remained unusually heavy the next week, and Honeywell common continued to show abnormal price gains.

Monday, May 1 to Friday, May 4: Principals from the stockholder group and Georgeson completed over 300 phone calls to major company stockholders, while Georgeson staff ensured that all of the group's proxies were properly executed and delivered on time. Trading volume was heavy all week.

Friday, May 5: Last-minute votes were telefaxed to the Honeywell annual meeting. Too close to call, the announcement of the vote results on the antitakeover proposals were postponed for a week. After the meeting, the stockholder group repeated its invitation to discuss value-enhancing strategies with management.

Friday, May 12: Honeywell announced that its proposals had been defeated. That day, Honeywell volume was nearly 700,000 shares, and Honeywell common rose $1.625, up over 2 percent from the day before.

Monday, July 24: Honeywell announced a major corporate restructuring. Honeywell stock jumped $3.88 on volume of 1.9 million shares.

Over the three-month period, Honeywell common stock moved 22 percent, from $73 to over $89 per share. We do not claim to be responsible for all of the gain – takeover rumors had been circulating throughout the entire period, and perhaps Honeywell management would have announced its restructuring even without external pressure. But we believe our demonstration of shareholder concern – and power – played a substantial part in the gains realized.

The 1989 Honeywell proxy solicitation was an historic achievement for several reasons:

- It was the first time that institutional shareholders defeated a corporation's antitakeover proposals without the presence of a controlling shareholder;
- It was the first time institutional shareholders joined forces with private investors for a proxy initiative; and
- It was the first time an institutional shareholder initiative helped achieve a substantial improvement in share value.

In short, the 1989 Honeywell solicitation demonstrates the value of strategic shareholder involvement in corporate governance.

VIII. Multi-national ownership groups

At the end of the day, the proposition is simply stated. There will be an increasing need for the effective governance of large corporations as the traditional capacity of law is diluted with the eradication of national boundaries. Law and tradition have inveterately and unchangingly based the legitimacy of corporate power on the self-interest of owners to assure that management pursues objectives that are compatible with societal interest. The recent American experience demonstrates on the one hand that there is no limit to the extent of potential deterioration of protection from law and on the other that involvement in governance is value enhancing.

Notes

First presented as a talk to the National Association of Pension Funds (NAPF) Investment Conference, Eastbourne UK, 22 February 1990. Reprinted here by permission of the author.

1 A Tale of Two Takeovers, *Wall Street Journal*, July 7 1989, p. A10. It is noteworthy that both the Takeover Panel and institutional investors in Britain have recently adopted new rules concerning MBOs.
2 Hicks, Sir John 1982: Limited Liability: The Pros and Cons. In Tony Orhnial (ed.), *Limited Liability and the Corporation*. Action Society Trust.
3 It is the practice in the US to engage a firm of "proxy solicitors" to contact the legal owners and to secure sufficient proxies for a quorum and approval of management proposals at the Annual Meeting.

10

Comment on Robert Monks:
Is Institutional Investor Hegemony
a Viable Legitimating Alternative?

Brenda Sutton

The perceived abdication of shareholder rights and responsibilities, which Peter Drucker called the "central institutional change of our times", has recently been countered by intensive activity among investors demanding a greater voice in the governance of today's publicly-traded corporation. Stimulated primarily by the wave of takeovers (or, more specifically, the defense mechanisms against them) in the 1980s, numerous activist groups are now addressing broader issues of management performance and accountability. The most influential of these groups in North America is Institutional Shareholder Services (ISS), founded by Robert Monks. ISS states its purpose as "defining and promoting an ownership agenda which will allow shareholders to reclaim their property rights".

The "managerial revolution" of the early twentieth century is being challenged by this new class of investor-owners, who believe their interests in the corporation are threatened by the agenda of top management. No longer content to (or able to, considering the large blocks of shares they own) exercise the "Wall Street Rule" – selling the shares of an unsatisfactory company – institutional investors see their emerging role as participative in ensuring the long-term viability of the businesses they invest in.

Monks' position, both in the essay presented here and in his recent book *Power and Accountability* (with Nell Minow, published by Harper-Business in 1991), is that legitimation of the corporation can be achieved in large part by making those organizations once again accountable to the shareowners: i.e., returning to the belief in private property rights as a basis for corporate and managerial legitimacy.

If this goal is achieved, it could radically change the structure and process of transnational corporate governance. It is a well-publicized fact that by the year 2000, 50 percent of all publicly-traded shares in the US and the UK will be held by institutions – public and private pension funds, investment banks, mutual funds, foundations, and so on. This is, to say the least, a formidable interest group, and one whose voice will not be easily ignored.

Despite the positive benefits foreseeable in such a course, a number of analysts have questioned the ultimate desirability, or even viability, of this new form of "investor capitalism" in the future.

Certainly one of the central issues in the corporate legitimacy debate is the power of professional managers, who wield great influence in society without the support of a democratic process to validate that authority. The overall issue of corporate legitimacy is, however, increasingly one of organizational as well as managerial power – or, put another way, the goals and outputs of those organizations vis-à-vis changing public values and needs.

To assume that legitimation can be achieved by redirecting that power into the hands of the investors on the basis of property rights is a view that precludes the notion of the corporation as a social institution, one whose entire sphere of evolving interrelationships are as important to the maintenance of legitimacy as its obligations to the shareholders.

In fact, confusion over the concepts of "private property" and the "rights of property" lie at the core of the corporate legitimacy problem. The diffusion or institutionalization of publicly-traded shares, the growth of speculation as opposed to production, and the increasing difficulty in differentiating "public goods" from "private property" have effectively disqualified traditional ideas of property rights as adequate rationalizations for concentrated, transnational corporate power. In addition, the development of the "knowledge-based" society has, and will continue to, transform our most basic notions of what constitutes "property" and "value". In other words, investor-based accountability invokes only part of the overall schema of social change, and the elements necessary for enhancing corporate legitimacy.

Alfred F. Conard outlined some pros and cons of the activist agenda as follows:

> As policymakers face the growing potential of institutional activism, they must address the question of whether this phenomenon is likely to enhance or impair the benefits that enterprises bring to savers, employees,

consumers, and communities. On the positive side, institutional activism might enhance the profitability of enterprises, reduce the waste of takeover wars, rationalize management compensation, and preempt shareholder suits. On the negative side, it might sacrifice long-term gains to short-term profits, entrench inefficient managers in their jobs, give institutions preferred access to inside information, and diminish the responsivity of enterprises to social demands.[1]

Probably one of the most important questions embedded in the negative side of these issues is, who would be empowered if governance models were to shift to institutional investor hegemony? And to whom, in turn, would those new leaders be accountable?

In answer to the first question, in all likelihood it would be the fund managers themselves and their representatives. One could argue that this is just a changing of the guard from one set of self-perpetuating autocrats to another – and even, perhaps, to a new set of managers whose agenda is limited to the traditional definition of profit, translated in dollar terms to dividends. As to the second question, this has yet to be satisfactorily addressed.

While enhanced profitability of portfolio enterprises is certainly a good thing for millions of pension-holders and other investors (and thus economies in general), the inherent risk from investor-driven companies is that increasingly important issues of social responsibility could become even more marginalized than they already are by the narrow view of the investor-owners. It is still unclear, from the discussions now underway, what importance institutional shareholders would attach to these issues and to other factors in long-term corporate decision-making.

In this century, the corporation has emerged as an entity embodying centralized control coupled with decentralized operating divisions and planning based on sub-group functions. The managerial revolution gave life to a large, bureaucratic and rational form of organization which pursues profits as its primary *raison d'être*. Until recent decades, this pursuit went largely unchallenged, and the corporation was perceived as serving its purpose well. Social values and vested interests have changed profoundly, however, and a single-minded drive toward short-term monetary gain at the expense of resources, the environment, and the "quality of life" in general is no longer accorded the legitimacy it enjoyed in the past. Corporate managers have, for the most part, accepted these changes as part of the business environment and have begun to seek strategies whereby such trends can be reconciled with commercial logic.

By virtue of its power and authority in society, the corporation has increasingly become the nexus for a *consortium* of interests. The governance process of the future will need to reflect that plurality for the maintenance of its legitimacy to all of its stakeholders and the public. The question remains whether or not the new *shareholder* agenda for governance, of performance based on profit alone, can respond in an effective and timely manner to changing social priorities.

Notes

1   Conard, Alfred F. 1988: Beyond Managerialism: Investor Capitalism? University of Michigan *Journal of Law Reform*, 22, 117–78.

Part III

Legitimacy and the Future of Corporate Governance

11

Business in the Ecosystem of Power

KENNETH BOULDING

Power takes many forms. In the remarks that follow, I first discuss power in the broadest terms. Second, I describe various kinds of human power. And third, I address the power exercised by business, exploring the implications of that process for business itself and for society.

The Ecological and Evolutionary Background

Power is a word not usually associated with ecosystems. It has been associated with business.[1] Power we associate with decisions, especially human decisions. Human power is part of the wider concept of power, which is the potential for change. Power in this sense is something, for instance, possessed by the fertilized egg. My own fertilized egg, somewhere in 1909, had the potential for producing a male *Homo sapiens* with a pale skin and blue eyes, originally black hair, about six feet tall, with an active brain, and so on. The potential was pretty much realized. The fact that my parents spoke English, that they were Methodists and lived in Liverpool, introduced cultural potential into the fertilized egg, though I did end up as an American and a Quaker. Virtually all potentials and forms of power represent a range of possibilities, not a single deterministic future. If my parents had died when I was an infant, I would certainly have lived a very different kind of life, even though I would have retained the same genetic potential.

Social potential, again, is part of a larger context that might be called "environmental potential." A wheat seed has the potential for growing into a wheat plant and producing a lot more wheat seeds if the environment is favorable. If it falls on stony ground or is strangled by weeds, as the parable suggests,[2] its life history will be different, though it will still be part of its genetic potential.

Environmental potential is what ecology, the study of ecosystems, is all about. An ecosystem contains interacting populations of different species, together with their physical environment. The ecosystem in which every fertilized egg or seed is placed determines, perhaps with some uncertainty, its set of probable futures. The critical concept here is the population of a species. A population could almost be defined as a set or list of individuals which are alike enough to be interesting. We can tie it down somewhat by defining a population as a set of individuals which can receive additions (births) and subtractions (deaths) and in which each individual has a life history from birth to death. A fundamental principle, which I have sometimes called the "bathtub theorem," is that the increase of any population, whether of humans, mosquitoes, automobiles, savings banks, or ideas, in any period, is equal to the number of additions minus the number of subtractions.[3] Additions include births, new members of a species added, plus immigrations if these occur in a particular area. Subtractions include deaths plus outmigrations. If additions and subtractions are equal, the population will remain constant. If additions are greater than subtractions, the population will increase. If subtractions are greater than additions, the population will decline. Additions and subtractions are functions of the size of the population itself and of the other populations and significant elements in its environment.

The idea that an ecosystem with interacting populations of various species can have an equilibrium is a useful one, though we have to be careful with it, for equilibrium in a strict sense is unknown in the real world, which is in a process of constant change. But equilibrium is at least a useful product of the human imagination. An ecosystem is in equilibrium when all populations in it are stable, with additions equal to subtractions, and when the underlying environment in terms of climate, materials, and the genetic potential (DNA) of all species in the physical environment, is also stable.[4]

The dynamics of such a system can be visualized if we suppose a particular population that is "too big," that is, above equilibrium. Its members will find food hard to obtain and will be open to being eaten by others. Deaths are likely to exceed births. If it is an open system, outmigrants may exceed immigrants. The population will fall. If the population is below equilibrium, "too small," its members will find food will be easier to get. They will be less likely to be eaten, immigration may exceed outmigration, and the population will rise. There will be some level of the population, therefore, between "too big" and "too small," in which additions are equal to subtractions and the population is stable. Looking at the dynamics of such a system over time, it is likely that there will be fluctuations about the equilibrium level. If fluctuations are too large, the equilibrium may be destroyed and the population, for instance, might become extinct, in which case the whole system would change.

Evolution is the process by which the equilibrium populations of an ecosystem change constantly, partly through genetic mutation, which creates new types of individuals and eventually new species, and partly through extinction as equilibrium populations fall to zero because of new competitors, climatic changes, ice ages, soil erosion, delta building, geological changes, and so on. In the last 100,000 years or so, the earth has developed a remarkable species, *Homo sapiens*, which has changed the whole world through its unprecedented capacity to produce artifacts.

An equilibrium population of a species in an ecosystem may be called a "niche." It is a fundamental principle, which biologists find a little hard to accept because they don't like studying what isn't there. They do not like the concept that all ecosystems have "empty niches," species that would have an equilibrium population in the system if they existed. Evolution, essentially, is the filling of empty niches by the development of new species. This can happen either through genetic mutation or by migration. It is very clear, for instance, that Australia had an empty niche for rabbits which was not filled until humans brought them there in boats, as rabbits could not swim across the seas that separate Australia from the rest of the world. Once they were brought into Australia, however, they expanded very rapidly into quite a large niche, to the detriment of many existing species, the populations of which declined. Australia also clearly had an empty niche in 1788 for eighteenth-century Europeans who had invented guns and were able to sail 12,000 miles to the other side of the earth, and this niche was occupied. It probably had an empty niche for Chinese for many centuries which was not filled. Indeed, if the Ming emperors had not discouraged sea travel so severely, it is quite possible that Australia would be speaking Chinese today and would be called something else. Empty niches are filled only with a certain probability. This is why evolution is a profoundly indeterministic process. The "big bang" had the potential for uncounted numbers of different universes, only one of which has happened up to the present. The one that happened developed because of a long succession of extremely improbable events.

Newtonian determinism has no place in evolutionary theory and the evolution of the human race conforms to this pattern.

With the human race, evolution goes into a new gear. Even though the genetic difference between humans and chimpanzees seems to be quite small, that small change has made an enormous difference to the earth, mainly because of the huge capacity of humans for knowledge, know-how, and the making of artifacts. Over much of the globe now, the mass of human artifacts is larger than the biomass (the mass of living organisms). This is certainly true in cities and even in land devoted to agriculture, for the crops that are grown, even though they are produced from biological genes, are in a very real sense human artifacts, in the sense that they would not have existed had it not been for the human race. The same could be said of domestic animals. It is only in the sea, the untouched forests, and in the unpopulated parts of the world that the biomass exceeds the mass of human artifacts.

The extraordinary capacity of the human race for producing artifacts derives essentially from the huge power in the human brain for developing what might be called "know-what," that is, very complex and fairly realistic images of the world and its relationships. The power of the biological genetic structure and the fertilized egg is "know-how." Genes know how to construct whatever form of life they are programmed for. This know-how can only change very slowly, for successful genetic mutation which perpetuates itself is quite rare. The capacity of the human race, however, for increasing know-what creates a continual increase in human know-how because of the mind's power to imagine changes in the human environment. Even the most primitive stone tools were probably not made by random hacking away, but by imagining what would happen if their maker did certain things. With humans, therefore, we get decision on a scale which is quite unknown in prehuman evolution and this leads to a conscious power over the environment. Decision, of course, is not confined to humans, for something that goes beyond mere automatic response to stimulus is characteristic of much animal behavior. But in humans the power of decision expands by orders of magnitude because of our capacity for forming complex images of the future derived from our images of the past and our capacity to select among these images of the future according to some system of values of better or worse.

Decision implies having a range of images of the future over which we believe we have some control or power and then selecting the one that we think is best and trying to bring it about. Our images of the future may, of course, be wrong in the sense that they cannot be realized and there will be many examples of failure in which the future does not correspond to the expectations of the decision maker. Even failure, however, is a very important learning process. Indeed it is essential to human learning, for it may change the way in which we create images of the future. If as a result failure is followed by successes, genuine learning will have taken place; if it is followed by further failure, more change is required in the way in which we construct our images of the future. There is, therefore, a process of natural selection here by which erroneous images tend to be diminished and correct images tend to expand. This process may break down if the real environment is changing rapidly, but ordinarily it works pretty well. The immense variety of human artifacts that now exist in the world – cathedrals, airplanes, nuclear weapons, computers, novels, operas, philosophies – is a result of this evolutionary process, the rate of which seems to have been increasing even more than exponentially, espiecially with the rise of organized learning cultures like science.

Human artifacts are by no means confined to physical objects. They include language embodied in certain structures in the brain and mind; in airwaves in the case of speech; in hieroglyphs, letters, pictures, diagrams, and graphs in the case of writing. What is significant here, however, is not the physical embodiment so much as the meaning and message contained. Language transfers a structure from one human mind into another and the transfers can be done in almost any language. There are as many ways for one human being to say to another "come and eat" as there are languages, but they all have the same result. This, incidentally, illustrates a fundamental principle of evolution, namely that it is essentially a process in information and the extensions of that process in know-how and know-what. Matter and energy are significant mainly as encoders and transmitters of information. There is something in the hypothesis of Benjamin Whorf[5] that the structure of a language affects what is communicated. The Indo-European languages with their subject–verb–object structure may tie their users too much to things and not enough to processes, and the use of mathematics may limit thought somewhat, simply because of its remarkable shortage of verbs. But in most cases one doubts that more than one percent of meaning is lost in translation, especially if the translation is explanatory enough. Poetry can never be perfectly translated, for the overtones of the words in one language are not necessarily those in another, but a good translator can certainly convey a large proportion of the meaning and impact of a poem from one language to another.

Another very important human artifact consists of organizations – families, corporations, churches, states, professional societies, and so on. These exist primarily as images in peoples' heads, though they may be embodied in part in buildings like churches, factories, office buildings, homes, or in documents, charters, though even these are important mainly as symbols and evidence of the existence of the organization in the minds of people. The 49th parallel is quite invisible from outer space and exists only in the minds of humans as a boundary, even if it has a certain embodiment in immigration and customs officers. Similarly, a corporation exists essentially in the minds of humans in a common belief in its existence, the evidence of which may also be embodied in charters and legal documents, shares of stock, bonds, and so on. A share of stock is not the paper it is written on, but is a belief in the minds of the right people that governs their images of the future and their behavior and decisions.

The Nature of Power

With humans, decisions become an essential part of the ecosystem and decisions involve power, that is, the ability to move into futures that we envisage in our minds. Human power might almost be defined as the potential for creating wanted change through decision. In the total ecosystem, which consists not only of all living species but of all human artifacts, all interacting with each other, power must be seen as a subtle and complex part of the environment. It is a very complex structure and perhaps because it is so complex it is very little understood. If you ask people to suggest a gesture that symbolizes power, the commonest is perhaps a bang on the table with a clenched fist. This, however, only symbolizes a small part of the total structure of power. Writing a check, especially in more developed societies, may be a much more important symbol than a clenched fist. Somebody who can write a check for a million dollars obviously has more power than some bully who can only write a check for $100. Giving an order over the telephone or by letter or document is also an important symbol of power. The smile and the handshake should also not be neglected. These also represent a form of power. In some sense, Albrecht Dürer's "praying hands" may be a more powerful symbol than the clenched fist, for much human history is hard to explain without something that might be called "transcendental power."

We can identify three major categories of power, each with important subcategories. These are destructive power, productive power, and integrative power. Destructive power is symbolized by the weapon, the armed force, but also by the devastating criticism or the snub or a rejected handshake. It is also represented by the bulldozer and the mill (whether flour mill or steel mill). These seem like diverse, contradictory aspects. Destructive power, however, does divide into two main categories: destruction as a prelude to production and destruction as an agent of threat. The miller destroys wheat in order to produce flour. The baker destroys flour in order to produce bread. The steel mill destroys ore to produce steel. Everything that we use depreciates and ages through the destructive powers of use and time. Here destructive power can be thought of as cost, that which has to be diminished in order that something else may be increased. If the value of what is increased is greater than what is diminished, we have profit either in the accounting sense or in the larger psychological sense – "For what shall it profit a man, if he shall gain the whole world, and lose his own soul?"[6]

When destructive power is used to back up a threat, a very different system emerges. Threat is a communication from one person, organization, or group to another that says in effect, "You do something I want or I will do something you don't want," the latter involving the exercise of some sort of destructive power, whether this is a bandit's threat ("Your money or your life"), a trade union threatening a strike, a nation threatening war, a state threatening criminals through the police, and so on. What happens then depends very much on the response of the threatened. A common response is submission, as when we pay our income tax or obey a traffic policeman, or make a bargaining concession. Without a threat–submission system politics would be almost impossible. It would be hard to sustain governments by voluntary contributions to a United Way fund.

Sometimes, however, the response is defiance: "I won't do what you want. Carry out your threat if you wish." This puts the action back in the hands of the threatener. It is often very costly to carry out a threat, so defiance sometimes results in the retreat of the threatener, and, of course, sometimes not, though it is often a difficult question as to whether carrying out a threat really benefits the threatener more than not carrying it out. Another response is flight, getting out of the range of the threatener. This is one reason why the human race has spread all around the world and is an important part of the explanation of why the United States speaks English. Another reaction is counterthreat – "You do something nasty to me and I'll do something nasty to you." This leads into deterrence, beloved of strategic thinkers, and an important aspect of military power. This is sometimes stable in the short run, as nuclear deterrence has been. But it can be shown that it cannot be stable in the long run or it would not deter in the short run. If the probability of nuclear weapons going off were zero, they would not deter anybody. It would be like not having them. If it is not zero, if we wait long enough they will go off and deterrence will break down. In the pre-nuclear era, indeed, the probability of deterrence breaking down seems to have been on the order of 4 percent per annum, rather like a 25-year flood.[7]

Productive power at the biological level is what the fertilized egg has. At the human social level this is the power of the artist, the craftsman who creates artifacts. It is the power of the manufacturer to produce his products, the power of the doctor to cure people, of the teacher to teach people. This is the power that is expressed somewhat imperfectly in that mathematical icon, the GNP, the gross national product. Productive power emerges fundamentally as a result of a learning process. This may be unconscious learning, as we see in biological evolution, where the random changes in DNA are selected through ecological survival in a process that has carried us from the DNA that only knew how to produce viruses and single-celled organisms, to the DNA that knows how to produce us. In humans, in societal evolution, the process is more conscious, though even here unconscious selection is by no means absent, as the rise and fall of empires, civilizations, and corporations suggests.

An important and very complex element in productive power is the control of property and the institutional and organizational arrangements which surround it. It is hard for production to take place unless the producer has control over the "means of production," the raw materials, the means of transportation, the buildings, the machines, and in some sense even the actions of workers and the network of interpersonal, interorganizational connections that may be necessary.

Control has two institutional aspects: ownership, which is continuous control, subject to some legal restrictions and definitions; and rent, which is the transmission of control from the owner to the renter for a specific period, in return for some payment, usually of money. Somewhere between rent and ownership is debt, which enables the indebted to control things which they do not own in return for a payment of interest to the debt holder. The great virtue of rent in all its forms is that it is a way of enabling those who have the skills of controlling to control materials, artifacts, and even human beings that they do not own, and of enabling people who own things that they are not skilled in controlling, to turn them over to a good controller for rent or interest. The productiveness of these arrangements depends on the fact that if they do not exist, property can be redistributed only through a threat system. This is very costly.

One aspect of productive power is economic power, part of which is purchasing power, reflected partly in the distribution of net worth among individuals, which involves the distribution of the total real assets of the society among the ultimate owners. Those who have a lot of net worth obviously have more economic power than those who have little or none. It is important to recognize, however, that net worth should, in some sense, include human capital, that is, the value of people's minds and bodies. What is recognized as legitimate or illegitimate is of great importance in the dynamics of productive and economic power. Slavery, in which the slave is the property of the slave owner, turned out to be a very inefficient system compared with the wage labor system, in which each person is his or her own property, but has the ability to "rent" this property in minds and bodies to an employer for a specific period for a given wage or reward. Under capitalism, whatever that is (for it is a continuous evolutionary process and changes all the time and we certainly cannot say when it began) there has been a constant development of complexity in these property and rental relationships involving the financial system, the labor market, the legal structure, and government intervention. In centrally planned economies, a much more direct threat system seems to be involved. The success or failure of either system depends in large degree on the extent to which the social institutions permit those who are skilled in the control of productive assets and resources to obtain this control without having to own them. The distribution of ownership rarely corresponds with the distribution of skills and control. This seems to be as true under public ownership as it is under private ownership.

Underlying the structure of both threat power and productive and economic power is a complex set of relationships in society which is all too rarely recognized as such. This may be called "integrative power," the power which is created and distributed by legitimacy, loyalty, love, a sense of community, respect, affection, and so on. It has a negative sense in terms of illegitimacy, disloyalty, hatred, alienation, disrespect, and so on, which diminish it. It is frequently expressed in symbols – a flag, a cross, even a bumper sticker or a lapel button. It is expressed in symbolic architecture, like the cathedral, the dome of the capital (the great tit of government), the erection of the Washington Monument, the robes of the emperor, the gowns of the faculty, even the orange hair of the punk. Art, literature, and music play an important role in it – national anthems, the B Minor Mass, and the Hallelujah Chorus, the chanting of Tibetan monks, the Sistine Chapel, "socialist realist art" under Stalin, epics and patriotic poetry . . . the list is long. Without integrative power both threat power and productive economic power are hard to generate and preserve. Without morale an army cannot march. Without the love of country, wars would be impossible. Without some sense of legitimation the tax system would collapse. Unless teachers are accepted as legitimate by students, formal education would collapse. Unless financial instruments and markets are regarded as legitimate, capitalism would be impossible.

It is surprising how infrequently integrative power is recognized as an essential, even dominant, form of power, perhaps because it is subtle and all-pervasive. We think of power in terms of volcanoes exploding, bombs going off, battles being won, and so on, but those phenomena are really quite minor. It is the slow, imperceptible shift of the continents that creates the volcanoes, and it is the slow, imperceptible shift of integrative structures that creates and destroys nations, empires, and even religions. Because threat power is visible and dramatic in the shape of armies and weapons, we overrate it. Without legitimation and integrative power threat is very ineffective. Very few people ever got rich by mugging. Empires cripple the imperial power economically.[8] This happened to Rome, to Britain, to France, and is now happening in the United States. The old Stock Exchange in Leningrad, where financial power lost legitimacy and became powerless, is now a Palace of Culture and Rest. There is a story that when the status of Poland was being discussed at Yalta towards the end of the Second World War Roosevelt is reported to have said "The Pope won't like this," to which Stalin replied, "How many divisions does the Pope have?" We might ask that question of the Poles today. Conquerors come and go. Integrative structures stay around. The Pope survived the Roman emperors, China turned all its conquerors into Chinese, military defeat often leads to an economic and cultural upsurge, as in Paris after 1871, in Berlin after 1919, and economically in Japan and Germany after the Second World War. Integrative power pervades everything, often very surprisingly.

If there is one dynamic in society which governs all the rest, it is the dynamic of legitimacy. This is very hard to explain and predict. It often comes out of very obscure places – "Can any good thing come out of Nazareth?" Medina and Mecca were obscure settlements. An unsuccessful academic by the name of Karl Marx in the British Museum stirred a third of the human race, but now his vogue seems to be passing into eclipse. An odd New Englander in upstate New York by the name of Joseph Smith created an integrative structure which has spread over the whole world, with its Rome in Salt Lake City. In the 1920s nobody in England even questioned the British Empire. We used to sing, "Wider, still and wider may thy bounds be set, God who made thee mighty, Make thee mightier yet."[9] And in one generation that empire dissolved. Legitimacy is an inconceivably unpredictable system. It is not surprising that we turn our minds away from it and concentrate on the more visible sources of power, but we do this at great cost to our understanding and to ourselves.

The Power of Business

Finally, let us get down to business. The delightful ambiguity of this phrase is highly significant. Business is at the same time an organizational segment of the world system, ranging from mom-and-pop grocery stores to General Motors – we might almost add the Soviet steel trust. It is also an aspect of all organizations and all human life. The family, the foundation, the state, the church, the Rotary Club, the symphony orchestra, the art gallery, all at some point or other "get down to business" and have to face some of the problems that businesses face. Even the hermit exhibits some aspects of a small firm.

Businesses, in the narrower sense, have certain characteristics in common. They have balance sheets, which governments and departments of defense rarely have, in which are listed the assets which they control on one side, and the way the total value of these assets is in some sense distributed among owners on the other side. They have income statements, which summarize the events that have happened to the balance sheet in the course of an accounting period. These events are of two kinds: exchange of assets, in which one asset goes up and

another asset goes down by an equal amount, at least according to the
cost accountant. This happens when assets are bought and sold. It
happens also when assets are transformed into one another, as when
wheat is milled into flour. Wages are a little tricky, but when wages are
paid, money goes down in the balance sheet, and the product of the
work, whether this is the sprucings up of the janitor or the transformations of the assembly line worker, goes up. Frequently, moreover,
assets are revalued at the moment of sale. If the product of the
enterprise is sold for an amount of money greater than its cost, total
assets goes up and net worth, however that is defined, goes up. This is
profit. Getting down to business involves profit making, revaluing
things above cost, whether as accounting profit or psychological or
even spiritual profit.

A critical question is, where does profit come from? This is by no
means easy to answer. Economists are really divided on the matter.[10]
The Marxists say that it comes out of exploitation, that is, not counting
some cost that ought to have been recorded and paid. In terms of
"simple-minded Marxism," labor is supposed to produce everything,
but it doesn't get everything. And what it doesn't get (surplus value, or
non-labor income), it should get. Mainline neo-classical economics, of
course, defends profit on the grounds that labor doesn't produce
everything, any more than raw materials do. Labor has to be organized
into productive processes which involve the manipulation of property
and balance sheets, which labor doesn't do and doesn't even know how
to do. Even neo-classical economists worry little about economic rent,
however we identify it, which seems to be the reward of the lazy owner
who does not do anything. How far interest is economic rent arising
out of the imperfections of financial institutions is still a tricky question.
At the moment we certainly seem to be in danger of becoming a *rentier*
society, in spite of Keynes' quite unfulfilled predictions about the
"euthanasia of the *rentier*."[11] Interest, in the United States at least, has
gone from about one percent of national income in 1950, to close to 10
percent today, with a consequent erosion of profit. This increase may
be ominous. Certainly the abolition of profit, as occurred in 1932 and
1933, when profits were sharply negative and interest rates were still
positive, had a great deal to do with the Great Depression and with
producing 25 percent unemployment. There seems to be a fundamental
principle that something can go wrong with anything, and certainly
something went radically wrong with the capitalist world in the early
Thirties, though not as dramatically wrong as in the Soviet Union

under Stalin's "First Collectivization." At least the Great Depression didn't kill six million people and create a famine. In fact, agricultural production rose slightly in the Great Depression. Very few people actually starved, though many went hungry.

There are technical economic problems here to which we still do not know the answer. Can capitalism, for instance, survive a stationary state? Or must it have continuous net investment in order to preserve profits? A possible answer to this question is yes, capitalism could survive, but not without some change in existing financial institutions. The problem is we would be quite unsure about which changes to make. But, clearly, the accumulation both of population and of human artifacts cannot go on forever. At some point something like a stationary state must emerge – unless, of course, we expand into the solar system, in which case this evil day might be postponed for a long time. It cannot be said too often – but mainly because nobody seems to be saying it – that the ability of the capitalist system to provide full employment has something to do with the gap between interest and profit. When an employer hires somebody, he or she sacrifices the interest that could have been obtained on the money spent on the wage in the hope of profit on the product of the work. When, as in 1932 and 1933, profits were negative and interest was still positive, anybody who employed anybody was either a philanthropist, a fool, or a creature of habit. The third alternative probably explains why the economy survived those two years. Certainly anybody who employed anybody during that period was bound to lose. Fortunately, the system turned around in 1933. Otherwise, the whole economy might have collapsed and unemployment might have approached 50 or 75 percent.

This raises the question of the integrative power of business and the business institution, that is, its generally recognized legitimacy and the loyalty that people have towards it. One of my mentors, Joseph Schumpeter, thought that capitalism was an excellent system in terms of increasing the standard of life, encouraging political liberty, variety, and opportunity, but he thought it probably would not survive because it was living on the eroding legitimacy of an earlier period, so the people didn't love it enough. Legitimacy, oddly enough, is somewhat related to the capacity of institutions to demand sacrifice. The blood of the martyrs is the seed of the church, the blood of the soldiers is the seed of patriotism and the national state, for it is hard for any of us to admit that sacrifices are in vain. Very few people ever died for General Motors or for the Chase Manhattan Bank. People do suffer when they get laid off, but they usually get other jobs. There is something inevitably impersonal about the market. It demands a certain amount of courtesy and trust. We smile at a salesperson and that person smiles back. Business people have lunch with their suppliers and financiers. But this isn't like going into battle or accepting celibacy as a priest. I once banked at a bank that had a motto, "the bank that puts people first," which it later changed to "the bank for my money."

Certainly labor relations involve much more than simple exchange. What the worker gives up is not what the employer receives. What the employer gives up is not what the worker receives. The labor relationship involves some reciprocity, and this inevitably involves integrative structures in terms of trust, respect, identification with the objectives of the firm. On the other hand, paternalism on the part of the firm can backfire very badly in terms of integrative power. Samuel Gomper's slogan, "an honest day's work for an honest day's pay," carried a clear message to the employer: "Don't follow me home!" The firm is not a family. Nonetheless, it does manifest some aspects of a community, simply because so many employees of the firm are usually together in one place. Even that is not always true, which perhaps explains the strange quality of the Teamsters' Union. On the other hand, the impersonality of the market has real social advantages. The trouble with communes is that they require an enormous amount of palaver, discussion, and agreement. The market, as Mancur Olson said,[12] economizes agreement, which is very important to economize. How do we economize agreement, however, without undermining that almost unconscious and subtle agreement that constitutes legitimation?

The Japanese are supposed to be good at creating industrial cultures which legitimate the corporate enterprise in the minds of the workers, and we have seen a few cases of such legitimation in our country. Du Pont is perhaps as close as we come to a Japanese *zaibatsu* [family holding companies]. There is a rumor that good Presbyterian business leaders have had their employees sing hymns in praise of the product before they start work, but if this practice ever did exist it was certainly rare.

The search for legitimation and integrative power, however, is by no means confined to business. Sacrifice creates integrative power only up to a point. At some point a revolt occurs. This, possibly, is happening with the national state. Small wars may legitimate the state, as the sacrifices of the American Revolution certainly did the United States. As the cost of war increases, however, particularly with the development of the nuclear threat, the whole legitimacy of the national state comes into question. Why should we love that which can only destroy us and cannot really defend us? We see something of the same thing happening in religion. The extraordinary change in the Catholic Church in the last generation reflects, perhaps, the struggle against declining legitimacy on the part of its members and their need for reestablishing the legitimation of the local community. We now see this happening in the communist world, where the obvious defects of centrally planned economies are becoming so apparent. A "this worldly" religion or faith like Marxism, which promises a better life for the grandchildren, is severly eroded when the grandchildren show up and the better life still seems some way off. "Other worldly" religions, like Islam and fundamentalist Christianity, may be less susceptible to erosion because they are hard to test over time.

Where then does this leave business? Can we learn anything about survival power either of individual businesses or the business species as a whole or as particular industries? Certainly from genetics and evolutionary theory some fundamental principles emerge. The ultimate survival power of a species is more related to its adaptability to changes in its environment, including other species, than it is to its adaptation to a particular environment at a particular moment of time. The too-well adapted may not be adaptable. There may be some tradeoff here, though it may be hard to say what it is. Learning is a very important component in survival, as adaptability is related to learning capacity. We find this also in social systems. The Jews have survived, as an identifiable group, for 3,000 years or more because they had a culture of learning and of adaptability which has enabled them to survive all sorts of persecutions and dispersals. The Romans as a culture and as an empire did not survive; they were transformed. Concentration on destructive power to the neglect of productive power and integrative power can easily lead to extinction. The cockroach survived much longer than *Tyrannosaurus rex*. The little mammals survived the catastrophe that exterminated the dinosaurs, perhaps because they had better brains and could learn to adapt to changing circumstances.

There are, clearly, lessons for business here, either for individual businesses or for the overall business community. An individual business survives if it produces quantities of things or provides services at an overall cost less than the price it can obtain for them in the market. The environment of individual businesses changes all the time and there must be a learning process to adapt to these changes. One of the fundamental tasks of management is to develop an information and learning structure which will inform managers about changes in the overall environment of a particular business. Productive power is increased by learning new processes for transforming assets of all kinds into forms which have a higher value. I have often told people exactly how to get rich: Always transform your assets into the form which is rising most rapidly in relative value. Then I go on to say that I offer this advice free, which is what it is worth, because it is hard to predict the future. The redistributions of net worth which are going on all the time in our society as relative prices change may be more the result of good luck than of good management. Still, there *is* such a thing as good management and it does involve a learning process which develops at least moderately accurate images of the environment and its possible futures.

Productive and evaluative power certainly are the most important elements in the success of individual businesses. Threat power is relatively minor for organizations which operate primarily in the market, but it is not unknown, especially in labor-management bargaining and sometimes in monopolies. The collapse of OPEC, however, is a good example of the instability of monopoly and the weakness of threat power. We see the same principles at work in the rise and fall of empires.[13] The general principle seems to be that a fairly spontaneous learning process leading to a rise in productive power results in the use of such power for purposes and threat and for building military might, which eventually diminishes productivity and leads to a decline of empire. This can be summarized in the statement that a rise in wealth often leads to a rise in military power, which destroys wealth. Threat is a poor means for getting rich. Few people have ever gotten rich by fighting, and becoming a great power usually impoverishes a nation. The economic success, for instance, of Sweden and Denmark from the 19th century on, and the relative economic stagnation of the imperial powers such as Britain and France, and the extraordinary economic success of Japan since the Second World War, and the relative economic malaise of the United States, are good examples of this principle. The same principle may even apply to businesses. Economic success increases the size of businesses to the point where they get illusions of grandeur and throw their weight around, which often comes back with a resounding, sometimes fatal, thwack.

Integrative power is also important in business. In the old days, accountants even recognized this in the balance sheet as something called "goodwill." Reputation is an aspect of integrative power, as the continued success of Bayer Aspirin demonstrates. Integrative power can be destroyed if it is abused. A case in point is that of the famous example of Gillette Razors, who under new management marketed an inferior product that failed to sell, in spite of their good name. A deserved reputation for honesty and decency is an important element in the survival both of individual firms and of the business community as a whole.

The legitimacy of the business institution has been challenged in the twentieth century. That institution has been replaced by centrally-planned economies for roughly a third of the world's population, not, however, with conspicuous success. This replacement of the business institution by centrally-planned economies can be interpreted as an undeserved collapse of integrative power, whereby a perfectly useful institution has lost legitimacy. Integrative power, however, is the ultimate power. No institution or organization can function if it loses legitimacy. And yet the dynamics of legitimacy, as noted earlier, are mysterious. Whether organizations representing the business community as a whole can foster legitimacy remains a question. It would be interesting to study whether, for instance, the Committee for Economic Development, which represented a much more integrative approach to the public image of the business community than did the National Association of Manufacturers, has had an effect in increasing the legitimacy of the business community as a whole. It certainly played an important role in the remarkable success of the great disarmament following the Second World War, an episode surprisingly neglected in business history.

Another question, which probably has some complicated answers, is that of the impact of business grants and foundations on the position of businesses in the integrative power structure. This is particularly important at the local level, where the support of United Way and other local charities by business creates an impression of benignity and goodwill. On the other hand, grants may create a sense of alienation on the part of the recipient towards the grantor, as placing the recipient too much in the grantor's economic power. Whether economic power can "buy" integrative power is a question that needs much further study. One element curiously absent in our society is organizations which study the total environment of business. Much work needs to be done in this area. A careful historical study of how business people have made bad decisions, mainly because of an inadequate image in their minds of their total environment, would be of great value. A good example would be the catastrophic decision on the part of public utility executives to build nuclear power plants, apparently under the belief that the demand for electricity was going to rise indefinitely at 7 percent per annum. The most important factor in human learning is the creative response to failure and this is all too much neglected.

Once the larger concept of power is taken into account, the possibility of creative historical and empirical research into these processes becomes very exciting – research that may make the business community more conscious of its potential for integrative power and hence increase its chances of long-run survival.

Notes

First published in *Business in the Contemporary World*, 1 (1) 1988. Reprinted by kind permission of *BCW*.

1 Robert Brady, *Business as a System of Power* (NY: Columbia University Press) 1943.
2 Matthew 13: 3–8.
3 K. E. Boulding, *Ecodynamics: A New Theory of Societal Evolution* (Beverly Hills CA: Sage Publications) 1978, 1981.
4 The mathematics of this is fairly simple. If the additions and subtractions to each species are regarded as a function of the population of all the others, and in equilibrium additions equal subtractions, then we have n equations, one for each population, and n unknowns, equilibrium populations, which under a wide range of circumstances will have a solution.
5 Benjamin Whorf, *Language, Thought, and Reality* (Cambridge MA: Technology Press) 1969.
6 Mark 8: 36.
7 J. David Singer and Marvin Small, *The Wages of War, 1816–1965: A Statistical Handbook* (NY: John Wiley & Sons) 1972.
8 Paul Kennedy, *The Rise and Fall of the Great Powers* (NY: Random House) 1987.
9 Edward Elgar, "Pomp and Circumstance."
10 Naturally there are those who agree with me and those who don't.
11 J. M. Keynes, *The General Theory of Employment, Interest, and Money* (London: Macmillan) 1936.
12 Mancur Olson, *The Logic of Collective Action* (Cambridge MA: Harvard University Press) 1965.
13 Kennedy, 1987.

12

Corporate Governance – A Burning Issue

F.-Friedrich Neubauer and Ada Demb

In the Western industrialized world – and particularly in the Anglo-Saxon countries – corporate governance has become an increasingly important theme during recent years. In its most general definition, corporate governance addresses the relationship between a company and society. This is a Janus-faced relationship: on the one hand it defines the role which modern society assigns a corporation, and how society ensures that this role is enforced; on the other, the life-space which society owes to a business must also be defined.

With the present state of affairs in the area of corporate governance both parties are dissatisfied. While corporations often feel regulated in an unacceptable manner, a widespread discomfort can also be registered in the general public, because the growth, the internationalization, and the broadly-based product/service offering of most companies have outpaced by leaps and bounds traditional governance mechanisms (including, but not limited to, the board of directors). "Watch dogs that didn't bark" was the telling headline of an article in the *Financial Times*, in which the question was raised why the control and regulatory authorities had failed to exercise their duties in a timely and efficient manner before the spectacular collapse of a UK bank.

Against this backdrop it seems appropriate to revisit the concept of corporate governance, and to raise some questions of our own on how one might improve its functioning.

I. Corporate Governance as a System

The concept of corporate governance has its origins in the last century, with the creation of the modern business corporation. This concept, seemingly adequate in earlier days, was based on the separation between capital (broken up into units of shares in order to allow a spreading of the risk) on one side, and professional managers on the other (the latter, as a rule, did not own substantial shareholdings). To assure that these professional managers heeded and fulfilled the will of the share-owners, the institution of a board was created. The job of this body was to exercise the governance function within the corporation.

As corporations grew and gained more influence, the governance task became more complicated. The significance of the impact of modern corporations can be illustrated by looking at just the ten largest companies in the world, using employment as a selection criterion. These organizations are responsible for the livelihood and support of between 15 and 20 million people, if one includes dependent family members in this calculation. This number corresponds roughly to the total population of the Scandanavian countries. An average of about 200 board members are ultimately responsible for the oversight of these 10 corporations, and thus for the well-being of those 15 to 20 million people – a burden which many of these board members neither expected when they accepted the position, nor did they ask for it.[1]

In light of these developments, it is hardly surprising that in govern-ments, and the public at large, the conviction has grown that the task of corporate governance could not be left to boards alone. Governments and the public (including specific interested parties such as labor) insisted on exercising a direct influence on corporations, and succeeded to some extent in establishing this right either formally, or as a moral claim. Among other measures, numerous regulations were designed, labor groups organized themselves and pushed through co-determination in some countries, capital markets refined their influence on cor-porations, and even the public at large (particularly in England and the USA) found ways and means to prompt companies to respond to society's needs. The result of this process was that the governance task became the mandate of an entire *governance system*.

How can we describe a governance system? According to Kester,[2] the term "governance system" is meant broadly to imply the entire set of incentives, safeguards, and dispute resolution processes used to control and coordinate the actions of various self-interested parties interacting in a bilateral exchange relationship (these parties will here-inafter be called "stakeholders"). For Kester, the construction of such systems may itself span a continuum bounded at one end by the writing of *explicit*, detailed contracts which may be enforced by court order in the event of an attempted breach by one of the parties. On the other end of that continuum, one finds a reliance on forms of *implicit* contracting, founded on trust relationships and possibly enforced by largely non-legalistic mechanisms structured to encourage compliance with informal agreements.

Who are the Stakeholders?

Stakeholders are individuals or groups who, in practical terms, have something at stake in a given corporation; for that reason they are vitally interested in the well-being of that corporation. Considering the scale and scope of corporate influence, this could include virtually everyone; but for the purposes of analysis, we commonly distinguish the following six groups of stakeholders:

The providers of funds (shareholders, banks, etc.)
The employees
The general public
Governments (linked with the general public, as its representatives)
The customers
The suppliers

All of these parties have a high interest in the performance of a corporation. In some cases, the fate of a company can determine the ultimate existence of a particular stakeholder, such as a supplier. These groups are therefore legitimately interested in whether or not a corporation is well managed.

It follows logically that the function of a governance system is to make sure that the corporations can be called to task by the stakeholders for their behavior. "Corporate governance is always a question of performance accountability," as we have written elsewhere.[3] Through these optics one can define a governance system as a process with which to make companies responsive to the rights and wishes of their stakeholders.

Such a governance system is, however, not to be seen as a one-way street. It also serves as a mechanism which is employed to secure a reasonable life-space for the corporation, i.e., providing sufficient room for a corporation to function in fulfilling its task. There are two aspects to this demand: First, the requests made by the stakeholders vis-à-vis corporate operations are frequently in conflict with each other. They therefore must be weighed against each other in the interest of the greater good, a task usually assigned to the board. Secondly, one has to make sure that the demands made on the corporation by the different interest groups, all together, do not strangle a company to such an extent that it cannot perform its main task, namely to create wealth.

There is no shortage of examples for this second notion, among them the following two illustrations.

A few years ago, those European manufacturers of building materials whose products contained asbestos struck a deal with German and Swiss government authorities which allowed these companies to replace the harmful asbestos fiber with a harmless one within a reasonable time frame (and, in the process, observing stringent security measures to protect employees); by doing so, these companies preempted the issuance of further regulation.

In a similar way, the board of Daimler-Benz had to fight the German *Kartellamt* (the German antitrust authorities) to secure a life-space for their company when their acquisition of a majority shareholding in MBB was contested by those authorities. The argument of the regulators was that a merger between Daimler-Benz (which already owned Dornier, a company with similar activities to MBB) and MBB would reduce competition in certain segments of the German market for space-related products and systems. Daimler-Benz argued (and eventually won) that the market for those products which the combined Daimler-Benz-MBB Group would produce is a *global* market, in which the new combination of firms would only be a minor player.[4]

These two frequently clashing currents, namely the satisfaction of stakeholder interests while at the same time securing the necessary corporate "elbow room", have to be kept in a reasonable balance. On a more fundamental level is the need to reach an equilibrium between the legitimacy of the corporation (which society has to bestow) and its economic survival. This equilibrium is a dynamic one, i.e., it cannot be defined once and for all; rather, it must be recalibrated again and again – a primary task of the governance system.

II.   Some Characteristics of the Relationships Between the Corporation and Its Stakeholders

Relationships between the corporation and its stakeholders can be extraordinarily varied: some are very simple and relatively clear, while others subtle and complex; some are direct, and others use intervening institutions. There can be no doubt that these differences will be heightened between countries, societies, and national cultures.

Similarly varied are the mechanisms which can be used in a given governance system to make it work. The following are a few arbitrarily-chosen examples:

- Customers and suppliers alike frequently secure their influence on a corporation with the help of *complex strategic alliances*, a concept that has lately found many international followers. In this context systematically structured vertical integrations represent an extreme form; it can exist *de jure*, but also simply *de facto*, as some Japanese companies demonstrate so convincingly.

- A subtle example of a relationship with a very important stakeholder are the regular, intensive *exchanges of information* between corporations and large *institutional investors* (pension funds, etc.), a growing practice in, for example, the USA, where institutional investors have often refused (with a few notable and noisy exceptions, such as the fight for representation on the board of Sears Roebuck) a seat on the board of a company in which they have invested. In these private information sessions, the representatives of a fund are thoroughly briefed about the state of the business, and they themselves are not shy about expressing their opinion on the way the corporation is managed. In other countries, similar exchanges of information take place with the major banks who have invested in the company. Analysts such as Alfred Conard have suggested that such interchanges may taste a bit of "inside information" swapping, but overall, some form of communication is increasingly necessary to offset potential conflicts over corporate strategy and direction. In the US, the Securities and Exchange Commission recently changed its rules on shareholder/management communication, expanding opportunities for discussion (*Wall Street Journal*, October 15, 1992).

- Another subtle yet powerful influence of the government on major corporations was achieved for decades in Japan through an unusual mechanism: on a routine basis, high-ranking functionaries of MITI became top managers in key corporations and vice-versa. This ensured that government officials and business leaders maintained a thorough knowledge of each other.

- Also important to mention here is the phenomenon of the "lender–owner" relationship as observed in Japan and the Federal Republic of Germany. In these cases, banks as important creditors of a corporation secure added influence by owning shares of the corporation in question. Some observers have posited that this arrangement has contributed to the longer-term view of corporate strategy held in those countries, due to the longer time horizons of a creditor as opposed to an investor seeking dividends. It should be noted, in this context, that German banks reserve the right to exercise proxy votes in shareholder meetings along with other shareowners.

- Many stakeholders also use the board to represent their demands. Among these are the shareholders, of course, but in countries like the Federal Republic of Germany, as well as other European states, labor and unions can also be included. Other stakeholders who make use of the board to communicate their needs include suppliers, customers, and creditors, who often secure themselves a seat on the board of firms with which they collaborate.

- Undoubtedly, cross-shareholdings among partners should be listed here as well.

- Among the other stakeholders, the general public and the governmental institutions who represent them should not be neglected. The public at large has developed a whole array of means at its disposal to prompt corporations to listen to their wishes and their rights. One example of the public's impact is the British company which, at the height of the campaign in America against South African apartheid, decided to dissolve its long-running stake in a South African company in order to keep a new and important investment in the USA out of the firing line. In the Federal Republic of Germany and around the world, "green" organizations have exercised a similar influence on companies.

The practice of government agencies to influence corporations does not have to be elaborated here; it is widely known. Regulation could be increased on a supranational level by such organizations as the EC, but the impact of that action may in turn be tempered by a neutralization of regulation on the level of the nation-state.

III. A Systematic Study of Major Governance Systems is Called For

A brief look at the above-mentioned forms of corporate governance results in two impressions:

- Large parts of these governance systems appear "accidental" in structure and content. This should not be surprising if one remembers that they are the result of historical waves of efforts to broaden governance systems in response to changing circumstances.

- At the same time, one gets the impression that hardly anybody outside of corporations can judge the cumulative effect of these different influences on the company, because they appeared in waves and were at the same time stimulated by interest groups who often operated in isolation.

This situation *per se* is unsatisfactory. It is, however, to be expected that it will worsen rapidly as the confrontation between the corporation and society intensifies. All signs indicate that on a more and more populated planet these relationships cannot continue to be managed antagonistically; partnership on a broad front (and not only with employees) seems to be the only way out. All of these observations make it mandatory to systematically research the governance systems in the leading economies, an inquiry aimed at taking stock of the prevailing important practices and their impacts on both the corporation and society.

This, however, would only be a first step. Governance systems change at an ever-increasing rate. It is therefore also necessary to identify the direction of some of these developments, and to interpret their meaning.

Third, one would have to raise the normative issue as to how the governance system in a country like the Federal Republic of Germany, for instance, should be changed in order to make sure that the basic values spelled out in the German *Grundgesetz* (Constitution) can be realized – to cite only one source of criteria with which to organize a governance system. A research project of this nature would, of course, be an immense task. It is very difficult to imagine that one could tackle it comprehensively, at least at the outset. As a starting point, it is probably much wiser to single out a few relationships that represent "virgin territory", that is, that have hardly been researched, but ones that at the same time are gaining dramatic significance.

A.   Examples of possible pilot projects

Two examples for pilot studies emerge which could be approached relatively easily.

1   *The role of institutional investors in the context of corporate governance*: It is widely known that institutional investors own roughly 70 percent of all shares traded on the British stock exchanges. In the USA, this percentage is approaching 50 percent. Behind the scenes are the British and American pension funds whose assets amount to £270 billion and $2.6 trillion, respectively.

On the European continent, the picture is somewhat different and, leaving aside a few examples such as the Dutch national pension fund, institutions do not play a comparable role. One of the reasons is the smaller stock markets: in Great Britain, the stock market capitalization amounts to 98 percent of the GNP; comparable figures for France and Germany are 20 percent, and for Italy 16 percent. In Europe, banks and insurance companies are important institutional investors, while in Japan the Keiretsus – Mitsubishi, Mitsui, Sumitomo – dominate the scene; although they represent only 0.1 percent of the number of Japanese firms, they are responsible for 78 percent of the value of all stocks traded at the Tokyo exchange.

This phenomenon is not only spreading worldwide (even if one concedes that there are marked differences in different economies), but it is expected that the English and American funds will become more active internationally. For example, American funds have boosted their foreign investments from practically zero in 1979 to around US$100 billion in 1990; these investments are anticipated to exceed $200 billion by 1994.[5]

The influence of these institutional investors vis-à-vis corporate governance should not be underestimated. The sheer size of their involvements, which cannot easily be sold off without depressing the markets, will make it necessary that the investors take an active interest in the companies whose shares are in their portfolios.

It is also expected that far reaching changes in the area of European institutional investors will emerge; national investment restrictions, some observers feel, may soon fall victim to the deregulation efforts of the EC.

The potential role of these institutional investors – the new, as well as the old ones – is as yet barely understood. To analyze their significance today and in the future requires the urgent attention of researchers on an international level.

2 *New forms of measuring performance*: A second badly needed pilot study should concentrate on the question of to what extent reporting systems on the "performance" of corporations are still in agreement with the information needs of society.

Practically all of our measurement systems turn out to be fragmentary if one takes a broader look at them, and important aspects of economic activity and corporate impact are not covered. This is true in the macro, as well as the micro-economic sense. Not only do we not know, for example, what the real cost of deforestation is; the things we thinks we do know, based on such venerable instruments such as corporate balance sheets and income statements are considered increasingly irrelevant sources of information by the public, and hence are somewhat limited for governance purposes. Suffering from this development are, among others, certified public accountants and auditors. After the collapse of large corporations whose statements had received the unqualified stamp of approval by respectable accountants up to practically the last minute, this criticism is gaining in intensity.

Obviously the providers of funds, employees, and other stakeholders are interested to know whether a balance sheet has been prepared in accordance with generally accepted principles; they are even more interested in receiving some assurance that the company is really a "going concern", i.e., whether it can still conduct its activities in a year's time, whether it can still generate a profit, and whether it is still able to provide jobs and pay taxes.

B.   The necessity of international cooperation

A research program of the dimensions spelled out above can only be undertaken if one succeeds in finding international partners on two levels: at the level of international researchers on corporate governance issues, and at the level of multinational corporations themselves.

Complex problems like the ones mentioned above can no longer be handled on a national level. In order to grapple with them, one needs the help of experts in all major economies as well as developing nations. The need for the involvement of corporate leaders is to guarantee the practical orientation of this research. These companies must be convinced that they should serve as "clinics" where the results of the research process can be tested at a very early stage. It would help if representatives of business could meet once or twice a year, in international working groups, to exchange experiences.

C.   Dissemination of the results

The insights gained in a governance project would not only be of value to the corporations and societies in the Western world. They also would be of immense value for the countries in the former East Bloc; these countries somewhat naively think that privatization will provide them with that marvelous capitalist tool called corporation which is going to produce the riches they need. Unless they are able to come up with workable, effective governance systems, they might discover before long that, by creating big corporations, they have unleashed monsters they can no longer control.[6]

IV.   Concluding Remarks

As we noted earlier, the concept of governance grew out of the felt need to safeguard the interests of the owners vis-à-vis the professional managers. As the interdependence between a wider group of stake-holders and the corporation grew, the concept of governance had to be extended to them as well. In such a constellation, antagonistic approaches have little chance to succeed. We suspect that all stakeholders should, rather, seek a kind of "common cause". Some observers of the German and Japanese models of governance may allow for just that, as John Plender[7] wrote in *The Financial Times*: "Where the twentieth century Britains now see conflicts of interest, the German employers, employees, suppliers and creditors are often making common cause," and "To many British observers the problem (of governance) is the divorce between ownership and control. . . . To the Germans, and more particularly the Japanese, this seems largely irrelevant. Ownership discipline has played no part in the Japanese success story nor is there no need even for two-tier boards in the system where employees of large companies are regarded as the real owners and the composition of the Japanese boardroom is seen as an expression of employee sovereignty."

Are these approaches the models for the future? Doubts are called for so long as we do not look into the matter much more thoroughly on an international basis. After all, as Queen Christina of Sweden (1626–89) once observed, "In the art of governing one always remains a student."

Notes

1 Ada Demb and Fred Neubauer, *The Corporate Board: Confronting the Paradoxes*. New York: Oxford University Press, 1992, p. 3.
2 W. Carl Kester, "Governance, Contracting, and Investment Time Horizons". *Working Paper*, 1991, p. 10. Quoted with permission of the author.
3 Demb and Neubauer, *op. cit.*, p. 2.
4 Demb and Neubauer, p. 15.
5 André Baladi, "The Growing Role of Pension Funds in Shaping International Corporate Governance, Benefits and Compensation". *International Magazine*, vol. 21 (3), October 1991.
6 Ada Demb, "East Europe's Companies: The Buck Stops Where?" *European Affairs*, June 1990. pp. 22–6.
7 John Plender, "A Quiz with no simple answers." *The Financial Times*, December 9, 1991.

13

The Emerging Corporatism: Business Executives as Social Managers

AHMET AYKAÇ AND MICHAEL GORDY

It has become commonplace in business circles to speak of the shifting role of corporate leaders. One of the least-examined aspects of this shift, however, is the movement of business executives into the role of explicit social managers, dragged by the logic of their activities into social matters that often extend far beyond the parameters of traditional commerce.

We believe this development to be symptomatic of something more profound happening with respect to governance both within the corporation and outside it. Briefly, we think it expresses a growing disequilibrium between two historically divergent but coexisting types of governance: corporatism and democracy. Moreover, this disequilibrium expresses a conjuncture of political, economic and ideological trends revolving around the internationalization of corporate activity and a need for the "de-localization" of social, political and managerial perspectives.

The idea of "de-localization" obviously depends upon the concept of "localness". By this we mean that reality, both social and natural, is structurally organized, and that within the structure of the whole there are sub-structures whose character shapes the way things look within them. Everyone lives, thinks, experiences, etc., within a sub-structure of the whole, and sees things from a perspective organized by the parameters of that sub-structure. Everyone, therefore, has a "local" perspective.

Yet insofar as one's local substructure is part of less-local substructures, and ultimately part of the structured whole, the localness of one's activities is ramified by the inter-relations with less-local substructures. These interactions cannot be perceived as such without broadening and deepening the structural perspective one takes, breaking with his or her own localness to take on a greater one.

Therefore the disequilibrium we mentioned above appears differently depending on whether one looks out on society from within the corporation or looks at the relationship of the corporation to society from the point of view of society as a whole. We shall examine each of these two optics and try to learn what we can from their perspective.

It will become clear as we go along that each of these points of view is informed by its own peculiar logic. Thus each optic will participate in a specific context of meaning whose criteria of significance shape what is observed.

Because what we are trying to understand is anything but straightforward, both our examination of it and the exposition of what we find will have to take on an organic, structural, dynamic character rather than one built upon the notion of linear causality or positivistic reduction. This means that instead of trying to analyze the situation into its constitutive elements and then building them back together again, we will look at the structure within which the elements are arranged without reducing them to one another nor to a central "cause". In this way we hope to preserve an understanding of their mutual interaction while looking at the way those interactions are shaped by the dynamic structure of the whole.

We will begin by taking on each of the two optics mentioned earlier, the one *inside* the corporation and the one *outside*. Then we will give a very brief historical perspective of the operant ideals of governance at work, showing the dynamic interaction of two ideologies both in their present disequilibrium and their possible re-equilibration, and placing these movements in the context of the dominant belief that politics and economics are, or should be, separate. Finally we shall investigate the political implications of all this considering what we see as current socio-economic and political trends in the West, specifically the "de-localization" of business activity.

Inside Looking Out

"Business as usual" is no longer usual from the point of view of corporate managers. The world is changing so rapidly, and along such conflicting and contradictory lines, that executives have found traditional commercial logic inadequate for providing the long-term insights upon which real business strategy depends. Managers have begun to feel that the rules of the game they play have changed; indeed, they may even suspect that it is no longer even the same game. Monitoring the business environment, and planning on the basis of the information received, is becoming increasingly difficult, leading to a loosening of the connection between projects and results.

One of the central features of this situation is that existing business metrics no longer appear capable of generating the appropriate information. Measurement of performance is inherently reactive, based upon reading responsibility into events *ex post facto*. When something desirable happens it is concluded that somebody did something right, yet when considering what to do in the present no such "right" answer can be found, particularly if it is sought by superimposing previous "right" answers onto present circumstances.

Perceived causal relationships have become so diffuse, with so many countervailing factors and temporal constraints at work, that even ascribing responsibility for previous "good" results has bordered on the arbitrary. Evaluating managerial performance after the fact implicitly assumes a measure of control over outcomes on the part of managers that is highly suspect. Thus evaluation of the past seems almost as murky as predicting the future from within traditional commercial categories of measurement.

Allied to this creeping sense of doubt about categories is the perception that there is a discrepancy between the skills that lead to corporate advancement and the skills managers find necessary when they have reached top positions. Competition must give way to creating co-operation, and the habit of toeing the corporate line must transform itself into the capacity for creating "vision". For some, this process is much like asking a bicycle racer to take up duties as a brain surgeon.

There is also an increasing contradiction between the pressures for empowerment coming from inside, as well as outside, the company and the hierarchical command organization under which most corporations operate. Control-oriented apparatuses tend to be unable to respond to these pressures with the requisite speed and flexibility, giving rise to reflections on the optimal governance structure for specific businesses and for corporations as a whole.

These reflections have been imbued with a sense of managerial loss of control within companies – i.e., the inability either to shape events or react adequately to pressures coming from society as a whole, pressures that are felt to be encroachments on legitimate commercial activity. Because of these pressures, top executives are having to spend more and more time concerned with issues apparently unrelated to business practice as traditionally defined, such as the social costs of buyouts and relocations, education and health care, long-term as well as short-term ecological issues, just to name a few. In some cases they are even being asked to participate explicitly in social management activities because of their expanding role as managers of business. The overt separation between business and social management is breaking down.

The meaning of all these developments is not yet clear on a broad social scale. We are in the midst of a paradigm shift in the so-called "hard" sciences whose implications for social values are only beginning to be experienced, a shift modifying the way we read meaning into events. The fundamental interconnectedness of reality, the structural relations amongst a plethora of events somewhat arbitrarily called "causes and effects", the impossibility of distinguishing the observer from the observed in any strict sense – all of these and many other related issues are being felt but not fully comprehended by managers facing the shifting variables and increasingly diverse contexts of their day-to-day activities. They are being felt particularly strongly concerning the changing values of corporate personnel, values that reflect changes in social perceptions in general, and values that must somehow be assimilated rather than rejected outright.

All the above points, which do not make up an exhaustive list by any means, indicate that a top corporate manager's life is becoming more *nuancée*, less straightforward, and increasingly filled with uncertainty about the information he is using, indeed, uncertainty as to whether what he is using is "information" at all. Within this context the notion of "efficiency" is an idea most open to question. More to the point, many business leaders long nostalgically for a simpler world where society's problems remained outside their area of managerial concern.

But what does the situation look like outside the corporation? If we shift our perspective to that optic there are certain things that emerge as important concerns with respect to governance.

Outside Looking In

First of all, it is fairly obvious from the point of view of society as a whole that the resources at the command of corporations of any size are very large and concentrated relative to their environment, and that the disposition of these resources is in the hands of a relatively small number of executives. This is to say nothing more than that the objective social weight of corporate activity is becoming widely apparent. These qualities are also being viewed in some quarters as evidence of "efficiency" and "success".

Within the above perspective it appears that the criteria used in decision-making by the managers of successful corporations have led to accumulation and power. Implied is the view that those who have power must somehow have made "right" decisions along the way to obtaining it. Hence the belief that business is at least marginally more efficient than government at "getting things done" is coupled with the belief that business leaders got to where they are by merit. Accumulation of financial resources *by* the corporation and accumulation of power *within* the corporation by certain individuals are both seen as marks of "efficiency", a term defined by business centuries ago and now deemed to be the appropriate criterion by which to judge all social decisions.

On another front there is growing frustration that government is not using efficiency as a criterion for decision-making, and that this is one of the central reasons for its purported ineffectiveness and wastefulness. The perception of government's bureaucratic inertia is conjoined with the belief that business is somehow less bureaucratized and therefore more "responsive". There is also a growing sense that governments in general, and democratic governments in particular, are becoming paralyzed in the face of rapidly evolving, interconnected global problems, problems that affect profoundly the resolution of local issues.

This growing discontent with democratic processes includes a belief, particularly in North America but with echoes in Europe, that democracy itself has become a spectacle. Political advancement is widely believed to be based on demagoguery, and voting has become an allegory for "shopping", an essentially consumerist activity with all the passivity that this implies. As pointed out above, this situation is usually contrasted with business, where advancement is believed to be grounded objectively on merit.

While these points all tend to work in favor of taking business practices and commercial categories as models for social practice in general, there are countervailing viewpoints at work as well. It is widely believed that it is just this business "success" in freeing itself from any constraints in meeting consumer desires that has led to the degradation of global and local ecosystems. There is also a sense that this environmental deterioration is rapidly accelerating along with economic and social decline, and that unchecked business activity cannot work towards solving these problems.

This position implies that since power and merit are in the hands of corporations, and because the social weight of corporate activity has become so preponderant, these corporate qualities must somehow be co-opted and made to fulfill a more socially responsible role. (Some take this position because they believe it to be a lesser of evils, while others think it to be a positively desirable move.) If only the efficiency of business could be harnessed to goals acceptable to and in the interest of the larger society, it is thought, the deteriorating global and national socio-economic and environmental situations could be ameliorated.

Yet even among groups seeking more social control over business there is a deep-seated belief that the resources necessary for establishing this control are all in the hands of business itself. Thus it is seemingly unimaginable that effective reorienting of corporate practices towards wider social goals – goals outstripping commercial logic – could take place without the active cooperation and participation of corporate leaders. This being the case, the idea of business leaders becoming explicit social managers makes sense.

But does it, at least in the way indicated above? It seems that just as top managers are beginning to doubt the efficacy and adequacy of traditional commercial categories, elements of the wider population want to widen the application of those very same categories in an attempt to resolve apparently intractable social and political problems. At the same time, managers are hesitant to oppose this wider application, if only because the business community has been so vocal and deter- mined in trying to inculcate these values amongst the populace for so many decades. Moreover, large sectors of society accept commercial categories but do so in parallel with a deep-seated distrust of corpor- ations. We shall have to step back and consider these equivocal points of view from a broader structural perspective if we are to hope to clarify the situation at all.

Diverging or Complementary Perspectives?

In order to see these two optics in a larger context we need to have a brief look at two divergent historical theories of governance that have shaped the ideological structure of Western political discourse for over a thousand years. These are corporatism and democracy. While this account must necessarily flirt with over-simplification, our aim here is merely to set out some landmarks for locating the question of governance as it relates to the internal and external social perspectives we sketched above.

One of the most important achievements of Western democracy has been the virtual elimination from the formal political scene of various elements of what is known as "corporatism". The term corporatism has several meanings. Historically it has designated a form of social organization in which corporations, chartered and given legitimacy by the government, have played an intermediary role between the public and the state. The origins of this form go back to medieval times where the great trade guilds controlled the activities of craftsmen and traders. At the height of their power the guilds represented a third force in society alongside the Church and the nobility.

What was significant in this form of social order was that simple alignment to a certain trade, or to the Church or to the nobility, gave one the right to meddle in, influence, or even run society's affairs. It was taken for granted that those who belonged to these groups were, merely because of their membership, better qualified than the average person to run society.

During the eighteenth century, which was arguably the most important century in the millennium, three great revolutions essentially decimated these forms of social organization and made possible the conceptualization of new ones. In the sphere of material production the onset of the industrial revolution radically transformed the forces of production and production relations. The rise of the use of machinery in the factory system effectively disempowered the craftsmen and gave control over the manufacturing process to the industrial capitalists, thus enhancing the social power of the latter and accelerating their political ascendancy.

The American revolution fundamentally changed popular political consciousness by joining an essentially anti-colonialist property-owners' movement to the ideas of popular control of government and liberation from corporatist constraints, ideas that served as well to organize and mobilize strata of society outside the propertied classes. Henceforth the American versions of the notions of freedom and equality (albeit in practice restricted to property-owners) came to serve as rallying cries inspiring anti-corporatist political movements throughout the Western world.

The French revolution signalled the expansion and refinement of the motivating force of these democratic ideals. Gathering the peasantry and the poor around the universal principles of freedom, democracy and brotherhood, the Third Estate was able to wrest political power from the nobility and the Church, and thus, among other things, accelerate the development of an industrial capital-based system in continental Europe. Freedom for capital was joined to freedom for the individual (specifically freedom of labor mobility and the right to sell one's time) in an objective conjuncture with the interests of the Third Estate. By breaking down the social and legal barriers to the movement of serfs away from the agricultural estates, the French revolution removed obstacles to urbanization and industrialization that had hampered the growth of capitalist production. In this way democratic ideology gave conceptual shape to socio-economic change and helped that change along.

This conjuncture of politics and economics was inverted in the political and ideological message inherent in these decisive historical developments. The message said that belonging to a particular group did *not* give one the right to run, meddle in, or otherwise exercise undue influence over society's affairs. That right was only to be gained through some mechanism, or form of suffrage, whereby the wishes of the people were aggregated and expressed by way of a parliament or some other representational apparatus.

Economic enterprise, on the other hand, was conceived of as separate from politics. It was to be exercised through the market, which often found itself in an adversarial relationship with the governing authorities but in any event operating according to a logic peculiar to itself – a logic, in fine, ill-suited to application outside the field of commerce. Democratic principles had no relevance to the internal structure of business, where advancement was to be based on merit, and merit was defined by quantitative measures of business success. While government, built on democratic principles, was meant to act as society's check on potential business excesses, business, with its hierarchical and meritocratic governance structures, was expected to promote and guarantee the expansion of society's wealth.

While the tenets of the historical democratic ideal include freedom of thought and speech, they also imply the freedom to be heard, which in practice has meant free elections to select some body to whom the legitimate exercise of political power is entrusted. Coincident with this freedom to be heard is the protection of dissenters from illegitimate reprisals by the majority, along with the possibility of modifying political decisions at regular intervals.

These tenets, abstract as they are, make no claim as to the efficiency of the political systems based upon them. Neither do they claim that the criteria used by the population for choosing their representatives, nor for deciding particular questions, have any particular merit aside from allowing popular participation in political life.

While these democratic ideals came to dominate political discourse and gave shape to formal political institutions, corporatism as an ideal was resuscitated in the work of sociologist Emile Durkheim. He essentially saw corporatism as a way of circumventing the problem of what he called "anomie" (alienation). His view was that industrial society, having alienated a majority of the people, needed some way of reintroducing the moral training and social discipline required to keep society together. This could not be done through the state, not because of the state's basic inability to deal with problems in general but because *it was too distant and emotionally neutral* to be able to deal with anomie. Therefore this task was to be carried out locally through corporatist institutions that, while no longer explicitly political, maintained an intermediary role between the state and the mass of population. Social clubs, private schools, trades unions, and in some respects political parties, to name but a few examples, served as two-way means of communication between the impersonal state apparatus and peoples' daily concerns.

In essence, representative democracy, the ideal of which was to allow everyone to participate in the affairs of state, by its very representative character became too remote from peoples' daily concerns to be positively owned by the people it sought to represent, particularly at the national level. Paradoxical as it may seem, corporatism, which had been weeded out as being antithetical to representative democracy, became the vehicle through which democracy could sustain itself by tending to local concerns.

Business, in contrast to representative democratic institutions, always has to act locally no matter how global its reach and therefore has become the ideal candidate for fulfilling the corporatist role foreseen by Durkheim. Business practices take place in specific markets, with specific client populations and specific work forces. Thus commercial logic requires generating employee loyalty along with the goodwill of local populations, states of affairs that can only be achieved through local action. For this, business requires informal corporatist structures to treat local problems locally while simultaneously reproducing business ideals. Local populations have to be "taken care of" in ways that reflect local power relationships and needs, something that cannot be achieved by democratic institutions alone.

In this way, corporatism has served an implicit function in governance while the explicit role has been filled by self-styled democratic institutions. Reproduction of values and ideals has taken place within local structures while formal governmental activities have remained in the hands of various non-local parliaments.

It appears, then, that two seemingly different avenues have conjoined into one for addressing the problem of political aggregation. That problem, which revolves around the question of how frequently conflicting individual interests are to be combined to become the general interest, was thought to have been resolved by representative democracy. But the workings of that democracy have depended upon corporatist structures that were found necessary by the business community as well. It was only in theory that a strict distinction could be maintained between political and economic life, since the two were joined by their dependency on informal corporatist institutions.

What Is Happening Now?

As the reach of business enterprise has become global, and as business has been able to move capital and enterprise more freely around the world, the problems of local populations have become increasingly tied to non-local developments. Likewise, there has been a tendency for managers in multinational corporations to move about from one locality to another in their climb up the corporate ladder, making their connections to a specific community increasingly abstract. Added to this has been a business-supported governmental attack on labor unions in the United Kingdom and North America that has significantly undermined the efficacy of those unions as corporatist structures at the local level, and has left many local populations with diminished power over events in their daily lives.

Local populations, faced with the breakdown of the traditional corporatist institutions that shaped their lives (the decline of labor unions being just one of many examples) have been left with the more abstract, non-local institutions of democratic government as the only avenue for expressing their concerns. But, as we have seen, these institutions cannot function locally without the inter-mediation of corporatist structures, and are themselves increasingly constrained by complex and often contradictory global forces over which they appear to have little or no control. Demographic explosions, population shifts, world-wide ecological developments and international financial crises are examples that come immediately to mind.

To put it more succinctly, with the uneven and accelerating spread of business enterprise and its attendant crises and dislocations, the problems confronting society have become increasingly non-local, although their effects are certainly felt locally. The ideals of freedom and individualism have become more abstract as control over the global deployment of productive resources has become more concentrated. Awareness of world-wide economic and ecological interdependence has given lie to the belief that society is composed of mechanistically separate and separable parts. Likewise, the issue of political aggregation has become increasingly pertinent as decisions taken on the basis of individualism move the world further toward political paralysis and chaos.

The void left by the internationalization of business activity and the associated decline of informal corporatist structures has given rise to a contradiction between the local needs and perspectives of the wider society and the global reach of business enterprise. This contradiction is beginning to be felt by some business managers in that their need to act in local markets is at odds with both the commercial exigencies of world-wide economic trends and the acceleration of social, political and environmental change.

People in all walks of life, including business, are beginning to recognize that local problems cannot be resolved locally without reference to the larger structures of social life.

It may be that, unconsciously or consciously, the movement towards an explicit social role for managers is really a demand for a political structure that makes the interdependence of all aspects of society explicit by implicating corporations in the wider social aspects of their commercial activities. Perhaps corporate leaders are being drawn to take responsibility for dealing with some of the consequences of what they are already doing or not doing, and are willing to be so drawn because they realize that those consequences feed back onto their ability to do business in the long run.

Optimism and Pessimism

To take an optimistic view of these developments let's entertain the possibility that this movement is an expression of the rise of a new theoretical paradigm for social relations: a paradigm involving the relativization of the Newtonian–Cartesian–Darwinian model of reality whose claim to absolute validity is being swept aside by theoretical breakthroughs in quantum physics and molecular biology. We might then want to point out that the traditional form of the democratic ideal, formulated as it has been in terms of individualism and the separation of economic from political activities (at least in theory), reflects the Newtonian–Cartesian–Darwinian paradigm in an inflexibly absolutist way and is being replaced by the recognition of the deep interconnectedness of social life and the need for flexibility in all forms of governance. If democratic ideals are to survive, on this view, they must be radically transformed to reflect the reality of this interconnectedness. That is the optimistic view.

The pessimistic view (and the two views may be complementary in the way wave and particle theories of light are complementary) is that the ideology of individual responsibility, an ideology crucial to traditional democracy, is breaking down in the face of the material interconnectedness of socio-economic forces and is making way for the rise of some form of authoritarianism. From this perspective it appears that the alternatives are either some new form of collective democratic responsibility, or an explicit dictatorship, probably a corporatist one.

When democratic institutions appear unable to respond to crises that threaten the reproduction of the existing social order, powerful elements of society often turn towards some form of explicit corporatism in an attempt to resolve their difficulties. The European fascist states of the 1930s are good examples of this, fascist parties having used corporatist structures to circumvent the last vestiges of democratic institutions on their way to power. More recent examples are the military governments in Greece and Chile, installed when dominant groups in those societies could no longer maintain their hegemony by democratic means. People in crisis tend to be unwilling to have their fate decided by what seems to them to be an uncontrolled lottery method of leadership selection.

In either case (or in both cases) business can be seen as the necessary intermediary between local concerns and global events, if no other alternative than corporate social management is seriously entertained. Only business is perceived as having both the resources and reach to deal with local problems within global structures, and business values have permeated social ideologies – at least in the developed countries – to the point where people are used to living with corporatist structures, at least informal ones.

Tentative Conclusions

From inside the corporation looking out there is a perceived need for the world to be ordered so that business can flourish, but this perception is coupled with the recognition that commercial logic is perhaps incapable of understanding the problem, let alone providing knowledge of how to deal with it. Traditional democratic ideals do not speak to the question of interrelatedness and common interest in any but the most abstract ways, so some form of corporatism, based on a new logic that prominently includes business interests is what would be most appealing from this point of view.

From the outside looking in, the apparent invincibility of corporate power, and the seeming paralysis of democratic governments in the face of the effects of that power, make some form of corporatism seem inevitable. In any event, it appears to many people that business is going to do what it decides is necessary to survive, and the social consequences will be there for all to see.

Any attempt to shape corporate practice along lines that transcend commercial logic will have to take advantage of the awareness among managers that they are not really in control of things, that their categories are inadequate, and then join this awareness to an attempt to show that real corporate interest lies in planetary survival. In the short term this may not be achievable.

In the short run democracy as it has been perceived and practised, we believe, will not survive; that much seems to us to be certain. It is also highly probable that some form of authoritarian corporatism will be tried in developed countries. But we also believe that the reality of planetary interdependence and global complexity will cause these attempts to fail in the medium-term. If it is then not too late, perhaps we shall see the rise of a new political culture, one based on interdependence and less-abstract democratic participation in society's decisions, one that embodies the localness of corporatism without its exclusiveness, one that, for want of a more elegant term, might be called "holistic democracy". It is not too soon to begin thinking about what this might mean.

14

Intuition in Managerial Decision-making: Codeword for Global Transformation

Willis Harman

Intuition, up through the mid-1970s, was not something tough-minded businessmen thought of themselves as using. Among businesspersons in the late 1980s, not only does the word "intuition" refer to an ability worth having – it is also likely to signal to the listener that the individual using it is open to the current re-thinking about the entire business enterprise.

Words like "intuition" and "creativity" are used to refer to certain capabilities of the unconscious mind in the service of the conscious mind. Other words are used as well, ranging from "hunches" and "gut feel" to "creative inspiration". In earlier times other terms, such as "revelation" or "Divine guidance" might have been used.

This realm of human experience is basically mysterious. The access to information and the capability of synthesis displayed by the unconscious intuitive mind are sometimes quite startling, in view of both "common-sense" and scientific assumptions about the nature of mental processes.

"Practical" persons are sometimes reluctant to gather all of these phenomena into one container. Some who are quite comfortable with "hunches", "creative problem-solving", and "instinct" are far less so with what they have heard about the "deep intuition" or "higher creativity". But however much one may want to honor such conservative feelings, we live in a time when as much truth-telling as possible seems called for. Our efforts to understand intuition will probably be most fruitful if we consider the whole vast spectrum of experiences that seem to fall within this category, and recognize that over the last quarter century a remarkable tolerance has developed for this entire area.

The close relationship between "ordinary" intuition and similar experiences which have for centuries been described in more overtly religious terminology highlights the fact that contemporary theories of cognition and perception are unlikely to yield very adequate ways of understanding intuition.

The Scientific Understanding of Intuition

We want to understand as much as we can about intuition – which is to say, we want to understand both scientifically and experientially. The greatest scientists have acknowledged their debt to the mysterious processes of intuition, and practically all the conceptual advances in science have been made in some intuitive leap. Despite this fact, however, science has neither made a concerted research effort into understanding intuition, nor has it come up with any very useful conceptual framework within which to understand the process.

One of the primary factors to be recognized in the scientific study of intuition is the strong psychological resistance *against* learning about intuition. As the American psychologist Abraham Maslow said in *Toward A Psychology of Being*, we all have both "a need to know and a fear of knowing." We recognize and acknowledge our own resistance to uncovering unsavory repressed material, unaccepted aggressive and sexual urges, unconscious fears, etc. But the force with which we resist that is puny compared to the force with which we resist discovering "the godlike in ourselves" (as Maslow put it).

It is important to note in this connection that historically, scientists have been reluctant to admit the reality of unconscious mental processes. The concept of psychosomatic illness, for example, knocked long at the door of scientific legitimacy before finally being admitted; the concept that positive emotions might have a beneficial effect on healing had to wait even longer (until the 1970s) for acceptance. The idea of unconscious mental operations similar to those taking place in the conscious mind was strongly resisted by the scientific community until roughly a quarter of a century ago, when research on subliminal perception and related topics made the proposition almost indisputable. Hypnosis researcher Ernest Hilgard's concept of the "hidden observer," a part of the unconscious that observes all, and is not fooled by the hypnotist's suggestions, was part of the turning of the tide in the 1960s and 1970s. Work of Jacqueline Damgaard and others on cases of multiple personality disorder, in the 1980s, discloses that one of the alternate personalities – one with unique characteristics, termed the "inner self-helper" – not only observes but actively offers help in the task of personality integration; it claims never to have been born and never to die, and hints at having access to information not ordinarily accessible to the conscious mind.

What this research on the unconscious mind makes clear is that the topic of intuition is in fact a fundamental challenge to the current scientific paradigm. Nobel laureate Roger Sperry, in a 1987 paper entitled "The Structure and Significance of the Consciousness Revolution," identifies one of the key issues. There are two types of causation evident in the universe. One is "upward causation," as when the movement of gas molecules in the cylinder causes the piston to move and your automobile to travel along the road. The other is "downward causation," as when you decide it would be nice to take a trip, and *that* causes your automobile to travel down the road. Science has dealt primarily with the former, and practically not at all with the latter. According to Sperry, a fundamental "consciousness revolution" is taking place in science, wherein the validity of consciousness-related, teleological, "downward causation" is recognized along with that of reductionistic "upward causation."

But the issue goes even deeper. It is not just a matter that contemporary science proves to be inadequate to deal with intuition in some strict research sense. Because society's official knowledge-validating system, science, has nothing to say about values, creativity, morals and ethics, aesthetic sense, and in general man/woman as a spiritual being in a meaningful universe, the influence of those aspects of life is muted when it comes to our most powerful institutions. Thus institutional decisions are made that squander irreplaceable resources, foul the environment, threaten the Earth's life-support systems, inhumanely use our fellow citizens, create chronic poverty and hunger, and imperil the future of civilized society on the planet – decisions that individual humans in those institutions know are unwise.

Thus there is a growing challenge to the adequacy of the economic, technical, and scientific authority system of modern society, a challenge which resembles the seventeenth century challenge to the ecclesiastical authority system of medieval society. The latter marked the shift from the Middle Ages to the modern era. The contemporary challenge marks a transition from the modern to some sort of trans-modern era. We shall return to this point a little later on.

Business Discovers Intuition

The word "intuition", found frequently these days in business and management publications, is a relative newcomer. Only since the late 1970s have business journals and books included reference to "hunches" and intuition in decision-making. Prior to that not only was intuition absent from the practical businessman's lexicon; one was unlikely to find the word anywhere without it being preceded by the adjective "feminine."

A recent book on intuition in business defines it as "a process of knowing without the intervention of reason or analysis." The idea of arriving at insight without a recognizable thought process was profoundly disturbing in a time when "rational man" was the ideal model. It was not a concept that the tough-minded business executive talked about comfortably. Yet it is now an open secret that the most successful executives have learned to trust their intuition – and have further learned that in the trusting it became more reliable and accurate, until in the end it becomes the most trustworthy guide available. The rational mind, still useful, is put in a secondary role with respect to the deep intuition.

In certain contemporary leadership development workshops, executives learn that all individuals can discover in themselves a deep sense of purpose. The emerging concept of management involves honoring that purpose in oneself and in others, allowing it full play in the organization and relying on the motivation associated with it.

Managers are being taught in many of today's training courses that the inhibiting effect of fear (of ridicule, of criticism, of failure, of success) can be abolished. One can learn to trust the total environment in such a way that all experience is merely feedback from the universe, and there is nothing to fear.

Not long ago I was in a meeting of a small group of corporate executives. One mentioned that a rather unusual set of coincidences had been instrumental in his being included in the meeting. Another remarked, "There are no coincidences." As though that were a code phrase signifying something understood but not spoken, heads nodded around the table.

One of the lessons stressed in some of these courses and meetings is that we are not entirely separate individuals as we may have assumed. At some deeper level of the mind we all interconnect, and that is why no one of us can really win unless we all do.

These examples illustrate how certain principles, which are being learned in preparation for effective leadership and executive functioning, are not really compatible with the picture of reality that has dominated in our most powerful institutions. That is not, in fine, a stable situation; either society's "picture of reality" is changing, or this type of training will eventually be dropped.

Whether we focus on these new insights in executive development, or on Roger Sperry's "consciousness revolution in science," or both together – the implications are the same. Modern society appears to be going through one of the most fundamental shifts in history. To redefine empirical science as radically as these examples imply is to deal with a change as basic as the one in the original scientific revolution. It amounts to a departure from the objectivist, positivist, reductionist assumptions that underlie most of modern science. It implies recognition that positivistic, reductionistic science intrinsically amounts to no more than a partial and inadequate understanding of the universe we live in and our place in it.

The Scientific "Heresy" and Its Consequences

Let us remind ourselves how modern times came about. The seventeenth century in Western Europe can reasonably be taken as the end of the Middle Ages and the birthdate of modern times. That century saw an "economic revolution" centered around the flourishing city of Amsterdam, with development of the early capitalist institutions and the concept of markets for both goods and labor. In that century there was also the first of the modern liberal-democratic revolutions, in England. And there was the "invention," with the Treaty of Westphalia, of the autonomous nation-state, free to do anything it has the power to impose. But most importantly, that is the century of the "scientific revolution."

From these developments stem the defining characteristics of modern society: centrality of the economic and technology-centered institutions, rising demand for democracy and equity, unbridled national sovereignty, and – most fundamental of all – "reality" defined by empirical science. By now these characteristics have influenced practically every other society on the globe. They account for the present dominance of Western (European) society. They are also the source of the global dilemmas we all now face.

The overall pattern of life in every society forms around some underlying picture of reality. Modern society differs from medieval society principally because its underlying image of reality is different. We have to look to that image both to understand the astounding successes of modern society, and also its present predicament.

For a person living in the medieval world (as in many traditional societies) life is a seamless whole. Rocks, trees, rivers, and clouds are wondrous and alive; the world is enchanted, infused with spirit. Events are explained by divine purpose or by their function in a meaningful world. Humans feel at home in nature; the cosmos is a place of *belonging*. The Earth as the centre of the cosmos is the seat of change, decay, and Christian redemption. Above it circle planets and the stars, themselves pure and unchanging, moved by some sort of intelligent or divine spirits and signalling and influencing human events by their locations and aspects. The universe is alive and imbued with purpose; all creatures are a part of a Great Chain of Being, with man between the angels and the lower animals. The working of enchantments, the occurrence of miracles, the presence of witches and other beings with supernatural powers, are – if not commonplace – assumed to be quite real and consequential. The kinds of dichotomies that come so naturally to the modern Western mind – man versus nature; facts versus values; science versus religion; intuition versus the rational mind – simply don't exist (Berman, 1981).

This image of reality was displaced by the scientific revolution – one of the great watershed epochs in history, marking the end of medieval times and the beginning of the modern era. The world perceived by the educated person in Western Europe in 1600 was still the world of the Middle Ages. By 1700 the "scientific heresy" had become so widely accepted that the informed person literally perceived a different reality, much more like today's. He saw essentially a dead universe, constructed and set in motion by the Creator, with subsequent events accounted for by mechanical forces and lawful behaviors. Man was seen as separate from, and potentially controlling of, nature.

Just as the hypnotized person may see things that aren't there or fail to see things that are, so "reality" is transformed when the "cultural hypnosis" shifts. It was not just that after the seventeenth century men now believed that the earth goes round the sun, and scientists began to explore the world around them. The change was far more fundamental. It essentially consisted of a different perceived universe, and a different basis on which truth is to be decided – a shift from the religious authority system of the Middle Ages to the authority system of empirical science. As we now know, as a result of this shift in the underlying picture of reality, every institution in society was affected by the scientific revolution. The spread of the scientific heresy affected not just scientists, but everyone.

A Crisis in Science, and the Rise of a "New Heresy"

As time went on, confidence in the "reality" of empirical science grew. It was astoundingly successful at providing the power to predict and control the physical world, as our present technological prowess attests.

Yet by the latter twentieth century it was becoming apparent that, however useful science might be for some purposes, such as generating new technologies, it had a serious negative effect on our understanding of values. Its effect was to undermine the common religious base of values and to replace it with a kind of moral relativism. Into the vacuum came, as a kind of "pseudo-values", economic and technical criteria – material progress, efficiency, productivity, etc. Decisions that would affect the lives of people around the globe, and generations to come, were decided on the basis of short-term economic considerations. The "technological imperative" to develop and apply any technology that could turn a profit or destroy an enemy endangered both the life-support systems of the planet and human civilization.

Spirituality and religiosity did not disappear, of course. The churches still played a role in peoples' lives, and privately many a scientist guided his or her life by deep spiritual beliefs. But *modern man was attempting the impossible*. That was to manage society, and the planet, on the basis of two conflicting and mutually contradictory pictures of reality – the mechanistic universe of empirical science, and the spiritual universe assumed in society's religious traditions.

The root of this problem was certain assumptions that had, over time, come to characterize the scientific enterprise. Three of these are particularly important:

- The *objectivist* assumption, that there is an objective universe which the scientific observer can explore and approximate, progressively more precisely, by quantitative models;
- The *positivist* assumption, that what is scientifically "real" must take as its basic data only that which is physically observable; and

- The *reductionist* assumption, that scientific explanation consists in explaining complex phenomena in terms of more elemental events (e.g., human behavior in terms of stimulus and response).

These characteristics have seemed so integral to the scientific method that it is hard to imagine they would ever be displaced.

And yet these assumptions set the stage for an almost inevitable crisis. Science became increasingly adept at exploring the external, physical world and increasingly neglectful of the world of inner experience. This was extremely serious, because it is from this deep intuitive experience that all individuals and societies have always derived their sense of ultimate meanings and eternal values. Industrial society became more and more like a ship with ever-increasing speed, but no compass or charts to guide it.

By the beginning of this decade the situation had indeed become a crisis. A "new heresy" was heard in the land. The scientific heresy of the seventeenth century had amounted to a widening group of people observing that reality is not the way the religious authorities had been telling it. The new heresy opined that reality is not the way the secular authorities had been telling it either. The controlled experiments of empirical science are not automatically the road to ultimate truth; and the technological accomplishments of science do not automatically lead to good effects.

Just as the modern perceptions of reality differ from the medieval, so a growing band of individuals today are betting their lives on a different picture of reality than that of reductionistic science. It is not just that some "New Age" values are spreading through the populace. Rather, a fundamentally different and competing picture of reality combines holistic mental and physical approaches, new concepts of business management, and people seeking to replace the lost meaning in their lives.

Making Intuition Fit Science and Vice-versa

The problems science has had in dealing with certain areas of human experience – for example, the intuitive, the creative, the aesthetic, the spiritual – are well known. Some of the controversies (e.g., free will versus determinism; positivistic science versus spirituality) have been going on for many generations. It is only very recently that several developments have appeared which both sharpen the challenge and point toward a resolution.

The realization that somehow science seems to miss important aspects of human experience has spread rapidly over the past quarter century. Although this quiet rebellion takes many cultish and bizarre forms, nevertheless the core of the "New Age" perspective now infuses much of mainstream society. Growing public interest in such areas as Eastern religious philosophies, yoga and meditation, paranormal phenomena, more natural approaches to education and healing, etc., points toward a widespread dissatisfaction with scientists' exclusive claim to valid truth-seeking.

Although in the historical development of science there were good reasons for an initial limiting of the scope of the new inquiry to those aspects of reality that are physically measurable, and to explanations that are non-teleological and reductionistic, nonetheless there were consequences. One of those consequences has been that a tremendous amount of effort has gone into defending the barricades against, or explaining away, a host of phenomena that don't fit within those limits.

The reassessment of that situation is an integral part of the "New Age" outlook, although it is not always clearly articulated. It amounts to, simply and brashly, a proposal that science can be reformulated. Instead of starting with a limiting bias and having to defend against the anomalous, what if we start with the assumption that *any class of inner experiences that have been reported, or of phenomena that have been observed, apparently in some sense exists?* The need, then, is for a scientific outlook that accommodates all that exists.

A key element of this response is the proposition of Roger Sperry, that science include "downward" as well as "upward" causation. Another key was offered by another Nobel laureate, Sir Karl Popper, in his concept of a hierarchical arrangement of sciences – an arrangement in which *emergent* qualities (such as consciousness) necessary for a science that deals with the human experience are not contradicted by the fact that they don't seem to fit in with the physical sciences.

The Impact of Changing Attitudes Toward Intuition

So what really are the implications of the fact that our society has apparently decided to honor intuition, in business and other practical sectors of society? There are several:

1 *It brings a new approach to decision-making.* Using intuition (together with the rational mind) amounts to using more of the mind. Because the "more" turns out to be extremely competent, decision-making should be more "successful" on the whole.

2 *It has implications with regard to values.* Our most important value commitments have their origins in the inclinations of the deep intuitive mind. Paying more attention to this brings about challenges to the economic and technical values which hold such powerful sway over modern society, and so strongly influence social choices. The influence of these values will tend to decline, as the valence of other values increases – particularly cooperative, altruistic, humane, ecological, aesthetic, and spiritual values.

3 *It amounts to a reassessment of the role of business.* As more and more of those involved in the business enterprise – executives, employees, customers – experience changes in the value structures that govern their lives, the basic questions of the role of business, the role of speculation (versus investment), relationships with the developing world, business involvement in the arms race, and so on, will all be reassessed. Furthermore,

4 *It amounts to a reassessment of the basic metaphysical assumptions that underlie modern industrial society.* Insofar as it does so, it amounts to the end of the modern era just as surely as the shift in assumptions (the scientific revolution) signified the end of the medieval era. In other words, the late twenty-first century will be as different from modern times as these times are from the Middle Ages.

It is in this fourth area, namely the *global implications of changing assumptions*, where the growing acceptance of intuition has its greatest potential significance. Our global problems – nuclear weapons, endemic arms buildups and armed conflict, terrorism, environmental degradation, extinction of species, human-induced climate change, chronic hunger and poverty, toxic chemical concentrations – are not the accidental product of bad decisions. Rather, they are deeply connected to the socioeconomic system of the modern world. *They are really the consequences of what we might call "the modern perception of reality."* If that perception is changing, then our whole approach to the most serious problems of our day will also change.

Assumptions are built into the whole social structure that reflect our basic perception of reality – or, rather, reflect the prevailing picture back when the institutions of modern society were shaped. These include the assumptions that

● Progress is in the direction of increasing involvement of individuals and their activities in the mainstream economy;

- Jobs in that economy must be generated at all costs because jobs are the main way people participate in their society;
- "Consumers" have an insatiable appetite for the products of that economic activity (whether or not they recognized it before being educated to the fact);
- Because of the cost of capital it is reasonable to take a short-term view of investments which will affect the lives of future generations (economists call this "discounting the future");
- That the Earth and its resources are there to be exploited for the benefit of the human species;
- That any technology that *can* be developed and applied, *should* be;
- That "national security" is to be found through the development of increasingly devastating weapons.

The end result of the ethic of mass consumption and "material progress" is the destruction of the environment despite attempts to counteract that through environmental protection legislation, etc. It is also persistent starvation in various regions of the globe despite the fact that there are excesses of food in other regions. It is continued arms buildup, despite clear indications that the planet is at risk as long as preparation for war is legitimated as national policy. It is the treatment of "resources" (including other creatures) as though they were placed here for our use.

Naturally enough, we all experience a psychological resistance to the proposition that our internalized assumptions about reality must change. It is not a comfortable feeling to be aware that some kind of fundamental transition is essential, and at the same time not know what that is likely to do to our accustomed way of life, our assumed "security," or indeed, our basic image of "how things are." Each of us has undoubtedly, to some extent, experienced this kind of discomfort.

Thus, on one hand, we can see an exhilarating time ahead. Business will be discovering new roles; unsolvable problems will appear solvable after all. Task number one is a global mind change, and many of us will feel ourselves to be at the vibrant heart of that change. On the other hand, this fundamental shift is going to feel threatening to many people, and some of them will respond irrationally. The things we can do to keep the level of anxiety down will be important in discounting the amount of human misery, as society goes through what will possibly prove a very wrenching transformation.

All things considered, we could summarize by observing that the current interest in intuition goes much deeper than it appears on the surface. It is, certainly, a message that augurs a major transformation of global society.

Notes

Paper presented at the IMI-Geneva Conference on Intuition in Business, Geneva Switzerland, February 19, 1988. Reproduced by generous permission of the author.

References

Berman, Morris 1981: *The Reenchantment of the World*. Ithaca: Cornell University Press.

Damgaard, Jacqueline 1987: "The Inner Self-Helper: Transcendent Life Within Life?" In *Consciousness and Survival*. Sausalito CA: Institute of Noetic Sciences.

Harman, Willis 1988: *Global Mind Change*. Indianapolis IN: Knowledge Systems.

Hilgard, Ernest 1978: *Divided Consciousness*. New York: John Wiley.

Maslow, Abraham 1968: *Toward a Psychology of Being*. New York: Van Nostrand.

Popper, Karl R. and Eccles, John C. 1981: *The Self and Its Brain*. Berlin and London: Springer International.

Sperry, Roger 1987: "Structure and Significance of the Consciousness Revolution." *Journal of Mind and Behaviour*, Volume 8 (1), 37–66.

Selected Bibliography

Arendt, Hannah 1958: *The Human Condition*. Chicago IL: University of Chicago Press.

Arendt, Hannah 1963: *On Revolution*. New York: Viking Press.

Baldwin, Fred 1984: *Conflicting Interests: Corporate Governance Controversies*. Lexington MA: Lexington Books.

Barker, Sir Ernest 1959: *The Political Thought of Plato and Aristotle*. New York: Dover.

Barnard, Chester 1938: *The Functions of the Executive*. Cambridge: Harvard University Press.

Becker, Lawrence C. 1977: *Property Rights: Philosophic Foundations*. Boston: Routledge & Kegan Paul.

Bell, Daniel 1974: *The Coming of Post-industrial Society*. London: Heinemann.

Berger, Peter L. 1981: New Attack on the Legitimacy of Business. *Harvard Business Review*, September/October, 82–9.

Berger, Peter L. and Luckmann, Thomas 1967: *The Social Construction of Reality*. New York: Doubleday & Co.

Berle, Adolf A. 1954: *The 20th Century Capitalist Revolution*. New York: Harcourt, Brace & World.

Berlin, Isaiah 1991: *The Crooked Timber of Humanity: Chapters in the History of Ideas*. Henry Hardy (ed.). New York: Alfred A. Knopf.

Block, Fred 1991: *Postindustrial Possibilities: A Critique of Economic Discourse*. Berkeley: University of California Press.

Boulding, Kenneth 1985: *The World as a Total System*. Beverly Hills CA: Sage.

Boulding, Kenneth 1989: *Three Faces of Power*. Newbury Park CA: Sage Publications.

Boulding, Kenneth and Mukerjee, T. (eds) 1972: *Economic Imperialism: A Book of Readings*. Ann Arbor MI: University of Michigan Press.

Brady, Robert A. 1943: *Business As A System of Power*. New York: Columbia University Press.

Briston, Richard J. and Dobbins, Richard 1978: *The Growth and Impact of Institutional Investors*. London: Institute of Chartered Accountants in England and Wales.

Capra, Fritjof 1982: *The Turning Point: Science, Society, and the Rising Culture*. New York: Simon & Schuster.

Clarkson, Max B. E. 1991: *The Strategic Management of Stakeholder Relations and Corporate Social Responsibilities*. Paper presented at the 11th Annual Strategic Management Society Conference, University of Toronto.

Davis, John P. 1905: *Corporations: A Study of the Origin and Development of Great Business Combinations and of their Relation to the Authority of the State* (2 volumes). Buffalo New York: W. S. Hein & Co.

Davis, Keith and Blomstrom, Robert L. 1975: *Business and Society: Environment and Responsibility*. New York: McGraw–Hill.

Donaldson, Thomas 1982: *Corporations and Morality*. Englewood Cliffs NJ: Prentice–Hall.

Drucker, Peter 1946: *The Concept of the Corporation*. New York: John Day.

Duverger, Maurice 1980: *The Study of Politics*. Robert Wagoner (trans.) Surrey: Thomas Nelson and Sons Ltd. [Published in French as *Sociologie politique*.]

Eells, Richard 1972: *Global Corporations: The Emerging System of World Economic Power*. New York: Free Press.

Eells, Richard and Walton, Clarence 1974: *The Conceptual Foundations of Business*. Homewood IL: Richard D. Irwin Inc.

Fama, Eugene 1980: Agency Problems and the Theory of the Firm. *Journal of Political Economy*, 88 (2), 288–307.

Fischel, Daniel R. 1982: The Corporate Governance Movement. *Vanderbilt Law Review*, 35 (6), 1259–92.

Freeman, R. Edward 1984: *Corporate Strategy: A Stakeholder Approach*. Boston: Pitman.

French, J. R. and Raven, B. 1959: The Bases of Social Power. In D. Cartwright (ed.), *Studies in Social Power*. Ann Arbor MI: Research Center for Group Dynamics.

French, Peter 1984: *Collective and Corporate Responsibility*. New York: Columbia University Press.

Fromm, Erich 1955: *The Sane Society*. New York: Rinehart Press.

Galbraith, John Kenneth 1983: *The Anatomy of Power*. Boston: Houghton Mifflin.

Galbraith, J. K. 1967: *The New Industrial State*. London: Hamish Hamilton.

Galbraith, J. K. 1958: *The Affluent Society*. Boston: Houghton Mifflin.

Harman, Willis 1988: *Global Mind Change*. New York: Warner Books.

Hayek, F. A. 1976: *Individualism and the Economic Order*. London: Routledge & Kegan Paul.

Heilbroner, Robert 1989: Reflections: The Triumph of Capitalism. *The New Yorker*, January 23, 98–109.

Heilbroner, R. 1988: *Behind the Veil of Economics*. New York: W. W. Norton.

Heilbroner, R. 1976: *Business Civilization in Decline*. New York: W. W. Norton.

Held, David 1989: *Political Theory and the Modern State*. Oxford: Polity Press. [Held offers an interesting counterpoint to Habermas's theory of "motivation crisis".]

Heyderbrand, Wolf von 1985: Technarchy and Corporatism: Toward a Theory of Organizational Change Under Advanced Capitalism and Early State Socialism. *Current Perspectives in Social Theory*, 6, 71–128.

Hirsch, Fred 1976: *The Social Limits to Growth*. New York: Twentieth-Century Fund.

Hurst, James Willard 1970: *The Legitimacy of the Business Corporation in the Law of the United States 1780–1970*. Charlottesville VA: University of Virginia Press.

Isaacs, Nathan 1925: On Agents and "Agencies". *Harvard Business Review*, 3, 265–74.

Jacoby, Neil H. 1973: *Corporate Power and Social Responsibility: A Blueprint for the Future*. New York: Macmillan.

Jensen, Michael 1989: Eclipse of the Public Corporation. *Harvard Business Review*, September/October, 61–74.

Julien, Claude 1991: La démocratie blessée par les injustices du système économique. *Le Monde Diplomatique*, June, 1, 16–17.

Karsten, Siegfried G. 1990: Quantum Theory and Social Economics. *The American Journal of Economics and Sociology*, 49 (4), 385–99.

Kempin, Frederick and Wiesen, Jeremy 1976: *Legal Aspects of the Management Process.* St Paul MN: West Publishing.

Küng, Hans 1991: *Global Responsibility: In Search of a New World Ethic.* London: SCM Press.

Kuttner, Robert 1991: *The End of Laissez-Faire.* New York: Alfred A. Knopf.

Ladd, John 1984: Corporate Mythology and Individual Responsibility. *International Journal of Applied Philosophy,* 2.

Levin, Lawrence Meyer 1936: *The Political Doctrine of Montesquieu's Esprit des Lois: Its Classical Background.* New York: Institute of French Studies, Columbia University Press.

Levy, A. B. 1950: *Private Corporations and Their Control.* London: Routledge & Kegan Paul.

Lippmann, Walter 1922: *Public Opinion.* New York: Free Press.

Lindblom, Charles E. 1977: *Politics and Markets.* New York: Basic Books.

Locke, John 1952: *The Second Treatise of Government.* Indianapolis: Bobbs–Merrill.

Loewenstein, K. 1966: *Max Weber's Political Ideas in the Perspective of Our Time.* Amherst: University of Massachusetts Press.

Manning, Rita C. 1984: Corporate Responsibility and Corporate Personhood. *Journal of Business Ethics,* 3, 77–84.

Marcuse, Herbert 1964: *One-Dimensional Man.* Boston: Beacon Press.

Mason, Edward S. 1970: The Corporation in the Post-Industrial State. *California Management Review,* 12 (4), 5–25.

Merquior, J. G. 1980: *Rousseau and Weber: Two Studies in the Theory of Legitimacy.* London: Routledge & Kegan Paul.

Midgeley, Kenneth (ed.) 1982: *Management Accountability and Corporate Governance.* New York: Macmillan.

Milgram, Stanley 1974: *Obedience to Authority: An Experimental View.* New York: Harper & Row.

Mintzberg, Henry 1984: Who Should Control the Corporation? *California Management Review,* 27 (1), 90–115.

Moulakis, Athanasios (ed.) 1986: *Legitimacy/Légitimité: Proceedings of the Florence Conference, June 1982.* New York: Walter deGruyter.

Ohmann, O. A. 1957: Search for a Managerial Philosophy. *Harvard Business Review,* September/October, 41–51.

Perlmutter, Howard V. 1991: On the Rocky Road to the First Global Civilization. *Human Relations,* 44 (9), 897.

Petrella, Riccardo 1991: L'évangile de la compétitivité. *Le Monde Diplomatique,* September, 32.

Pfeffer, Jeffrey and Salancik, Gerald R. 1978: *The External Control of Organizations: A Resource Dependence Perspective.* New York: Harper & Row.

Pols, Edward 1982: *The Acts of Our Being: A Reflection on Agency and Responsibility.* Amherst: University of Massachusetts Press.

Pratt, John W. and Zeckhauser, Richard J. (eds) 1985: *Principals and Agents: The Structure of Business.* Cambridge: Harvard Business School Press.

Rawls, John 1972: *A Theory of Justice.* Oxford: Clarendon Press.

Reidenbach, R. Eric and Robin, Donald P. 1991: A Conceptual Model of Corporate Moral Development. *Journal of Business Ethics,* 10 (4), 273–84.

Riley, Patrick 1973: How Coherent is the Social Contract Tradition? *Journal of the History of Ideas*, 34 (4), 542–62.

Rosenberg, Nathan and Birdzell, L. E. 1986: *How the West Grew Rich*. New York: Basic Books.

Russell, Bertrand 1967: *Power: A New Social Analysis*. London: Unwin Books.

Ryan, Alan 1984: *Property and Political Theory*. Oxford: Basil Blackwell.

Schlusberg, Malcolm D. 1969: Corporate Legitimacy and Social Responsibility: The Role of Law. *California Management Review*, 12 (1), 65–76.

Scott, John 1986: *Capitalist Property and Financial Power*. New York: New York University Press.

Silk, Leonard and Vogel, David 1976: *Ethics and Profits: The Crisis of Confidence in American Business*. New York: Simon & Schuster.

Stokman, Frans, Ziegler, Rolf, and Scott, John (eds) 1985: *Networks of Corporate Power*. Oxford: Polity Press.

Stone, Christopher 1975: *Where the Law Ends: The Social Control of Corporate Behavior*. New York: Harper & Row.

Velasquez, Manuel G. 1983: Why Corporations are not Morally Responsible for Anything They Do. *Business and Professional Ethics Journal*, 2, 1–18.

Weber, Max 1954: *Law and Economy in Society*. Max Rheinstein (ed.). Cambridge: Harvard University Press.

Weisskopf, Walter A. 1971: *Alienation and Economics*. New York: EP Dutton.

Whitley, Richard 1987: Taking Firms Seriously as Economic Actors: Toward a Sociology of Firm Behaviour. *Organization Studies*, 8 (2), 125–47.

Williamson, Oliver E. 1981: The Modern Corporation: Origins, Evolution, Attributes. *Journal of Economic Literature*, 29, 1537–68.

Index